The Porn Report

ONE WEEK LOAN

The Porn Report

Alan McKee,
Katherine Albury &
Catharine Lumby

MELBOURNE
UNIVERSITY
PRESS

MELBOURNE UNIVERSITY PRESS
An imprint of Melbourne University Publishing Limited
187 Grattan Street, Carlton, Victoria 3053, Australia
mup-info@unimelb.edu.au
www.mup.com.au

First published 2008
Text © Alan McKee, Katherine Albury & Catharine Lumby, 2008
Design and typography © Melbourne University Publishing Limited, 2008

Designed by Alice Graphics
Typeset by J&M Typesetting
Printed in Australia by Griffin Press

National Library of Australia Cataloguing-in-Publication entry:
Alan McKee.
 The porn report / authors, Alan McKee; Katherine
 Albury; Catharine Lumby.

Carlton, Vic.: Melbourne University Publishing, 2008.

9780522853407 (pbk.)

Includes index.
Bibliography.

Pornography.

Albury, Katherine.
Lumby, Catharine.

363.47

Contents

Acknowledgements

Alan

I'd like to thank all of the researchers who worked on this project. Without their hard work, enthusiasm and skill it would never have happened. Particular thanks are owed to Jenny Burton and Denise Durrington, the two project managers, who demonstrated great organisational abilities, leadership skills and big brains. Thank you also to Martin Chadwick, Victoria Creevey, Angela Greenshill, Lisa Kennedy and Andrew King. I am also extremely grateful to Jeremy Angelis, Mike Emmison and Jason Sternberg for support with the project. Stephen Cox in particular changed the nature of the research, for which my profound thanks. The research would have been much less colourful and human without the voices of the consumers that we interviewed—thanks to everybody around the country who took the time to complete the survey or agreed to be interviewed by us. Their bravery and honesty is admirable. And thank you to our wonderful band of interviewers who recorded their voices—Jason Bainbridge, Rosemary Cooper, Terry Evans, Clifton Evers, Anne Fawcett, Glen Fuller, Ryan Griffith, Cary Lee, Paul Levett, Nadia Mahjour, Pam Martin, Colin Parton, Kimba Scorpecci and Dion de Wild.

Thanks to my co-authors, Kath and Catharine, who inspire me and make me think that academics can do something worthwhile. And finally, to John Hartley, who is, I think, a genius.

This book is based on the findings of the 'Understanding Pornography in Australia' research project, funded by the Australian Research Council.

Kath

For research assistance, thanks to Anne Fawcett, Katrina Fox, Fiona Giles, Rebecca Huntley, Anna North and Matthew Thompson.

Thanks to all the organisations and individuals that facilitated my research, particularly to those who invited me to present my work in progress: Carol Queen and Robert Lawrence at the Center for Sex and Culture, San Francisco; Gary Dowsett and colleagues at the HIV Center for Clinical and Behavioral Studies, Columbia University; the Australian Research Centre for Sex, Health and Culture; Juliet Richters and her colleagues at the National Centre for HIV Social Research, University of New South Wales; Gail Hawkes, John Scott, and their colleagues at the University of New England; the Australian Society of Sexuality Educators, Researchers and Therapists, New South Wales; Dr Gabrielle Morrissey; the Ideas at the Powerhouse Festival, Brisbane; the State Records Gallery, New South Wales; the This Is Not Art Festival, Newcastle; ABC Radio National; the departments of Critical and Cultural Studies and Media and Communications, Macquarie University; the Creative Tropical Industries Forum, Charles Darwin University; the organisers of the Revelling 05 conference; the Cultural Studies Association of Australasia; and Michael Flood. Thanks, too, to all the media outlets and community organisations that directly or indirectly assisted with promotion and recruitment, particularly: ABC Radio National and Triple J; Lizz Kopecny and Glenn Vassilos of bi.org.au; and Craig Donarski and Jackie McMillan of the Sydney Hellfire Club.

Special thanks to my friends and colleagues in the departments of Media and Communications, and Gender and Cultural Studies at the University of Sydney, and in the School of Media, Film and Theatre at the University of New South Wales.

I am extremely grateful for the openness of all our interviewees, and to all those (too many to name!) who generously offered research materials, and food for thought of various kinds throughout this project, especially my fellow panellists and crew members at ABC Television's *The Einstein Factor*.

Extra special thanks, of course, to my family in Australia and the United States, and to Lamia Dabboussy, Clif Evers, Sean

Goodwin, Dan Hirst, Linda Jaivin and Tobin Saunders for your friendship, support and love.

And last but not least, to my co-authors!

Catharine

Many thanks to the Australian Research Council who funded this project. I would also like to thank Anna North for her research assistance. Pornography is a contentious area of research and the support and advice of colleagues and friends has made navigating this difficult topic easier. For conversation and the occasional robust debate, I am grateful to Kate Crawford, Clifton Evers, Fiona Giles, Robert Hughes, Rebecca Huntley, Megan Le Masurier, Carrie Miller, Jane Mills, Frank Moorhouse, Richard Neville and Elspeth Probyn. Finally, and most importantly, I'd like to thank Kath Albury and Alan McKee for being such intellectually and personally generous colleagues.

INTRODUCTION

Why Study Pornography?

When did you discover pornography? Catharine's first brush with the stuff was in Year 5 when a group of schoolboys at the back of the bus started reading out passages from *The Joy of Sex*. The book may have been intended as an earnest hippy ode to the beauty of lovemaking, but the ten year olds on that bus thought it was pure, delightful filth. Kath was seven when she discovered one of her father's *Playboy* magazines. She lived in a very bohemian feminist household so she wasn't fazed by the pictures of naked women. What really got her attention were the cartoons. Alan discovered an abandoned magazine in the woods behind his house when he was in his early teens. It was a heterosexual magazine, and his main reaction was disappointment that the women were naked but the men still had their clothes on.

Love it, hate it or just feel ambivalent about it, porn is something the majority of us have encountered before, often at a fairly young age. Pornography, as we know it, didn't arrive with the internet or the VCR, even though new technologies have certainly increased its availability and the ease with which it can be accessed. Passionate debates about the cultural, social and moral effects of pornography have a long history. These debates have once again become particularly heated in the wake of the internet, a medium that gives many people unprecedented access to pornography.

In March 2006, the Australian Labor Party announced that a Federal Labor government would introduce compulsory internet filtering to 'shield children from graphic pornography'. Every site that was potentially pornographic—including anything that presented sexually explicit words, or pictures with lots of skin in them—would supposedly be automatically filtered by every Australian computer.

Measures like this have been attempted or promised across the world, though with little success, except in states that exert totalitarian control over online media. In China, for instance, access to sites considered politically subversive or immoral is routinely blocked. The problem is that many pornographic sites are hosted overseas and are not easily regulated by national censorship regimes. Filtering software is improving and is undoubtedly a very useful tool for parents and educators who want to protect children from inappropriate material. But the reality is that, for the present at least, we live in a world where pornography is widely available. The authors of this book believe that we need to have an informed debate about its role in our society, and that means knowing more about what's in popular forms of pornography, who consumes it, how it affects their lives and how we can protect children from unwanted exposure to sexually explicit material.

Sex is a perennially popular and interesting subject, and most Australians will have views on the issue of porn. Yet despite the fact that the media is full of claims about pornography and the damage that it allegedly does to society, until recently no basic empirical research had been done into what is in most of the pornography consumed in Australia, and who the consumers are. Most discussions of pornography to date have relied on anecdotal experience or on very selective surveys of material. And when it comes to consumers, the general approach in media debates has been to portray them in stereotypical terms as sad old men or misogynist misfits, despite the fact that the most conservative estimates suggest that up to one-third of adult Australians consume pornography and that a significant proportion are female.

The Porn Report is the first piece of serious research carried out to provide basic information to anybody who wants to know the facts about pornography in Australia. This book is based on a three-year Federal Government–funded study by three academics called Understanding Pornography in Australia (see the Appendix for a full account of our research project). We did the study because we believe that the issues raised by pornography are important and that public debate and policy in the field needs to be based on information, not just on moral and ideological positions. We recognise that pornography is a subject on which people will always hold strong moral or political or religious views. We respect their right to do so. We come to this study with our own personal views and values. But the purpose of this book is not to challenge any point of view directly or to persuade others to adopt a position that any of the authors currently hold on pornography. Our central aim is to provide factual information about pornography and its consumption because we believe that informed debate is the foundation of healthy discourse and policy.

Too often, debates about pornography are circular and emotive. The same well known figures put forward the same well known views. And yet there is evidence that the majority of Australians may not share the objections to pornography that are persistently raised in the media. Surveys on attitudes to the availability of non-violent, sexually explicit material of the type found in the X video category consistently show that around three-quarters of Australians are comfortable with the idea of non-violent erotica being available to adults. This statistic suggests that there's a chasm between the views of some of pornography's most vocal opponents and the attitudes of a largely silent majority. We believe it's important to know why there is a such a gap between what's said about pornography and what many Australians think. Is the general public deluded about the reality of what's in porn and its effects on consumers? Or are public debates about porn out of touch with reality?

Part I of *The Porn Report* details a large-scale analysis of the place of pornography in Australian culture. We look at all aspects of pornography including what is actually in mainstream

pornography in Australia. Is it full of violence, rape and bestiality, as newspaper commentators and journalists often assume
it is? Is that really what pornography consumers are watching in
Australia?

We also look at the important question of how women are
represented in mainstream pornography and about their attitudes
to being porn consumers. We examine the production of sexually explicit material to find out if women are being exploited or
harmed by their involvement in making it.

We study the consumers of pornography. Who are they? How
many are there? What kinds of people are they? What part does
porn play in their lives? To get this information we directly asked
more than 1000 porn consumers to tell us what kind of pornography they like, what their social and political attitudes are and
what role they think porn plays in their lives and their relationships. In doing so, we have treated porn consumers in exactly the
same way that other researchers treat consumers of advertising
or newspapers. Some commentators will suggest that there is no
point asking pornography consumers about themselves because
anything they say has already been tainted by the process of
consuming pornography. Our response is to note that the consumption of pornography is so widespread that it makes no sense
to treat porn consumers as an aberrant group. Like it or not, porn
consumers make up a mainstream group in society.

In Part II, we look at the impact that feminism has had on
the porn industry, and at examples of porn made by feminists.
We also look at the vast amateur porn industry and at why so
many ordinary individuals and couples are now producing and
distributing their own sexually explicit material. The disturbing
subject of child pornography and the question of how to protect
children from exposure to pornography is tackled in Chapter 7.
We conclude our book with a surprising question: can porn ever
be ethical? And if it can, what would 'good' porn look like from a
consumer and a producer's point of view? We look at practices in
the porn production industry and examine what conditions porn
performers work under, what is best practice from a health and
safety point of view and how consumers of pornography can make

choices that deter the exploitation of anyone associated with porn production.

From the beginning of this project, we've liaised with the adult industry in Australia, which has made available its mailing lists, copies of bestseller lists, and so on. We can honestly say that nobody in the porn industry ever tried to influence our findings or control what we published. The people we dealt with were simply pleased that someone was trying to find out about the facts of the issue.

All of us have previously published articles on porn, in academic circles and the popular media. Our views are on the record and can be summed up as follows. While we are not anti-porn, we do not support misogyny, homophobia, racism, non-consensual sex, bullying or the disregarding of fair occupational health and safety measures in *any* workplace.

We regard any material that portrays non-consensual sex, any assault of another person and any other criminal act (such as the abuse of a child) as abhorrent. Such material is sometimes distributed for pornographic purposes. It is first and foremost the documentation of a crime. Our research shows, thankfully, that this kind of material is on the absolute fringes of the market for pornography. We also see porn photoshoots and film sets as workplaces, and consequently we expect them to be places where workers are treated fairly and decently.

We believe that porn consumers should be treated like any other media consumers: and that we need to know a lot more about their political values, their attitudes to women and men, and the kinds of relationships they have. For this reason, we've done what researchers have been doing with every other kind of media consumer: we've asked porn consumers to tell us what they think about the effect of porn on their lives.

Everyone has the right to have a say about pornography and to argue their case. But in order to have a meaningful say, we all need to work from the facts. Are the dirty old men we hear about in the newspapers really typical of the Australians who consume pornography? Is today's porn more 'feminist' than that produced in the 1970s? Why are so many ordinary Australians making their own pornography now?

Whatever your opinions on the issue, we hope that when you finish this book you'll be able to say that you understand more about pornography in Australia than you did when you picked it up.

PART I
The Survey

1

A Brief History of Pornography

Let's start with a slightly odd question.

What is pornography?

At first it seems obvious. *Playboy* is pornography. *Playschool* is not. But what about a photograph by a widely acclaimed photographic artist such as Robert Mapplethorpe that depicts a man in a suit with his penis exposed? Should these kinds of images be available to an adult public in an art gallery? And where do we draw the line? At the exposed penis? Or at some of the more confrontational images made by Mapplethorpe—a gay and HIV-positive man—which include images of sadomasochism and anal sex?

To some, the answer to these questions is obvious. Any material of this kind, regardless of whether it's in an art gallery or on a website, should be banned. Others argue that there's a big distinction between art and pornography. There are still others who claim that the division is irrelevant and that there should be very few restrictions on what adults can see or read.

If we're going to talk about pornography, then we need to find out more about the history of how people in the Western world have understood what is and isn't pornographic. This is because when you look at the history of censorship, it becomes very clear that what is regarded as obscene in one era is often regarded as culturally valuable in another. Whether something is pornography or art, in other words, depends a lot on who's looking and the cultural and historical viewing point from which they are looking. In short—and even though it seems an odd thing to say—you can't tell if something is pornographic just by looking at the thing itself. Just because an image is sexually explicit doesn't make it pornographic. It might fit into another category—it could be regarded as art, or as an illustration in a medical science textbook, or it could be material used for sex education purposes.

How are decisions made in any given society about what is pornographic and what isn't? What criteria have been used in the past and are used in the present to make those decisions? And how much have attitudes changed over the centuries?

We all know how heated debates about the nature, effects and purposes of pornography can become. What interests us about them, for the purposes of this book at least, isn't who's right and who's wrong but what these debates tell us about the way different groups express their social, moral and political views through the claims they make about pornography. For religious conservatives, pornography is the desecration of an act designed by God to be enjoyed in private between a husband and wife. For anti-porn feminists, pornography is a type of hate speech so vicious that it constitutes an actual assault on women. For free speech advocates, the availability of pornography symbolises the right of adults in a civil society to choose what they see or hear. In every case, claims about pornography are equally claims about the proper role of women, about what should remain private and about what is sexually normal or abnormal. The authors of this book obviously have their own opinions on these issues—opinions that have changed over time and may change again in subtle or even radical ways. Something we all share is a concern not to be smug, self-righteous or dismissive of other views or regimes for understanding and regulating pornography. There is no ideal or universal position for understanding what pornography is or what it does. There is always something new to be learnt in this field. In that spirit, then, we want to examine the history of pornography to learn more about the genre. What kinds of things have historically been called pornography? And what kinds of arguments have people made in favour of censoring particular kinds of culture?

The term 'pornography' was first used, in its modern sense, by nineteenth-century art historians to describe the erotic paintings and statues found by the archaeologists who unearthed Pompeii and Herculaneum from the volcanic ashes that buried them in AD 79. The response of museologists and historians to these graphic images was to ensure that these items were locked away from the gaze of women, children and other allegedly morally frail beings. Sexually explicit material can be found in all cultures. What varies is a given community's attitudes to how strictly such images or works should be censored and who should and shouldn't be allowed to see them. For example, a painting we regard today as a great work of art—Manet's *Olympia*—was decried as abominable filth by commentators writing in the late nineteenth century when the painting was first put on public display.

In the 1960s and 1970s, scholars studying the way different societies treat sexually explicit images began to question whether the whole idea of pornography wasn't, in fact, a nineteenth-century invention. They asked whether pornography was really a category 'created over time by police and judges, readers and librarians who relegated certain texts and artefacts to a separate category of representations labelled "pornographic" or "obscene"'. US historian Lynne Hunt puts it this way: 'Pornography was not a given; it was defined over time and by the conflicts between writers, artists and engravers on the one side and spies, policemen, clergymen and state officials on the other'. And Walter Kendrick, who wrote a cultural history of pornography, says that the term pornography always 'names an argument, not a thing'.

The idea that pornography is an invention of legal institutions, psychiatrists and doctors, readers and viewers, librarians and anyone else with an interest in what is and isn't obscene seems, at first blush, ridiculous. The common sense response to such a claim is to laugh and say: 'Pornography is made by pornographers.

Everyone knows pornography when they see it. It's always the same—a bunch of dirty pictures or words designed to sexually arouse the viewer or reader'.

In fact, history shows us that the kind of material regarded as obscene has varied widely, as have views of its purpose and value. A lot of what we consider high art in Western terms today once had more explicitly pornographic purposes. Paintings such as Titian's famous *Venus of Urbino*, which shows a young nude fixing the viewer with an inviting gaze while her hand rests suggestively across her vulva, were often originally commissioned for the private rooms and pleasures of elite gentlemen patrons. Today, they are on public display in our finest art museums. They're not seen as pornography anymore—not according to art historians, at least. But even today there are still some who would argue that fine art nudes are pornographic and exemplify either immoral or misogynist attitudes to women.

Images that seem to the modern eye bizarre as well as erotic often graced the margins of twelfth-century illuminated manuscripts produced in monasteries. Marginalia included portrayals of priests with erections, masturbating nuns and sexual couplings that saw clergy consorting with demons and animals. The purpose of this marginalia in documents intended for religious instruction is still not well understood. Is it pornographic in intent? It seems unlikely, given the nature of the manuscripts. Then did they, as some art historians have speculated, have a religious purpose?

In 1991, acclaimed American novelist Bret Easton Ellis published *American Psycho*, a work which contains astoundingly graphic descriptions of sex and violence. Ellis intended the book as a scorching critique of what he saw as the brutality and emptiness of a consumerist capitalist society. Many literary critics saw the book the same way. But others saw the novel as a pornographic incitement to rape and murder women and called for the book to be banned.

The range of material that has been attacked for being pornographic is astounding. And so is the range of apparently innocuous material that has been used for erotic purposes or banned on the argument that it might corrupt the public. The Roman author

Pliny tells us that Praxiteles's modest sculpture of Aphrodite was so sexually charged that young men were given to assaulting it. In the nineteenth century, a host of famous works promoting sexual health and contraception were banned on the grounds that they were pornographic. In Australia alone, the following have all been held to be obscene: US comic books, pulp fiction crime novels, a TV host's imitation of a crow call, and a plaster cast of Michelangelo's *David*, which toured department stores in 1966.

There is also a long history of writers, artists and photographers producing material specifically and explicitly for the purpose of giving people sexual pleasure—and for no other reason. Famed diarist Samuel Pepys is one of the few seventeenth-century writers who actually describes buying and reading an early French classic of the genre, *L'Ecole des filles*. After recounting in, well, pornographic detail his response to the book, he also recounts burning it so it would not disgrace him if found in his library. His oft-cited and rather transparent excuse for reading such a 'mighty lewd book' was to 'inform himself in the villainy of the world'.

But if erotic material, intentionally created for that purpose or not, has been with us for so long, why did it become such an issue in the nineteenth century? Why did it come under such close scrutiny and why were so many people and groups concerned with regulating or banning it?

Faith and Politics

When we look at the history of censorship and pornography in the Western world, one key theme is apparent: it is most often the history of dominant groups in society trying to protect groups they perceive as vulnerable from being corrupted by exposure to the wrong kinds of material.

The ability of dominant groups to regulate pornography or any material they regard as having the potential to corrupt the masses is bound up with the evolution of technologies for producing and disseminating images and texts. As the major institution controlling knowledge in a feudalistic society, the Christian Church was one of the key bodies regulating what people could read. Its power to censor was bound up with its power over the production and dissemination of handwritten manuscripts made in monasteries, at least up until the invention of the printing press in 1436.

The advent of Gutenberg's press, coupled with a slow but steady rise in literacy, eroded the power of the clergy to control what people read or knew. It's not surprising, then, to discover that in the sixteenth century, the Catholic Church tried to reassert its control over the masses by drawing up lists of banned material. According to the Church, books 'which professedly deal with, narrate, or teach things lascivious or obscene are absolutely prohibited, since not only the matter of faith but also that of morals, which are usually easily corrupted through the reading of such books, must be taken into consideration'.

As literacy grew and the first rumblings of the revolution that hailed modern liberal democracies began to sound in Europe, royalty joined the Church in the censorship game. In eighteenth-century France, for example, the royal censor had absolute power to grant or deny permission to print a book. As a result, most authors, not wanting to lose either favour with the king or their heads, published their works anonymously abroad and smuggled them back into the country.

A turning point in the history of censorship came in the early eighteenth century when the publisher of a book that had been freely available for nearly forty years—*The Nun in Her Smock*—was prosecuted for obscene libel. This changed the censorship landscape profoundly because democratic government was brought into the censorship equation. This eighteenth-century prosecution, as the authors of a key book on obscenity law note, brought morality within the sphere of government and cut across the old division between civil and ecclesiastical courts. For the first time, the state was involved in deciding what could and couldn't be read. The significance of this shift was that as democratic governments are required to represent the people who elected them—limited as that group was in the eighteenth century—they needed to justify their decision to ban this or that book.

A key argument that began to be articulated by public commentators and policymakers at this time was the claim that mature societies need to censor literature or images to protect their weaker members against corruption or harm. In the eighteenth and nine-teenth centuries, it was the working classes and women who were the focus of protection campaigns. Oddly enough, from a modern point of view, children were not a major focus of protection until the mid-nineteenth century, when political movements against child labour and child abuse represented a growing consensus that those under the age of twelve (defined as the age of sexual consent at the time) deserved special treatment.

One prompt for this shift, historians argue, was the develop-ment of a public market for pornographic works as a result of both the rapid growth in print literacy and the expansion of the popular book trade. The new urbanised working classes were increasingly able to read. And so, for the first time, they could make their own decisions about what kinds of things they might want to read. This presented a real challenge to governments, churches and other groups who wanted social control over what the masses read, what pleasures they enjoyed and how they lived their lives. Censorship laws from this period on were not so much directed at banning particular works, as at ensuring they didn't fall into the wrong hands. The right sort of reader was the educated, upper middle class gentleman, whose refinement and education allegedly pro-tected him from moral corruption. In his groundbreaking book *The Other Victorians*, Steven Marcus revealed the extent of the trade in erotic books and images in Victorian England. It is clear from his work, and that of other scholars, that the vast majority of collectors were middle and upper class gentlemen. They were safe, apparently, from the influence of this material, and could be trusted to use it wisely—unlike the working classes.

In the nineteenth century, spurred on by a plague of cam-paigns to eradicate 'vice', Western governments began to draw up laws that proscribed the production and distribution of porno-graphic material. In the United States, one of the leading crusaders against lewd material was Anthony Comstock, who founded the New York Society for the Suppression of Vice. In 1873, Comstock convinced the US Congress to pass a law that made it illegal to mail 'indecent' materials, which included information about sexual health and birth control. In England, many similar campaigns were waged, culminating in the 1857 *Obscene Publications Act*. As noted by the author of a history of obscenity law in Britain, Alan Travis, the law 'was to provide the legal framework for the banning in Britain of some of the greatest literary works of the twentieth century'. In 1868, in a case involving an anti-Catholic pamphlet somewhat floridly titled *The Confessional Unmasked Showing the Depravity of the Romish Priesthood, the Iniquity of the Confessional, and the Questions Put to Females in Confession*, Lord Chief Justice Cockburn devised an obscenity test that was to influence the common law in the United States and the Commonwealth for at least a century. He formulated the Hicklin test, as it became known, this way: 'The test of obscenity is whether the tendency of the matter charged as obscenity is to deprave and corrupt those whose minds are open to such immoral influences and into whose hands a publication of this sort might fall'.

Even at the time, it was clear that there was more than a little snobbery involved in these campaigns. A contemporary of Cockburn's, the Reverend Sydney Smith, had this to say about anti-vice advocates: 'They are members of a society for suppressing the vices of persons whose incomes do not exceed five thousand pounds'. History shows us that some judges and others in authority thought—and may still privately think—that the working classes were akin to children when it came to such a test.

And it wasn't just the working classes—women, too, had to be protected from the corrupting influence of sexually explicit material. The best example of the grip this view had in the nineteenth century was the spate of prosecutions of authors and publishers of books that dared to give information about contraception to ordinary women. For example, Charles Knowlton's *The Fruits of Philosophy*, published by famous suffragette Annie Besant in 1877, included advice for women about their bodies, sexual pleasures and ways of preventing pregnancy. It was sexually explicit but had a specifically educational purpose. This didn't matter, however, to those who sought to prosecute the people involved in its publication. Men might be able to deal with such material but women, they claimed, simply weren't capable. Both Knowlton and Besant were sentenced to jail for publishing the book and the book itself was defined, by law, as obscene. In case after case, prosecutors argued that any book that tried to give women sexually explicit information would corrupt them. In one typical seizure, a policeman gave evidence that the books seized were the 'most obscene' he'd ever come across and were clearly calculated to encourage women to disregard virtue and condemn chastity.

Women were so weak-minded, legislators thought, that they even had to be protected from novels. As US historian Thomas Laqueur has shown in his history of cultural attitudes to masturbation, the rise of the novel in the eighteenth and nineteenth centuries was accompanied by a very public debate about the dangers of allowing women to indulge in such a fantasy-provoking item. The novel, it was said by many esteemed commentators, caused women to retreat into their own private world; it awakened dangerous romantic and even sexual passions; it played havoc with their nerves; it irritated their internal organs and eventually drove them mad. And if a host of erotic images from the same era is to be believed, reading novels also encouraged women to masturbate. An eighteenth-century engraving, *Midday Heat*, based on a gouache by Pierre-Antoine Baudouin, shows a woman collapsed in a kind of ecstasy, her book flung to one side, one hand resting under her gown and between her legs. The cloud over fiction, Laqueur writes, was the same cloud that hovered over pornography, which 'represented in its purest form the power of literature to arouse the imagination and make itself felt on the body'. Female readers, Laqueur observes, were the embodiment of the enthralled, corrupted and misguided reader, always ready to give themselves over to flights of fantasy. So even non-sexually explicit novels, by encouraging women to have fantasies, were thought to be a form of pornography in the nineteenth century. Once again, we see that it isn't the content of the object itself that tells us whether something is pornography—it's the cultural context that frames it.

Art or Smut?

A foundational belief underpinning obscenity laws and trials in Western countries, as Australian academic Barbara Sullivan writes, was the assumption that a 'direct (and uncontroversial) relationship' existed between 'exposure to obscene publications and moral harm—and between individual moral harm and harm to the community—for those who did not have the necessary "cultural competencies" to deal with this material: that is the majority of the population'. Highbrow literature and art was never meant to be the target of obscenity laws, even in the Victorian era.

Throughout the nineteenth century, anti-censorship advocates saw themselves as doing battle with philistines on behalf of literature and art. Certainly, many of the works banned under a variety of laws and legal precedents in the first half of the twentieth century were books now regarded as literary masterpieces. The rollcall of authors whose works have been censored over the past 150 years includes Emile Zola, James Joyce, Oscar Wilde, Radclyffe Hall, Ernest Hemingway, DH Lawrence, F Scott Fitzgerald, Walt Whitman, Gore Vidal, Philip Roth, Henry Miller and Bret Easton Ellis. The great majority of free speech advocates did not see themselves as *for* pornography, which they regarded as explicit material that lacked any higher artistic or moral purpose. Rather, they were *against* restricting artistic expression and *for* the right of the cultivated reader to decide what was good to read. The problem for authorities charged with the duty of applying obscenity laws was how to decide when something was art and when it was pornography. As the century wore on, and novelists and artists grew bolder in dealing with sexual material, the line between art and porn grew ever blurrier.

The unfortunate result was that policemen, magistrates and politicians were often required to act as de facto literary critics, with predictably hilarious results. A wonderful Australian example involves an obscenity trial in which Max Harris, the publisher of a progressive literary magazine, was forced to defend the publication of a series of modernist poems that turned out to be written as a hoax. The poems were published as the work of an undiscovered genius, one Ern Malley. In fact, they were written by two staunch critics of modern poetry, Harold Stewart and James McAuley, using deliberately arbitrary phrases and with an intentional disregard for narrative or theme. Their aim was to show that modernist publications like Harris's *Angry Penguins* would publish any old tosh if it sounded progressive. In one famous court exchange, prosecution witness Detective Vogelsand gave evidence that an Ern Malley poem titled 'Night Piece' was obscene because it was set in a park at night. He told the court: 'I have found that people who go into parks at night go there for immoral purposes'. He acknowledged, rather touchingly, that: 'My experience as a police officer might, under the circumstances, tinge my appreciation of poetry'.

At the heart of many, though by no means all, discussions of the effect and regulation of sexually explicit material in the first half of the twentieth century was an implicit division between erotic art and smut. A classic example of this opposition is the 1967 claim of an Australian parliamentarian that it is possible to draw a clear legal line between 'adult, mature type literature' and 'yellow gutter-snipe material' that is 'not literature at all'. As Barbara Sullivan, the author of a history of the politics attending the regulation of prostitution and pornography, observes, this position is a classically liberal one that gained momentum as the century progressed. Conservatives tended to be far more sceptical about claims that artistic merit should override concerns about the potentially corrupting influence of open references to sexual practices or desires.

This opposition between highbrow erotica and lowbrow porn is one that perpetuated the class-driven hierarchy that saw Victorians begin to police the trade in erotic material only when it became clear that the masses were at risk of consuming it. By the mid-twentieth century, there was less concern about the class or gender of the reader. The focus had switched to authorial intent. A writer like Henry Miller could get away with lurid descriptions of his one-night stands, yet *Playboy* magazine could attract penalties in many jurisdictions for showing any hint of inner labia.

As the 1960s wore on, and what is loosely called the 'sexual revolution' began spreading across the Western world, new voices, new problems and new politics began to define the censorship debate.

From Sexual Revolution to Feminist Revolt

British poet Philip Larkin once quipped that:

> Sexual intercourse began
> In nineteen sixty-three
> (Which was rather late for me)

Larkin was satirising the so-called sexual revolution that, it's often claimed, swept the Western world in the 1960s and 1970s and either enlightened or corrupted society, depending on who you ask. Larkin's target was the self-congratulatory spirit he detected in the liberationists. He has a point. Sex is a complex personal business and there is something extraordinarily patronising about any individual or group claiming they are 'liberated' in ways that others aren't. As we'll see, the question of who needed to be liberated from what formed the epicentre of debates about pornography in the latter half of the twentieth century. Arguments about 'protecting' various groups in society still survived, but alongside them emerged a new set of arguments about a positive need in society for everybody to be sexually liberated. This idea certainly didn't have a dominant position in nineteenth-century debates about censorship.

A myriad of social and political forces came together to form a critical mass of dissension about the laws, policies and social norms that policed expressions of sexuality. The 1970s saw a flood of changes that affected ideas about gender roles, sexual behaviour and moral attitudes. One of the most important was the availability of reliable contraception and sexual health advice. By the mid-1970s, premarital sex was becoming less stigmatised, sex manuals like *The Joy of Sex* were runaway bestsellers, some heterosexual couples began openly living together before marriage, and gay and lesbian rights movements were gathering steam.

The 1970s also saw pornography enter the mainstream, most visibly in film. As Linda Williams records in her definitive history of pornographic movies in the United States, the earliest porn films were stag movies that were almost exclusively watched at private parties, in brothels or in sex shop booths by men. The technology for producing or viewing films was obviously very primitive for much of the twentieth century compared to contemporary standards. Today, anyone with basic computer literacy can download porn films and watch them on a home computer. For that matter, they can make them using a mobile phone and email them to friends. By contrast, the earliest porn movies were not only disjointed and amateurish, they were far less widely available than other kinds of erotic material.

In the early 1970s, a host of films with an explicit pornographic purpose debuted on the popular market. The most infamous film of this era is *Deep Throat*, which opened in the United States in New York's Times Square in a theatre Williams describes as catering to the '"raincoat brigade"—furtive, middle-aged men who went to see the exploitation fare … and so named for their presumed masturbatory activity under their raincoats'. Had *Deep Throat* attracted only this audience, it would, Williams suggests, have been consigned to the trash bin of porn history. What set it aside was its crude attempt at a narrative.

The early 1970s were marked by a strong shift in social attitudes to sexually explicit material across the Western world. Censorship became a major political issue and, as Barbara Sullivan notes, there was a growing feeling that censorship practices were 'outmoded and undemocratic'. Sullivan writes that opposition to censorship was no longer solely focused on highbrow literature or art: 'On the one hand, many modern novels, such as *Portnoy's Complaint* adopted pornographic codes of representation. On the other hand, adult citizens were increasingly demanding the right to consume pornography as a sign of their cultural and sexual freedom'.

In Australia, a progressive Labor government came to power in 1972 and the following year announced that it was abandoning the century-old policy of using Federal Customs to prevent obscene publications from entering the country. The decision marked a shift from outright and often arbitrary censorship towards a system that emphasised classification. Though laws varied from state to state, the guiding principle of the new system was that adults had the right to see what they wished, excluding material that depicted sexually violent or criminal acts, as long as children and people who did not wish to consume pornography were protected.

In the United Kingdom, this spirit of the times was echoed in the report of the Williams Committee, which had been commissioned by a Labour government in 1977 to report on obscenity laws. The committee suggested a new definition of obscenity that recognised that many people found cruelty or violence far more offensive than sex. The report concluded: 'Only a small class of material should be forbidden to those who want it, because an objective assessment of likely harm does not support a wider prohibition'.

However, the Williams Committee report was received by a very different government from the one that commissioned it. Margaret Thatcher's neo-conservative regime was extremely libertarian on economic matters but was much more concerned with limiting choice when it came to issues it saw as matters of public morality.

The election of Ronald Reagan in the United States saw a similar change in the political climate in that country. Reagan, who owed an electoral debt to the Christian right, allowed Attorney-General Edwin Meese to set up a commission into pornography. The agenda was clear: Meese wanted to discredit the findings of a panel of experts who had been commissioned by President Lyndon Johnson in 1967 to study the operation of US obscenity laws. Following three years of careful research, the National Commission on Obscenity and Pornography found no empirical evidence that pornography was causing the social harm some claimed. Rather, they reported that the real issue was 'the inability or reluctance of people in our society to be open and direct in dealing with sexual matters'. The Meese Commission, as Marjorie Heins observes in her history of obscenity law in the United States, was chaired by 'a zealous anti-pornography prosecutor named Henry Hudson, and heavily weighted with people whose minds were made up on the subject'. The transcripts of the allegedly objective hearings are in stark contrast to the measured and scholarly approach of the 1967 commission. As Heins reports, 'Any pretense of impartiality dissolved as the Meese Commission hearings degenerated into a parade of witnesses recounting stories of sexual abuse by men who said they had been inspired by pornography'. Sexual assault and all forms of domestic violence are clearly horrific crimes that we should all work to eradicate. But, as we'll show later in this book, there are compelling scholarly reasons to question the view that pornography causes such crimes, despite constant and emotive assertions to the contrary. Indeed, research suggests that the problem with such claims is that they potentially divert government resources and social attention away from the real causes of such violence.

The election of neo-conservative governments in the United States and the UK heralded a backlash against the sexually liberal trends of the 1970s. A new political alliance was formed in many jurisdictions between two very strange bedfellows: religious conservatives and radical feminists. The concerns of most religious conservatives are fairly straightforward. They believe that sex is something that should be done in private between a heterosexual couple whose marriage has been sanctioned by their particular god. Radical feminists, on the other hand, tend to believe that marriage and heterosexual intercourse are patriarchal institutions that position women as the property of men and trade them as sexual currency. It's worth noting here that we are not using the term 'radical feminist' in a pejorative sense. The term is an accepted descriptor for a particular strand of feminism that dates back to the 1970s and is characterised by the belief, among others, that heterosexuality in a patriarchal society is in and of itself an oppression of women.

Far too many critics of both the religious conservative and radical feminist views of sexuality and pornography have chosen to parody them. We believe this is a lazy and simplistic approach. Both views deserve careful attention and understanding and both positions have been carefully argued by, respectively, eminent theological and feminist scholars. It is also important to note that many who have joined forces with former opponents in the debate about pornography have done so with the best motives. Concerns about the assault of children and women became increasingly publicised as a result of feminist campaigns against rape and domestic violence in the 1970s and 1980s. One of the strongest critics of pornography, a woman who has compared the damage done to women by pornography to the Holocaust, is Andrea Dworkin. She once summed up her deep sense of impotence about the status and chronic mistreatment of women, even in Western societies, this way:

> It has plagued us to understand why the status of women does not change ... Laws change but our status remains fixed ... Rape, battery, prostitution, and incest stay the same in that they keep happening to us as part of what life is.

The alliance between religious conservatives and radical feminists was ostensibly, if informally, struck on the grounds that both groups believed that pornography was one of the prime causes of the sexual and physical assault of women and children. The 1980s saw movements such as 'Take Back the Night' and 'Reclaim the Night' launched in the United States, the UK and Australia, drawing hundreds of thousands of women and men to protest male violence. These rallies frequently spotlighted the alleged role of pornography in promoting such violence.

The invention of the VCR only poured oil on the fire of concern about the growth and reach of hardcore pornography, particularly when it came to concerns about children being exposed to sexually explicit material and whether ordinary adults were at risk of becoming 'addicted' to porn.

Feminists like Andrea Dworkin and Catharine MacKinnon sit at one end of the anti-porn coalition. In her book *Intercourse*, Dworkin argues that all heterosexual sex is a kind of violation of women by men. MacKinnon believes that pornography is a form of sexual discrimination against women. In 1979, MacKinnon published a landmark book, *Sexual Harassment of Working Women: A Case of Sex Discrimination*. In it she pioneered the notion that sexual harassment is a form of gender-based discrimination—a laudable notion now widely accepted and enshrined in law and corporate policy in many Western countries. In the 1990s, MacKinnon sought to expand the definition of sexual harassment to include pornography, believing it to be one of the primary tools for the subordination of women. As she wrote in 1987: 'Gender is sexual. Pornography constitutes the meaning of that sexuality'. For feminists who support MacKinnon's views, pornography reveals and reinforces the savage misogyny at the heart of patriarchy. In pornography, they see a script that reduces women to sexual objects for the pleasure of men and reduces their humanity to so many body parts and orifices. Leading radical feminist scholar Sheila Jeffreys puts it this way: 'Pornography is the propaganda of woman hatred' that 'teaches the second class status of women'.

By the mid-1980s, the radical feminist critique of pornography had begun to have a mainstream impact. A good example of this was the debates in the Australian parliament over how to regulate the classification, sale and rental of pornographic videotapes. In 1983, a meeting of the Commonwealth and state ministers responsible for censorship agreed that a new X classification should be developed for videos that were more sexually explicit than movies currently classified R. The classification specifically excluded sexually violent material, child pornography and bestiality. Nonetheless, the debate that ensued focused almost entirely on claims that X-rated videos showed extreme cruelty towards women, and other abhorrent material.

In 1984, British conservative Mary Whitehouse toured Australia with her Australian counterpart, Reverend Fred Nile, and lobbied premiers and ministers to ban the X category. In a speech to the National Press Club, she spoke emotively about the horrors of 'video nasties' that, she said, contained material which 'sickened and distressed' ordinary people, including scenes of dismemberment and decapitation. The fact that this kind of material had nothing to do with the Australian X category seemed to get lost in the ensuing outrage.

The premier of New South Wales changed his stance and decided to condemn X-rated material after receiving advice from his Women's Advisory Council, which objected to any material that portrayed women as 'things, commodities or objects'. This advice was grounded in a very different logic to the one that spurred Mary Whitehouse and Fred Nile to condemn the X category. Yet when the premier chose International Women's Day to announce that he thought the whole issue of legalising the X category should be re-examined, he spoke in the same terms as the conservatives, invoking the spectres of pack-rape and extreme violence.

For some, but by no means all, feminists, almost all images of women and men having sex are misogynist at heart. Some feminists would even argue that there is no such thing as consensual heterosexual sex, because the entire process is grounded in the eroticisation of unequal power relations under patriarchy. This is clearly not a view that the majority of the community share. But it is one that deserves to be treated as least as seriously as claims by some religious leaders that sex outside of marriage and all same-sex contact is always wrong. These are arguments that are indeed still presented by some anti-pornography campaigners. Neither view represents mainstream sentiments today, but both have their serious and articulate advocates. The problem, from the point of view of rational public debate about pornography, is that these two very different positions have not only dominated the framing of the issue, they have been conflated, leading to the impression that a broad spectrum of people on the left and the right are in agreement about why pornography harms society. This conflation also means that many of the valid and specific concerns a large group of feminists have about the representation of women in pornography have not been clearly heard.

Pornography Goes Mainstream

The past two decades have seen an enormous growth in the diversity and quantity of pornography, in the ease with which people can access it and in the range of audiences for it. The era when most people first encountered porn under a bed or behind a tree in the local park is long gone. Today, pornography is downloadable from millions of websites. It has become one of the most successful global media industries. And, as we'll show in this book, the audience for pornography is not confined to the so-called raincoat brigade who used to slink into grotty cinemas in the 1960s. A growing number of young women consume pornography, often with their partners. More people are making their own porn and sharing it online. There is also far more diversity in pornography than ever before in the range of sexual acts and fantasies being catered for. At one end of the spectrum, a small but extraordinarily dangerous group of child pornographers is using the internet to advertise and distribute the results of its criminal activities. At the same time, there is now a far wider range of pornography being made by women or for women that is careful not to portray them as mere objects for indiscriminate male pleasure.

The new landscape is an extremely confronting one for anyone who opposes all pornography, whether for feminist or moral reasons. Even in countries like Australia, where non-violent porn films showing consensual adult sex are still banned for sale and rental in all states (although it is legal to possess them and many people do order them from the ACT where they are legally sold), pornography is readily available online.

The challenges for governments wanting to regulate this material are enormous. The classification systems that dominated approaches to censorship in the latter half of the twentieth century are impotent in trying to regulate a virtual tsunami of material, some of it produced commercially, but a growing amount made by people in their homes using handicams and via personal blogs. Short of simply pulling the plug on the internet, there is very little current governments can do to systematically classify and censor such material. There is simply so much of it that the cost of submitting it to a board is prohibitive and current filtering systems remain notoriously clumsy.

Accompanying this rapid growth in the output and consumption of sexually explicit material has been what UK media studies scholar Brian McNair refers to as the mainstreaming of porn. In a number of books, he has written about the way the culture of pornography has gradually become an acceptable subject and has been explored as a subject and a genre in recent Hollywood films, in advertising and fashion, in literature and in scholarly debates. McNair sees this mainstreaming as being closely linked to the sexual liberalisation of Western societies, including the rise of feminism and gay and lesbian rights movements.

While anti-porn feminists would strongly dispute the view that the growing visibility of porn has anything to do with women's liberation, there are many feminists who would agree with McNair. Angela Carter, for instance, has argued that pornography is one of the few genres that reflects the fact that the vast majority of women enjoy sex and that women do not engage in sex for the sole purpose of reproduction. Sex-positive feminists certainly do not condone all pornography, any more than they are likely to condone all advertising or all public health policies targeting women. They acknowledge that women are still discriminated against even in Western societies and, particularly, in many developing countries. Sex-positive feminists, however, do not believe that all sexualised representations of women are automatically degrading or that pornography is at the root of women's oppression. They approach pornography on a case by case basis and believe that debating the ethics of different porn practices and genres will do much more to change products than simply forcing them underground.

Pornography not only stirs our bodies, it stirs our ethical and political selves. Pornography draws out our beliefs about gender and sexuality, race and class, power and selfhood. Pornography is about much more than sex. Whatever you think of pornography, whether you consume it or abhor it, or both, it is now a highly visible part of our world and one we all need to discuss and deal with. Whether as a parent who needs to decide how to deal with their teenager potentially accessing porn on the internet, or whether as a citizen voting for governments who have to reinvent the regulatory landscape, we are all, today, involved in the pornography debate.

To return to one of the key questions in this book, should we censor pornography? As we've shown in this chapter, we first have to define pornography—and that's not as easy as it first seems. The answer depends on the period you're discussing—it's not likely that many people would argue these days that Michelangelo's *David* is pornography. But then it also depends on who you ask. Right-wing Christian groups might argue that art films showing real sex are pornography, but most film critics would disagree.

You could write dozens of books about these different subjects but because we're only writing one book, we've decided to focus on the material that there's not much disagreement about—sexually explicit material that's produced for the purpose of giving people sexual pleasure.

The other thing that we've tried to show in this chapter is the kinds of debates that have been had about pornography, including who have been the main commentators in public discussions over the years, and what kinds of things they have said. This is important because in the past, there were various assumptions about pornography that aren't seen to be true anymore.

Historically, the main argument for censoring material in the eighteenth and nineteenth centuries was that helpless members of society, particularly the working classes and women, weren't sufficiently educated or civilised to avoid corruption by exposure to pornography. This argument leads to confusion about art: some people argue that art should be excepted from censorship because it's likely to be consumed by educated people who can deal with it; other people argue that everyone should be treated the same and that art is no different from any other kind of sexually explicit material, and it should all be censored equally.

The idea of protecting women from pornography has survived, with an unlikely coalition of feminists and Christians coming together to argue that pornography causes harm to women—although nowadays they are less likely to argue that pornography corrupts women, and more likely to argue that it turns men into rapists.

And a new idea has emerged in the last fifty years as well—that there is a positive side to pornography in terms of sexual liberation, and that this is an argument against censorship.

If you read the newspapers you might get the impression that there's a simple gender division in Australia: men like pornography and women don't. The cliché is that women are appalled and upset by pornography, that it destroys their relationships and leads men to abuse them. You'd never imagine, from what's offered by much of the media, that some women might actually like pornography. And yet, as we discuss in the next chapter, the reality isn't as simple as the stereotype.

2

Dirty? Old? Men?
The Consumers of Pornography

Mike likes to get a particular computer station in the back corner
of the 24 hour Internet café he visits often—more often than a man
without a job can afford. The cubicle feels familiar and is margin-
ally more secluded than the others that line the walls. Late at night,
which is when Mike usually arrives, the café is not as busy or bright
as during the day. He finds his spot, logs on and starts looking at
pornography. And sometimes he's still there 24 hours later. 'They
have snack food in the place, and that's all I feed myself on—a soft
drink, a packet of chips', he says … Mike … believes he's addicted
to pornography … [and that] his dependence on porn is impacting
on his ability to lead a normal, balanced life.

Is Mike, sitting in his internet cubicle with his chips and cans of
soft drink, a typical porn user? Who uses pornography? What
kinds of people consume sexually explicit material in Australia?

How about we start with a slightly different question. Do
you use pornography? If you do, would you be willing to admit it
while down the pub talking to your mates, or at a party, or to your
partner, or if a researcher telephoned you and asked, or if your
mother brought it up over dinner?

According to a Roy Morgan survey, and similar surveys in other Western countries, about 33 per cent of adult Australians use some kind of sexually explicit materials—videos, DVDs, magazines or on the internet. That's about five million people. Yet when was the last time that you heard anybody admitting in the media that they use porn themselves? While millions of Australians quietly live their lives and use pornography, the only people we hear from in public debates are church leaders, social scientists, politicians and commentators—people whose claim to expertise on the issue is the very fact that they themselves don't watch porn, aren't friendly with anybody who watches porn, and don't know anything about the everyday use of porn.

This isn't seen as a problem. In fact, it seems to be the first qualification you need for speaking about porn in public. The only porn users you ever hear from in the media are people who call themselves 'addicts' and are trying to stop using it.

Perhaps this explains why there are two such contradictory images of porn users in Australia, which sit comfortably alongside each other.

On the one hand, everybody knows that the stereotypical porn user is a normal bloke, having a bit of fun. Every ordinary man likes porn. We know this because of magazines like *Ralph* and *Loaded*, semi-pornographic men's mags that are all about 'booze, babes and balls', the three key interests of every normal, red-blooded Australian male.

But on the other hand, everybody who reads newspapers knows that the people who use pornography are sad, dirty old men—like poor Mike in his internet cafe. Unable to have a proper relationship with a woman, they are deviant, slightly suspect and probably addicted. As one expert puts it, '[n]o man who regularly uses pornography can have a healthy sexual relationship with a woman'.

Both of these pictures seem obvious and commonsensical. But surely they can't both be true. They can't both be the typical porn user. So who is?

Unfortunately, there's not a lot of research out there that tells you about porn users. That's surprising, because pornography is one of the most researched media genres. For thirty years now, social scientists have been studying it. There are literally hundreds of articles and pieces of research investigating the effects of porn (we discuss these in detail in Chapter 4).

But for some reason, social scientists have been very reluctant to find out who actually uses pornography in the real world. Most research into pornography has been done in the laboratory, using people who don't normally watch pornography. So we know a lot about people who *don't* use pornography. But scientists have done very little work to find out what kind of people actually do use it.

So apart from the fact that they comprise up to one-third of the adult population, what do we know about the Australians who consume pornography?

The first point we can make is that, based on sheer numbers, they can't be that deviant. This is just a matter of statistics and definition. Deviancy implies marginal, extreme practices. If one-third of your adult population is doing something, then it can't really be deviant. In fact, it's getting pretty close to being mainstream.

There are really only two detailed surveys of Australian consumers of pornography. In 1996, Hugh Potter surveyed 380 consumers of sexually explicit materials. And in 2003, we conducted the largest ever survey of Australian pornography consumers—more than 1000 of them. (For all of the social-science information about how we got in touch with people, how we worded the questions, and the limitations of surveys as ways of gathering information, see the Notes.)

The results were interesting, mostly because they showed that consumers of pornography are like you and me: ordinary Australians from every age, level of education, voting preference, almost every religion, and walk of life. The only thing that makes them significantly different population-wise is that they're overwhelmingly male. Would you like to see some numbers? We've got numbers.

Demographics

When it comes to gender, porn is still largely a male hobby, although this is changing. Of the respondents to our survey, 82 per cent were male and 17 per cent were female (with a few people not answering the question). That's a big gender bias. But it's less biased than in the past. A full 90 per cent of the porn consumers who responded to Potter's survey in 1996 were male, so it seems that women are increasingly consuming sexually explicit materials these days.

Apart from this, we found out that consumers of pornography are pretty representative of the average Australian.

Potter found that the average age of consumers in his 1996 survey was thirty-nine years old, compared with an average age of thirty-five for the general population in 2001. In our survey we didn't gather exact ages but asked people to nominate a category: 1 per cent were under eighteen; 21 per cent were aged nineteen to twenty-five; 33 per cent were twenty-six to thirty-five; 24 per cent were thirty-six to forty-five; 13 per cent were forty-six to fifty-five; 6 per cent were fifty-six to sixty-five; and 3 per cent were over sixty-six (they add up to 101 per cent because of rounding figures to the nearest 1 per cent). This means that there were consumers of pornography in all age categories, but they tended to drop off in their fifties and sixties. This was similar to the 2003 survey, which showed that younger people were more likely to have viewed a sexually explicit film in the preceding twelve months than older adults.

In our survey, 77 per cent of the consumers were heterosexual; 17 per cent were bisexual, gay or lesbian; 4 per cent were BDSM (into bondage and domination, and sadomasochism); and there were small numbers of other sexualities (such as 'celibate'). The government census doesn't gather information about people's sexualities, but a common figure that's bandied around is that about 10 per cent of the population is gay or lesbian—there's no common figure for how many are bisexual.

We had respondents from every state and territory in the country, with a particular bias towards New South Wales (361) and Queensland (222), and the fewest respondents from the Australian Capital Territory (32), the Northern Territory (6) and Tasmania (26). Victoria (155) and Western Australia (119) pro-vided plenty of consumers, and South Australia less so (69). NSW has the largest population of any state, so it's not surprising that we got the most responses from there. Queenslanders and West Australians consume more pornography per head than any other state. Also, as Alan works in Queensland, the local press coverage of the survey there got more people on to the internet to complete it. The low response rate from the ACT and NT might be because there are fewer people living there than in the states. We also used mail-order catalogues as one way of getting the survey out and, of course, porn consumers in the territories don't need catalogues—they're allowed to buy porn legally from their local adult shops (although in the NT, as we note in Chapter 3, some Indigenous people are now not legally allowed to possess pornography).

Consumers had a broad range of incomes. The average annual income before tax in Australia for people in full-time employment in 2003 (when our survey was administered) was $38,168. In our survey, 51.5 per cent of respondents had earnings under $40,000 a year, so they were pretty typical. However, the porn consumers who responded to the survey had higher levels of formal education than the Australian average. In 1999, 27 per cent of twenty-five to sixty-four year olds had a tertiary qualification. But 49 per cent of the surveyed consumers had a tertiary education, and 16 per cent had a postgraduate qualification.

We don't think that this means that porn consumers are better educated than the average Australian. Another survey found that the biggest users of porn tended to be men who hadn't gone to university or who had blue-collar jobs. The most likely explanation for the highly educated nature of our sample is that we used a written survey form, and people who go on to university tend to be comfortable with formal writing. Those who are not so comfortable with written English or filling in forms are unlikely to have gone to university.

Is pornography an inner-city hobby? With the image of areas like Kings Cross, you might think so. But according to our survey, you can find porn users everywhere in Australia: 23 per cent lived in inner-city locations, 51 per cent in suburbs (where most Australians live), 10 per cent in towns, 7 per cent in small towns,

7 per cent in rural locations and 1 per cent in remote locations; five people lived in 'other' locations, including one on a battleship.

Debates about censoring pornography in Australia are often conducted around party lines. Right-wing parties usually want more censorship, or even to make pornography illegal. Left-wing parties tend to argue against censorship and for freedom of expression, although there are some on the left who oppose pornography because they believe it is a kind of hate speech against women.

But does that match up with the politics of porn users? This was one of the biggest surprises of the survey. Roughly equal numbers of porn users vote for the Coalition and for Labor. You wouldn't guess that from listening to the politicians.

In his 1996 survey, Potter found that 36 per cent of his sample voted for the Coalition and 44 per cent for the Labor party. Our results were slightly different: 24 per cent voted for the Coalition and 28 per cent for Labor, with 9 per cent voting for the Democrats and another 3 per cent voting for One Nation. The biggest surprise was that 16 per cent voted for the Greens, significantly more than the national average. That said, Labor and the Coalition were still the major parties being voted for, and there was not much difference between them in terms of attractiveness to consumers of pornography. Finally, 14 per cent were swinging voters, or didn't vote, and 6 per cent gave no answer or were uncodable.

We were also surprised by the results about religion. Again, from listening to public debates, you wouldn't imagine that churchgoers would use pornography. The only time you ever hear a religious leader speak about pornography is in order to condemn it as sinful, evil and perhaps the cause of all crime in society (as George Pell once claimed). Imagine our amazement, then, when we found out that almost 60 per cent of porn users were religious: 15 per cent were Catholics, 10 per cent were Anglicans, 2 per cent were Methodist, 11 per cent were 'other Christians', 3 per cent were Buddhist, 32 per cent were committed atheists, 9 per cent were agnostics, and 17 per cent described their religious beliefs as 'other'. The total of 58 per cent with some kind of religious belief is lower than the Australian average: the 2001 Census found that 74 per cent of Australians claimed a religious affiliation. But the majority of consumers of pornography either see no contradiction between their religious beliefs and their consumption of adult materials, or they find a way to reconcile them.

Only three Muslims—0.3 per cent of respondents—took part in the survey. Either Islam is more successful than other religions at stamping out pornography use among its followers, or Muslims are less willing to admit using porn.

Our survey shows that porn users live across Australia, in all states and territories; they drink lattes in inner cities and beer in the remote outback, and live in all the suburbs and towns in-between. They belong to all age groups, although users tend to drop off as they get into their fifties and sixties. They earn about the same as the people who don't use porn, they vote for mainstream political parties—including the right-wing parties that campaign against pornography—and the majority of them have religious beliefs, as do the majority of other Australians. They are overwhelmingly male, but this seems to be changing.

What else do we know about them?

We were interested, given the image of poor Mike in his internet cafe, to find out what kind of relationships and social lives porn users have. Again, the information we found was surprising. Are they lonely and cut off from human relationships? Obviously you can't ask that directly in a survey—'Are you a sad bastard?'— so we asked them, 'When you have guests in your home, are they mostly family, friends, work colleagues, or "I don't entertain people in my home"'. In replying, 70 per cent said that it was primarily friends who came round, 32 per cent said family and 2 per cent said work colleagues. Only 5 per cent said, 'I don't entertain people in my home' (some ticked more than one box, which is why the numbers add up to more than 100 per cent). We also asked them how often they go out socially: 30 per cent go out more than once a week, 41 per cent about once a week and 29 per cent less than once a week.

Putting these two sets of figures together, we would interpret them scientifically as saying that, basically, porn users do have social lives.

Do people turn to porn because they can't have real sexual relationships? We asked consumers, 'How would you describe the status of your current sexual relationship?' We found that 55 per cent were in monogamous relationships (married or partnered), 28 per cent were single, 9 per cent were in open relationships (3 per cent of those were open marriages), 2 per cent were celibate and 6 per cent described their sexual relationships as 'other'. Again, these numbers add up to more than 100 per cent as eighty-one people ticked more than one box, having more than one sexual relationship in their lives. In 2001, 59 per cent of Australians over the age of fifteen were either married or in de facto relationships. So it seems that the people using pornography are in relationships about as much as any other Australians. Again, poor Mike, sitting by himself, is looking less and less like the typical consumer of pornography.

Do the people who consume pornography also consume other media? It might seem like a strange question, but when people are worrying about the 'effects' of pornography, they usually treat it as something entirely separate from other media—as if people might consume nothing but pornography and so miss out on all the other messages about relationships, sex, politics and attitudes towards women that are carried in books and newspapers, and on radio and television every day. Nobody has ever asked consumers of pornography if they also read newspapers or listen to music, so we thought it would be interesting to find out. We asked them what TV channel they watched most often, and 6 per cent said they didn't watch any television. This is a higher figure than you might expect, as very few people in the general population go without watching any television. The explanation for this may appear when we look at the figures for the most watched TV channels. The ABC comes on top with 22 per cent, which is not the typical answer—the ABC would love it if it were. This percentage and the one relating to those who don't watch TV at all can be explained by the fact that our sample had a disproportionately high level of tertiary education. People with postgraduate degrees are the least likely to watch television, and if they do, the ABC is overwhelmingly their channel of choice.

Still, 94 per cent of the porn users that responded to our survey do watch television, so they're also plugged into the wider culture, not just living in a ghetto of nothing but sex. The next most popular channels after the ABC were Ten (20 per cent), Nine (14 per cent), SBS (11 per cent), Seven (9 per cent), regional channels (4 per cent), Fox 8 (3 per cent) and Fox Sports (2 per cent).

We asked porn users about the kind of music they listen to, asking them to tick as many boxes as they liked. Rock music came out top (52 per cent), then came 'Top 40' (30 per cent), 'easy listening' (25 per cent), dance (25 per cent), classical (23 per cent), jazz (22 per cent), metal (19 per cent), hip hop (17 per cent), country (11 per cent) and opera (6 per cent). We're not sure exactly how this fits into stereotypes of porn users, but the fact that they listen to classical music and jazz more than heavy metal or hip hop might raise a few eyebrows, perhaps because porn is so often associated with trash culture rather than high culture.

Only 6 per cent of porn users didn't read any books, while the 94 per cent that did again reflected the unusually high level of formal education among them. The top specified genres were thrillers (36 per cent), science-fiction (35 per cent), biographies (33 per cent), literature (27 per cent), crime (26 per cent), lifestyle (such as cooking and gardening books; 25 per cent), horror (17 per cent), poetry (9 per cent) and romance (7 per cent). The top genres are exactly what you would expect—thrillers and science-fiction, crime, biography and lifestyle are the genres of books that really sell. The presence of literature and poetry would be surprising were it not for the high level of formal education in the sample. Once again, this might disturb a few stereotypes about trash culture, as we see this sample of more than 1000 porn users reading more literary novels than horror.

When we asked if they read a newspaper, 15 per cent said they didn't. The top paper was the *Sydney Morning Herald* (22 per cent). The various other state newspapers reflected the sizes of their populations in the survey: the *Courier Mail* (19 per cent), *West Australian* (8 per cent), *Daily Telegraph* (7 per cent), *Age* (5 per cent), *Herald Sun* (7 per cent), *Adelaide Advertiser* (4 per cent), *Hobart Mercury* (2 per cent) and *Northern Territory News* (0.5 per cent). Regional newspapers were read by 14 per cent of respondents, while 8 per cent read the *Australian* and 3 per cent the *Australian Financial Review*. Journalists consistently write media stories about pornography as if they are speaking to an audience who are ignorant of and shocked by it. It turns out that many of their readers are actually consumers of pornography.

Of the 1023 participants, not a single one said that they didn't watch any television, read any newspapers, listen to any music or read any books. Whatever messages they might be getting from their porn, they are also getting other messages about society from other media. They are linked to wider culture, not cut off in a ghetto.

How Pornography Is Consumed

What part does pornography play in these people's lives? Are they, like Mike, addicted to it, watching it for hours on end? Is it a hobby? An interest?

Another interesting fact that came out of our survey is that there isn't one typical way to use pornography. People use it in a range of different ways.

We asked users how much money they spent on pornography each month, and 45 per cent said they didn't spend any money on pornography at all. Of these, 31 per cent only viewed or down-loaded free material from the internet; 8 per cent borrowed or exchanged material with friends, or used exchange schemes; and 6 per cent did not access any new material.

Of those who did buy material, 45 per cent of the sample spent between $1 and $50 a month. Not many people spent more than this: 7 per cent spent between $51 and $100 a month; 2 per cent spent between $101 and $150; and only seven people (less than 1 per cent) spent $151 or more a month.

Videos were the most popular medium for pornography (44 per cent), while 34 per cent used DVDs. The internet was the next most popular medium (42 per cent); however, only 6 per cent used fee-paying websites. Pornographic magazines were used by 27 per cent and 6 per cent read erotic novels. There were gender differences in these choices. Only 2 per cent of men read porno-graphic novels, as opposed to 15 per cent of women. Conversely, a greater percentage of men (83 per cent) than women (73 per cent) consumed pornographic videos or DVDs. This is still a sig-nificant majority of female porn consumers who consume explicit visual material, particularly when compared with the relatively small percentage that consume novels.

When asked, 'How large is your current collection of pornography?', 5 per cent of the sample had no items, 26 per cent had under ten items, 23 per cent had eleven to twenty-five items, 13 per cent had twenty-six to fifty items and 33 per cent had more than fifty items.

We also asked consumers, 'Do you use your pornography only once, or do you use it more than once?', to which 13 per cent replied that they only used each piece of pornography one time. However, the majority (85 per cent) re-use their material: 45 per cent said they sometimes go back to favourite pieces of pornography, and 40 per cent said they often went back to favourites.

As to how they consume pornography (where survey participants could pick as many options as they wanted), 76 per cent consumed their pornography alone, but 46 per cent also responded that they consumed it with a partner. Meanwhile, 5 per cent watched it in sexual situations with more than one partner and 6 per cent watched it with a crowd of friends. There was a range of practices, but watching pornography alone or with a partner were by far the most popular ways of doing it.

We asked two questions about the amount of time spent consuming adult materials: how many times a week consumers usually consumed these materials, and how much time they actually spent doing it. There was an even spread of answers to the first question: 28 per cent consumed pornography less than once a week, 21 per cent did so about once a week, 29 per cent did so up to three times a week and 21 per cent did so more than three times a week. As to how long they spent with these materials, there was slightly more consistency here. The largest groups spent less than one hour per week (41 per cent) or one to three hours per week (35 per cent) consuming pornography, while 12 per cent spent three to five hours and 9 per cent spent more than five hours. The majority of users were spending less than three hours a week with sexually explicit materials—a long way from poor Mike's experience of twenty-four-hour marathons.

In researching what kinds of things porn users like to consume, we asked them, 'Do you think there are any "classic" porn videos,

DVDs, novels, internet sites or magazines?', to which 38 per cent said 'yes', 45 per cent said 'no' and 16 per cent didn't answer. The most common nominations for the classics were the videos *Deep Throat* (107 mentions) and *Debbie Does Dallas* (96).

We asked users how they decided what pornography to buy, offering a range of suggestions but also space for 'Other (please describe)', and asking them to tick as many boxes as they wanted. The most popular responses all related to packaging and marketing. The largest single response was 'description in catalog' (37 per cent), then 'cover photo' (33 per cent) and 'description on back cover' (32 per cent). The next most popular reason for choosing a pornographic item was the 'star' involved (27 per cent), with 11 per cent choosing because of the director (videos), 4 per cent choosing because of the author (novels), 15 per cent choosing based on magazine reviews and 12 per cent on internet reviews. Only 11 per cent made choices based on personal recommendations by friends; 11 per cent were informed by adverts in magazines and 6 per cent by adverts on the internet. Of the 117 consumers who gave 'Other' reasons, the most common were the production house involved (2 per cent) and the kinds of sex involved (2 per cent).

We also asked these consumers what they thought made for good pornography, again asking them to tick as many boxes as they wanted. The top answer was 'attractive actors/actresses' (69 per cent), but it is interesting to ask what respondents consider 'attractive' when we see that the third most common answer for what makes good pornography was 'real-looking bodies' (51 per cent). Also interesting is that just behind 'attractive actors/actresses' was 'enthusiasm in sex scenes' (69 per cent)—it seems that pornography consumers like material in which people are seen to be enjoying themselves.

Forty-five per cent of the survey said they liked 'good production values', 44 per cent wanted 'realistic settings' and 41 per cent liked 'particular kinds of sex'—particularly anal sex (8 per cent), lesbian sex (6 per cent), group sex (6 per cent), oral sex (5 per cent) and BDSM (bondage and discipline, sadism and masochism; 5 per cent). Having a good story-line was important for 32 per cent and the writing was deemed important by 24 per cent—these categories were kept separate in order to cover both videos and pornographic novels. Good acting was nominated by 28 per cent, and 20 per cent nominated other aspects that make for good pornography, the most common of which was that the actors should obviously be genuinely enjoying themselves (3 per cent), then amateur pornography (1 per cent).

We asked consumers how happy they were with the porn that they consumed. The majority of people were happy (52 per cent) or very happy (13 per cent), while 25 per cent had no strong feelings, only 7 per cent were unhappy and only 2 per cent were very unhappy. We asked those respondents who were unhappy with the pornography they consumed to suggest how it could be improved. The most popular suggestion (2 per cent) was that the pornography should be of better 'quality' (production factors such as lighting, camerawork, editing, sound, writing and acting), followed by suggestions that the stars should have less plastic bodies and more realistic body types (2 per cent), and that it should be less male-oriented and take more account of foreplay and women's pleasure (1 per cent).

We asked respondents if they had ever applied anything they saw in pornography to their own sex lives: 59 per cent said 'yes', 27 per cent said 'no' and the rest did not respond. The most common practice, by a very large majority, was different sexual positions (reported by 23 per cent). The next most common practices were sex toys (6 per cent), anal sex (6 per cent), BDSM (6 per cent) and oral sex (5 per cent, of which 1 per cent specified that this was cunnilingus).

Finally, we asked respondents at what age they first encountered pornography. The majority of respondents (63 per cent) first saw pornography when they were under sixteen years of age, while 28 per cent saw it between the ages of sixteen and twenty, 6 per cent saw it between the ages of twenty-one and thirty, and 2 per cent were over the age of thirty.

Is the age of first exposure changing over time? We often hear concern in the media that the internet is making pornography available to children in a way that simply wasn't possible in the old days. Because we have researched people's ages now, as well as the ages at which they first saw pornography, we were able to make the comparison. The results were interesting (see Figure 2.1).

Figure 2.1: Are we seeing pornography at a younger age than in the past?

Current age	Under 16 when?	Percentage who first saw pornography under the age of 16
66+	1950s or previous	36.7%
56–65	1950s, early 1960s	22.8%
46–55	1960s, early 1970s	35.7%
36–45	1970s, early 1980s	58.7%
26–35	1980s, early 1990s	77.4%
19–25	1990s–2001	79.2%

It seems that, with the exception of those aged sixty-six and over (who were a small sample in our survey), each generation sees pornography earlier than the generation before it.

Speaking for Themselves

The typical porn consumer is still male, but he could live in any state or territory, be of any religion except Muslim, and vote for any political party. He watches television, reads books and newspapers and listens to music, like most other people. He has a social life and is likely to have a monogamous sexual partner. He spends less than $50 a month on porn and less than three hours a week watching it. He likes porn that has attractive actors, with bodies that look real, and who genuinely seem to be enjoying themselves.

That's a lot of numbers. But you might be thinking that surveys don't give you any feeling of what these people are really like, what they sound like, how they live—in short, who they are.

We agree. So after we did the survey, we went on to do a series of detailed interviews with some of the consumers. Our survey was anonymous, but at the end of it we told the consumers that if they were interested in doing a follow-up interview, they should provide their contact details; 32 per cent of the consumers did so. From this list, we interviewed forty-six people. We wanted to get the widest possible range of voices and the widest possible range of perspectives on the issue: across gender, geographic location, age, level of formal education and sexuality. We spoke to twenty-six male and twenty female consumers of pornography, who had the following characteristics.

Two were aged under eighteen, eight were aged nineteen to twenty-five, fourteen were aged twenty-six to thirty-five, eleven were aged thirty-six to forty-five, five were aged forty-six to fifty-five, two were aged fifty-six to sixty-five and four were aged over sixty-six. Fourteen people lived in Victoria, eleven in NSW, seven in Queensland, four each in Tasmania and South Australia, three in Western Australia, two in the ACT and one in the NT. Twenty-six were straight, five were gay or lesbian, nine were bisexual, five were into BDSM and one was celibate. Ten lived in urban areas, twenty-six in suburban areas, two in towns, one in a small town, six in rural areas and one in a remote area. Education-wise, seven had completed postgraduate study, twenty-two had done tertiary studies, eleven had done secondary studies and six were still studying. We didn't specifically weight respondents based on their voting preferences, but we ended up with fourteen Labor voters, eleven Liberal–National voters, nine Greens voters, six Democrats voters and six 'Other' (including issue-based voters, those not registered and those too young to vote).

We sent out a team of interviewers around the country to speak to these people. The consumers could choose if they wanted to be interviewed in their own homes or in a public place. All of the interviewers were people who had a knowledge of the area and some interviewing skills. Men interviewed men and women interviewed women. We had some couples in the sample and we didn't specify a gender for their interviewers.

You might think it would be quite an odd experience going into a stranger's house to interview a person or a couple, knowing very little about them except that they consumed pornography. Jenny Burton was our tireless project manager, who organised the group of interviewers and also did four of the interviews herself. She explained that although she was careful to ensure that the interviewers were safe at all times—including giving them mobile phones with our numbers programmed into them, and making sure that she had a record of the time and address of every interview that was conducted—she wasn't particularly worried about the process. She did three of her interviews in public places and one in a woman's house, and she wasn't concerned about going to the home of a porn user: 'I'd spoken to the girl whose house I was going to several times on the phone. She was quite young, and she was really bubbly. And she wanted me to go to her place— she was an artist and she wanted to show me her artwork as well. She wasn't embarrassed or anything about me going over there. She lives with her parents, and her parents knew what I was interviewing her about. Her whole family knew. I'm surprised they weren't there, actually, to listen in'.

Jenny never thought it could be dangerous: 'Just because people watch pornography doesn't mean they're any more dangerous than anybody else', she says. 'Well, she [an interviewee] was dangerously talkative'. The interview process for the book turned out to be a really positive experience for everyone concerned, Jenny says. She met up with one woman at a local pub: 'We had a pizza and a bottle of wine. It was more like going out with somebody and having a social [chat] with them than making conversation. I interviewed one woman in Noosa Heads. We went down to the river and sat and watched the seagulls and talked about pornography and sex. They were all really open, wanting to talk to me. It was fun. Women never get a chance to sit around talking about pornography and sex together. We all agreed at the end of it how much fun it was to be able to sit down and talk openly about sex. Women don't do that'.

So what did we find out from these interviews? In answering this, we've included a lot of quotes from the porn users because we thought that it was important to give the consumers a chance to speak in their own voices, particularly as you never hear them speaking anywhere else in the media. There's a stereotype that women aren't interested in pornography, which is simply not true. Some women are, but how often do you hear their voices in the news? Several of the women that we interviewed were very articulate and explained in detail what they like about the genre.

It's been interesting that since we did this research, a number of people in the public sphere have dismissed it, suggesting that consumers of pornography are not reliable witnesses. In one example, a letter in a newspaper equated consumers of pornography with weapons manufacturers, saying: 'Academics would have us take the words of porn users as grounds to support purveyance of pornography. By the same token, let us survey … weapons manufacturers in order to justify war'. Similarly, one academic claimed that 'just because a self-selecting group of pornography consumers say that pornography is good for their mental health and marriages does not make it so'. We are often accused of 'remarkable other-worldliness' for actually listening to what porn users say, which makes us wonder where the real world is if five million Australian consumers of pornography aren't part of it.

Of course, you can never take interview responses on face value. These consumers of pornography might be liars (they might know that porn is hurting their marriages but don't want to say it). They might be stupid or deceived (they might think that their partners like it, but in fact they don't). But asked to choose who knows themselves better—the people we spoke to, or an academic who's never met them—we're going to give the benefit of the doubt to these consumers, at least until we get any convincing evidence to the contrary.

Besides, the consumers didn't strike us as immoral or stupid. In fact, they made very sensible and clear arguments. For instance, they realised that just because porn was good for their relationships, it didn't mean that the same was true for everybody. One woman said: 'I might be a more sexual person than another girl might be. You know other people might be shocked by their partners asking them, but I wasn't. It's not shocking to me'.

Porn consumers told us about the place of pornography in their lives. By definition, of course, the people who would offer themselves up for interviews are the kinds of people who are happy to talk about their use of pornography. So it's not surprising that none of them hid their pornography use from their partners. In fact, many of them consumed porn with them. One woman said: 'It's one of the things that actually got us together, finding out that we had similar interests and tastes, and we're both quite willing to look at stuff online'. Another woman told us that it's something she looks for in a man: '[It's] the kind of thing that, at least for me, comes up quite early in a sexual relationship with someone, and the kind of person who is going to be shocked by the fact that I like pornography is probably not the kind of person who would be sexually compatible with me'.

These consumers said that using pornography had made their relationships stronger. One woman said that: 'I think he [her partner] was quite happy that he could share with me and we could go to sex shops together and have a look at ... which magazines we like and which videotapes we like and we could discuss a bit more openly our fantasies, I guess. And then it could be a together thing rather than something that would separate us, so I think in that, it's good'. Other consumers talked about 'spicing up' their sex life. One older man said that it allowed him to maintain an active sex life: 'I watch it to—especially my age now, it takes a lot for me to get (pause) ... stimulated'. And as for whether pornography made them lose interest in or judge their partners, as one man put it: 'I got my own star. She's my star and that's all there is to it'.

We asked the consumers to elaborate on what they like in pornography. Many of them used the term 'quality' to describe what makes for good pornography. More specifically, one key issue that several interviewees spontaneously mentioned was that the best pornography is where 'you can see real enjoyment'. The word 'enjoyment', or the idea of people 'enjoying' themselves, was used by several interviewees, along with 'genuine interest', that 'the people are there because they want to be there', that they 'like what they're doing', and that there's 'enthusiasm' or 'genuine chemistry' between the actors.

How could the users tell if the actors were genuinely into it? There seemed to be agreement that the people in porn films generally aren't very good actors—that's not really their primary skill set—so if they're not enjoying it, it's quite obvious: 'You can just tell that they aren't into it. They are just waiting for their pay cheque, that's it'. One man told us that 'in watching porn I always tend to sort of look at the background and if you notice things that look like they're drug related, or someone may be dependent upon drugs, it sort of kills the ability to be able to enjoy it'.

As we discuss in Chapter 3, there is a binary division in mainstream pornography. One dominant trend is 'fantasy'-based, with idealised bodies and romantic story-lines. The other dominant trend is 'naturalistic', with realistic bodies and without story-lines—it's just about the sex.

Some interviewees said that in their pornography they like the actors to have idealised bodies. Surprisingly, this was particularly common among the female consumers. As one woman said, in pornography: 'we're talking fantasy so we're talking the ideal body. Yeah'. Another woman said that: 'I like the style, like the *Playboy* style with all the big done-up hair and breasts and everything and the good looking guys ... I like the glossy, glitzy glamour style, not the dirty sort of old people stuff ... [a] classy feel with good looking people, just like you want to see good looking people in the movies. And you can have your fantasies'. Another woman told us that: 'What I absolutely *hate* is *ugly men*!! Like, hello people! No, it doesn't work like that'.

But other porn consumers said exactly the opposite, arguing that what they wanted to see in pornography was actors with 'realistic' bodies. As one person said: 'Real people are sexy and they're all so different and they're all beautiful in different ways'. One woman said of her sexual partners: 'I've found that the kind of pornography that my partners like to watch is the kind of pornography that contains women that look like *me*; they don't want to watch some skinny blonde tart, they want a *real* woman who's older ... [and] got a bit of sexual nous'. It's also interesting that eight of the men told us specifically, without prompting, that they don't like breast implants.

One more surprise was that some of the women that we spoke to mentioned the importance of clothing in the genre: 'That's what I really love about porn models', said one. 'They always have the *best* shoes! It's true! ... if you don't have great shoes, you can't have great sex!' None of the male consumers we spoke to mentioned clothing or shoes in their assessments of good pornography.

The porn genre is not famous for its story-lines, although, as we discuss in Chapter 3, upmarket 'couples' porn videos, which are aimed at women as well as men, are increasingly introducing more sustained story-lines and even complex character psychology. Again, we found two contradictory positions on story-lines in our interviews. Some consumers said that they disliked the 'lack of plot' or 'lousy story' in pornography. There was a definite gender bias here. Ten of the women we spoke to used the word 'story-line' when they were talking about what makes good porn. They also made fun of the problems they see with plots in traditional pornography: 'There's always like the rich person and the poor boy. The person breaking into a house and "ooh I tripped over" … on somebody. They're really ridiculous. Then there's the office one with either the female boss or the male boss, and what else is there … the broken-down car'. Or how about the classic, 'the pool guy' who turns up and says, 'I'm here for no apparent reason'.

On the other hand, there were several consumers who told us that not only was story unimportant, it actually got in the way of their viewing pleasure. Many of the men made comments like: 'Fuck that! I fast-forward through that. Once you've got an idea about it I just go to the good bits'. Although few heterosexual male consumers mentioned story-line as being important in pornography, several women challenged another stereotype by saying that they were not interested in plot. As one woman said: 'Get rid of the crappy story lines and just get down to it'.

In Chapter 5 we note that one strand of feminism has argued that it isn't pornography itself that's a problem for women—it's bad pornography that focuses more on men's sexual pleasure than on women's sexual pleasure. And as we will see in the next chapter, the content of mainstream pornography, although not exclusively about male pleasure, still has more fellatio than cunnilingus. Consumers of pornography are well aware of this gender bias in the genre, and they don't like it. The women, in particular, worried that most pornography was 'very focused on men and men's desire'. As one woman put it: 'You always see the male being pleasured, orgasming, but quite often it's not obvious that the woman is coming, so you assume that she's not … it's quite male-focused, cock-focused … vaginal intercourse-focused'. Another woman said that in her experience, a lot of porn is: 'Men's fantasies, so they can be slobs with tummies and whatever, and the women tend to be perfect, just kind of caricatures of women ... big boobs and tanned and have everything shaved and huge amounts of make-up on, because that's the male fantasy that they're ful-filling ... it's really weird as a woman watching it—you have to sort of identity with the woman, but the woman's not really like you ... Whereas it is acceptable for a guy to have this fantasy of being the plumber or being the ordinary bloke and just scoring with this young sexy thing'.

For these women, again, the problem is not pornography itself: 'It doesn't mean that porn in itself couldn't be a positive thing'. Some of the female interviewees said that they 'would like porn that's made by women that's for women', saying that female directors have a 'female perspective', which 'is less "wham bam thank you ma'am"' and 'not just focused on ... men coming'.

Tying in with our discussion of the history of public debates about this issue, several of the women also spontaneously raised the issue of feminism's attitudes towards pornography in the interviews. One woman, thinking about what makes good pornog-raphy, noted that: 'It depends on whether you see porn as being intrinsically degrading to women, and I don't think it necessarily is—although [some porn] can be. You can also see porn as being empowering for women, so it's sort of ... a murky area. I mean I am not a feminist in the way Andrea Dworkin is a feminist, but I guess I'm ambivalent about the intersection of pornography and feminism'. Another woman said: 'I think a lot of it [feminism's attitude towards pornography] comes from ignorance, not [being] interested in viewing the other side of the story ... I would hope that the majority of feminists nowadays are a little bit more liberal about it'. Another woman noted that: 'A lot of feminists absolutely abhor pornography ... [but] there's this whole other generation of feminists, women who like sex, porn, that stuff, simulated rape'.

One woman told her own story of reconciling her feminism with her use of pornography: 'Until recently [I] felt like, "Oh no, not porn, that's exploitative and anti-feminist" ... And only in the last five years [have I] gone, "Well actually, hang on a minute you know, it can be more open and it can be different things within it" ... I'd just been brought up to think that it's totally anti-feminist and it's wrong ... [by] my mum and uni probably as well ... the two together. So then me kind of thinking, "Well is that actually the case?" ... I'm ... thinking about it as well as enjoying it'.

Another woman argued that: 'I've never actually seen any porn where women look like they haven't chosen to participate. I think the whole idea that women are innocent things that need to be protected from the big bad world is the ultimate in sexism and absolutely ridiculous. So I think that expressions of female and male sexuality aren't oppressing anybody ... unless they're rape or obviously non-consensual things. I think it's just a misconstrued view of what women are'. Another woman said that: 'They say that pornography ... is degrading to women but again I don't agree because if the women choose to do it then they're not being degraded ... to me saying that they're degrading themselves isn't giving them ... the intelligence to make their own choices, it's almost like they're trying to baby-sit some women and what they say is right for you ... how can they know what you are better than you do?'. Yet another woman argued: 'We talk about a lot of equality and freedom and so on ... if you [a woman] can choose to be a dentist or a doctor or a lawyer ... [but] I don't think you can go, as a modern professional woman, "Well, I choose to be a porn star". Why do you have to be made to feel guilty and made to feel like a dirty person or slut, and made to feel like you were forced into it simply because you want to be a sex industry worker? And I don't like that, I really don't like that. I think if you enjoy it you should be allowed to. You're allowed to stay home and have kids, and you're allowed to go and work for twenty years. Why can't you go and have sex on camera?'

One woman argued, in terms familiar in feminism, that the idea that women are not supposed to be interested in pornography, or in sex more generally, is itself sexist: 'You're told if you're male ... you can go sow your seed and you can live it up to the max ... and part of that manly thing is that you have the God-given right to masturbate as much as you like and watch as much porn as you like. Whereas as a girl you're told ... don't have sex, put your thoughts onto something else like stitch-craft, or go play hockey!' Another woman said that: 'Women don't often look at pornography because we're all told that's not what nice women do ... it's always been such a taboo subject really, hasn't it, especially concerning women, about what they like and what they want. It's not something that you often hear about. I'm one of these [who say] "Power to the women! We want something too!"'

The men who were interviewed also made comments about gender and pornography. Several of the men argued that in pornography, far from being objectified, it's the women who hold the power: 'In porn generally it's the woman that has the right, she's the one that controls the act ... she tells him what to do'. Similarly, one man argued that: 'It's the guys that are actually used as the tools. You know the women get paid a lot more to do it, they're the centre of attention'. Another pointed out: 'The people with the big pay-packets are women'. And another man agreed that pornography shows women as sexual subjects rather than sexual objects: 'It's okay for the woman to be the sexual protagonist ... So in terms of gender politics, that's where I'm coming from. I think women should also be able to be sexual protagonists. I think porn has gone some way toward making that more acceptable'.

The men also made comments about body image. One man suggested that in pornography: 'The women are often a fair bit bigger than in magazines and other fashion model ads. But I guess most guys get off on big boobs and round arses'. Another said: 'In some ways the anti-porn voice has a point but I think mostly they miss the real issue ... that porn is so diverse. There are so many different types of porn with all different body types. It's impossible to generalise I reckon'.

Who Uses Porn?

Porn users are mostly men, but there are an increasing number of women who enjoy the genre. They live in cities, suburbs, towns and in the country, in every state and territory. They vote for all of the mainstream political parties and subscribe to many religions—though few follow Islam. They are of all ages—although they are mainly young—and of all income levels. Our sample was unusually highly educated, but we suspect that that was because we used a written survey form.

Importantly, users of pornography are human beings with everyday lives in which pornography plays a part. They have relationships, hobbies and ideas. They think for themselves. They can explain in interesting and informed and sometimes very funny ways why they enjoy pornography, and how it fits into their lives.

The image you may have of pornography from reading media reports is of a genre that's full of violence against women, and objectification—the kind of stuff that could cause consumers to have really negative attitudes. So we continue our study by looking at the actual content of mainstream pornography in Australia. What is in it, and when Australian consumers watch porn, what kinds of things do they choose to watch?

3

What Does Debbie Do?
The Content of Pornography

Step into any newsagency in Australia and chances are that you will find copies of *Picture* magazine, and *People* magazine, and probably *Playboy* and *Penthouse*—everyday pornography, distributed across the country. If you connect to the internet you can find pornography there too: according to some estimates, up to 372 million pages of sexually explicit material. And, as we note later in this chapter, although you can't legally *sell* sexually explicit videos in any state in Australia, you can *buy* them from mail-order companies such as Adultshop, which are involved in a market that is conservatively estimated to be worth $230 million per year. A Roy Morgan survey revealed that 33 per cent of Australian adults consume some kind of sexually explicit material each year.

That's a lot of pornography circulating in Australia. What are all of these people actually looking at?

If you listen to what many commentators are saying in newspapers, you get the impression that most of these consumers are watching violent and disturbing images:

> We're talking about a whole new world of extreme and violent images, including Internet sites specialising in rape, incest, coprophilia and bestiality ... the sex depicted in standard porn is wholly

devoid of intimacy and affection. Women are uniformly portrayed as the passive objects of men's sexual urges.

Is this true? Is mainstream porn really full of 'rape, incest, coprophilia'? Are women 'uniformly portrayed as the passive objects of men's sexual urges'?

What kind of pornography is the most popular in Australia—what, in pornographic terms, is mainstream? To answer this question we got copies of fifty of the bestselling pornographic videos and DVDs in Australia (see overleaf) and our team of 'coders' (research assistants) watched them to find out what was in them.

We chose videos and DVDs because they are still the most commonly consumed forms of pornography in Australia, according to our 2003 survey of more than 1000 consumers—and this despite the increasing presence of the internet in our society. Sixty-three per cent of respondents used videos or DVDs—44 per cent of the total sample watched videos and 33 per cent DVDs, with some obviously watching both. By contrast, only 42 per cent of consumers used the internet to view pornography and only 6 per cent accessed pay sites.

The fact that more people consume pornography on videos and DVDs than via the internet might seem surprising—after all, it's so easy to find pornography on the Net, compared with the trouble of ordering a video or DVD and having it delivered, or seeking out under-the-counter videos or DVDs for sale illegally in sex shops. But even in these days of increasing cyberconnectedness, not everybody has a broadband internet connection at home, and you really need broadband if you're looking at pictures. If your only access to the internet is at work, it's pretty stupid to look at porn there when your company's computer nerds are probably keeping track of every click that you make (the South Australian Industrial Relations Commission ruled in 2006 that it was fair for bosses to sack staff who were looking at pornography on work computers). Even if you have broadband at home, if you live with other people the chances are that the computer will be in a public area where a number of people may have access to it, and you might not want them seeing your pornography, for all kinds of reasons: because your mother might not approve, your wife might not be interested, or you are protecting your children from it.

Fifty of the Bestselling X-rated Videos/DVDs in Australia in 2003

- *100 Sex Scenes 4*
- *Action Sports Sex*
- *Anabolic World Sex Tour*
- *Ancient Secrets of the Kama Sutra*
- *Awesome Asians*
- *Awesome Asians 2*
- *Bad Wives*
- *Big Natural Tits*
- *Blue Movie*
- *Bonnie and Clyde: Outlaws of Love*
- *Buttbanged Naughty Nurses*
- *Conquest*
- *Consenting Adults*
- *Debbie Does Dallas*
- *Debbie Does Dallas '99*
- *Dripping Snatch*
- *Euphoria*
- *Faust Fucker*
- *Girls Who Take It Up the Ass 5*
- *Gushing Orgasms*
- *Hairfree Asian Honeys*
- *Half and Half*
- *Homemade Amateur Videos 2*
- *Jenna Ink*
- *Jinx*
- *Masseuse 3*
- *Nasty Girls*
- *Nice Rack*
- *Nineteen Video Magazine*
- *Overtime Vol 30: Pierced and Penetrated*
- *Paul Norman's Nastiest Multiples*
- *Pick-up Lines 40*
- *Puritan Video Mag*
- *Ready to Drop 16*
- *Rocco Never Dies*
- *Russian Teens 3*
- *Search for the Snow Leopard*
- *Seven Deadly Sins*
- *Sex Island*
- *Sex with Older Women*
- *Sorority Sex Kittens 1 & 2 (double tape)*
- *Supercum 3*
- *Sweet 18 Babes from Budapest 3*
- *The Best of Rocco*
- *The Girls of Summer*
- *The Hardest of Hardcore*
- *The John Holmes Collectors Edition*
- *The World's Greatest Anal Penetrations*
- *World's Largest Cocks 3*
- *Xtreme Scenes 25*

Unlike the United States, Australia has no national audit of bestselling pornographic videos and DVDs. But because of the slightly odd nature of censorship legislation in Australia, we were able to get information about popular titles. It's illegal to *sell* X-rated videos in any state in Australia—although many sex shops do sell them, they are actually breaking the law every time they do. They can only legally be sold in the Australian Capital Territory and the Northern Territory. But it is legal to *buy* X-rated videos in every state and territory (although, with the Coalition's emergency intervention in the Northern Territory in 2007, some

Indigenous people in the NT are now the only Australian citizens who are NOT legally allowed to possess pornography), so there is a massive mail-order market for pornographic videos and DVDs. At the time of our analysis, the majority were sold by two companies, Gallery Entertainment and Axis Entertainment, who agreed to give us lists of the bestselling titles. By merging these samples, we compiled our list of the fifty bestsellers.

Our objective was to map, in broad terms, mainstream pornography; to find out what was in it and who watched it. We looked particularly closely at whether violence or the objectification of women, both issues that many Australians are concerned about, were common in popular pornography. However, as we discuss below, these were not the only interesting issues that came out of the analysis.

Violence in Pornography

There is widespread public concern in Australia about violence in the media, not just in pornographic material but also more widely in films and television. So it's no surprise that it's illegal in Australia for X-rated, sexually explicit material to have any violence in it. Indeed, the category 'X' in the National Classification Code applies to films that 'contain real depictions of actual sexual activity between consenting adults in which there is no violence, sexualised violence, coercion, sexually assaultive language, or fetishes'. As the majority of pornographic videos and DVDs in Australia are legally classified material, distributed by reputable businesses who would find it against their profit-making interests to handle illegal material, our analysis took the nature of a test of how well the law was working. There should be very little that could be classified as any kind of violence in mainstream pornography in Australia.

So we asked our researchers to count how many of the scenes in these videos had violence in them.

Straightaway we hit a snag. How do you define violence?

This is one of the head-scratchers that academics come up against all the time—issues always seem straightforward and simple until you look at them up close. We'll give you an example of why this gets difficult. Take spanking. Some people get their sexual thrills from being spanked. If you watch a video where a woman puts a man over her knee and spanks him, is that violence? He asks her to do it, and he's obviously enjoying it, and she's obviously enjoying it. But all the same, she's spanking his buttocks. So is that violence?

This isn't an abstract, unimportant issue. We know that Australians don't want violent pornography to be available. So we need to have a definition—how do you spot violence, to make sure that such videos aren't legal?

Many previous academic studies decided that they should count spanking as violence, no matter if all the people involved are enjoying themselves and have specifically requested the behaviour.

That didn't make sense to us. It's not common sense. When people say that they're concerned about violent pornography, we don't think that they mean consensual spanking. They mean rape. They mean people being beaten, scared, forced to have sex. That is what worries them.

We eventually agreed on a social science definition of violence that is accepted by researchers as properly objective, and that matches that common-sense understanding of what concerns people. Robert Baron's definition of violence is: 'Any form of behaviour directed toward the goal of harm; or injuring another living being who is motivated to avoid such treatment'. Rape is violence. Spanking someone's bottom when they ask you to is not violence. That seemed like common sense, as well as good science, so we asked the coders viewing the videos to take that definition as their basis. If it was absolutely clear that everybody involved in a scene was consenting to what was happening, it shouldn't count as violence.

At the same time, we wanted to be very careful that we weren't being naive, and that we didn't ignore any possible coercion. If at any point it looked as though the actors weren't enjoying themselves, or if they seemed to be uncomfortable, or if the actors were being forced to do anything they didn't want to, then the researchers should count that as violence. Also, even in consensual sadomasochism, we decided that if there was any point where the actors or actresses ended up doing anything that could cause lasting physical damage—drawing blood, for example—then that should be counted as violence too. In doing this, we were erring on the side of caution, trying to make sure that we counted every possible instance of violence in these videos.

There was still one more issue that we had to sort out before we began counting how much violence was in these movies. If you punch somebody in the face when they're struggling to get away from you, that's obviously violence. Physical violence is easy to spot. But in recent years, our society has expanded its definition of violence to include other kinds of behaviour, such as verbal and emotional violence. So if you scream obscene abuse at a person, is that a kind of violence? In the National Classification Code used by the Office of Film and Literature Classification (OFLC), 'assaultive language' is as illegal in X-rated videos as physical violence. And the social science definition of violence that we used included 'any form of behaviour', not just physical violence. So we told the coders to count aggressive language as violence. Again, though, we thought about consent. Sometimes people enjoy 'talking dirty' during sex. They like being called, or calling each other, 'dirty' or 'nasty', or even stronger names. Of course, some people find this kind of talk abhorrent, but equally, some, in their private sexual lives, take pleasure from it, and pornography reflects this. So we told the researchers that vulgar language should only count as violence if the person who was spoken to appeared to be upset by the language used. If they seemed to be enjoying it, it didn't count as violence.

There were 838 scenes in these fifty bestselling porn videos. Of these, sixteen scenes—2 per cent—contained an element that might be described as violent. This is lower than some other researchers have found. Various surveys of American videos, for example, have found that between 5 per cent and 27 per cent of pornographic video scenes contained violence. This is because the surveys all used different definitions of violence. Some included spanking as violence, or counted any use of dirty language as 'verbal aggression'.

Seven of the scenes included what we could broadly call physical aggression. In scene sixteen of *Debbie Does Dallas*—a 1978 pornographic movie that is still on the bestseller list—a school principal puts (the initially reluctant) schoolgirl Debbie over his knee and spanks her (the scene begins 56 minutes/0 seconds into the video). This becomes sexual. In *The Best of Rocco*, scene eight (1h/4m/14s), Rocco attends a karate fight at a boxing ring with a woman. She fantasises about being in the ring with him, wrestling and having sex. He handles her roughly, pulls her hair, pushes her to the floor and has sex with her. Also in *The Best of Rocco*, scene twelve (1h/27m/36s), Rocco has sex with a woman in a hotel room. He forces her head down the toilet while he is penetrating her. In *Action Sports Sex*, during a scene in a surf clothing shop (4m/59s), it appears that a woman may be hit in the ribs by a man who is having sex with her; this isn't entirely clear. In *Rocco Never Dies*, scene eight (46m/39s), during a foursome in a hotel room, one of the men slaps one of the women in the face while they are having sex. In *Bad Wives*, scene fourteen (41m/19s), a woman has sex with her husband. In the course of this the sex becomes rough, with extreme hair pulling and the couple throwing each other around. In *Bad Wives*, scene fifteen (48m/49s), another woman is having sex with her husband, and again it moves into rough sex play. In each of these two scenes the woman initiates sex and demands it rougher, stating that this is what will give them orgasms. But in the actual performance of it, it is not entirely clear that every rough moment is consensual.

There was also a scene in the videos that included violent language where there was no reciprocity or pleasure. In *Seven Deadly Sins* (7m/3s), a female fan who is obsessed with a female pornography star fantasises about meeting the star in a surreal fantasy landscape. In her fantasy they end up arguing viciously and then having sex, before realising that they are actually both the same person—two sides of the same personality.

Eight scenes included sexual contact which might have been non-consensual. Five showed men forcing women into sexual acts, two showed women forcing men and one showed a male/female couple forcing a woman. But again, the individual cases were ambiguous.

In *Sorority Sex Kittens 2*, a male spy for a right-wing think tank is investigating Upsilon Sigma, a female sorority house whose motto is 'The world is ruled by the power of the pussy'. In the film's single instance of non-consensual sex, the spy is drugged and kidnapped, then presented to and swamped by a crowd of naked women (2h/37m/15s). Nothing sexual is seen apart from the spy being mobbed; exactly what happens to him is hidden behind a wall of naked women. The instance is brief and occurs as a joke—it is the final humiliation in his hopeless fight and a final insult from the sorority, of which he has a crazed hatred.

In *Seven Deadly Sins*, a man pretends to be a born-again preacher so he can sleep with lots of women (1h/40m/7s). He bets his friends that he can use his spiel to trick three attractive women into sleeping with him. But when he does he gets more than he bargains for as they drag him into an alternative dimension, where they use him to satisfy their sexually voracious appetites: 'Holy hell, ladies, where you taking me?' As they have sex, more and more women keep appearing in this hellish dimension, all demanding sexual fulfilment. When he tries to escape, the women drag him back, screaming, and he vanishes under a pile of female bodies. This is his punishment for his greedy sexual desires.

In *Faust Fucker*, scene two (2m/44s), a doctor chatters to the camera while trying to grope his female nurse. She pushes his hands away, smiling broadly all the time. This lasts for a number of seconds. In *Debbie Does Dallas*, scene eight (21m/53s), Debbie is reluctantly persuaded into letting her boss at the store where she works look at, then fondle, then lick her breasts. She is reluctant all the way through the scene and finally has to threaten to 'tell my mother' to get him to stop. Also in *Debbie Does Dallas*, scene twelve (28m/49s), a young woman, Roberta, is working in a candle store. The wife of her boss, Mrs Hardwick, comes back and finds her masturbating with the candles. Mrs Hardwick then starts to grope and fondle Roberta. Roberta tries to push her away. Mr Hardwick enters the shop and sits beside them. She protests. They continue to cajole her and grope her. We see a close-up as she decides to have sex with them, and it becomes consensual. She has sex with both of them.

In a fantasy sequence in *Ancient Secrets of the Kama Sutra*, we hear a woman reading from the Kama Sutra while we see the story played out. It tells of a king who had his guards escort his two princess daughters on a journey (1h/0m/27s). When they stop at night, by the campfire, 'the guards unwisely seduced the girls. They used the technique of the Sutra to overwhelm the women and show them pleasures the like of which they had never seen'. We see the two princesses being seduced. One actress plays the role as though the princess is thoroughly enjoying being seduced. The other plays it as though she is resisting, pulling her head away from the guard kissing her neck; but she quickly begins to enjoy it. The scene continues with both princesses enjoying the sex.

In *Bonnie and Clyde: Outlaws of Love*, the outlaws stop their car so that Bonnie can 'pee in the bushes'. They argue about whether to continue their 'glamorous life of crime'. Clyde grabs Bonnie and starts kissing her. She fights him off: 'Stop it! We're too close to the road! Someone might see! You'd like that, wouldn't you, boy?' As she talks about this, she begins to get aroused and she starts pressing against him: 'You'd like someone to come by and see you sucking me. That would just make you hot, wouldn't it? It arouses you, doesn't it: the fear, the danger?' (5m/11s). They start having sex against the side of the car.

In *Jinx*, a pimp goes into a bar (1m). He hassles the barmaid, groping her, and she struggles to get free of him. After a few seconds she stops struggling and begins to fellate him.

When we reviewed these results, two points were manifestly clear. The first is that pornography really has changed over time. Much anti-pornography writing emerged in the 1970s and, if our sample is anything to go by, the writers were quite correct: things were a lot worse in those days. Pornography was aimed at men and didn't take much account of women's pleasure. Today, with women emerging as a market for pornography, capitalism has followed its logical course and started to remove the elements of pornography that are offensive to this new market. Three of the moments of sexual violence occur in a single video: *Debbie Does Dallas* (1978). This is the only video that shows a woman being spanked against her will, and starting to enjoy it. This variation on the 'rape' theme—women say 'no', but they really like it when it's done to them—has vanished from recent pornography. In fact, in comparing the original *Debbie Does Dallas* with its sequel, *Debbie Does Dallas '99*, we can see how much pornography has changed over two decades. In the original, a cheerleading team wants to get the money to travel to see their team play, and so take on a variety of low-paid and humiliating jobs, many of which end up in sexual encounters that they do not seem to enjoy. As we have already described, several of the scenes rely on the women's powerlessness. By contrast, the story of *Debbie Does Dallas '99* is very different. Here, a cheerleading squad want their team to win. They decide to help by tracking down all the members of the opposing team and having lots of very energetic sex with them until they're too crippled to play properly, and thus lose to the cheerleaders' team.

The second point is that there is now a strong market in 'couples pornography'. These are pornographic films that are aimed explicitly at a joint viewership of men and women. They are still as sexually explicit as earlier videos but appeal to traditional notions of female pleasure, and have much higher production values and more complex story-lines and characters. There were many examples of couples porn in the bestsellers list. *Bad Wives* is about women who are unsatisfied with the sexual performance of their husbands and explore the pleasures of different kinds of sex. *Conquest* tells the story of a headstrong young woman and her best friend, who join a pirate ship to seek out and enjoy sexual pleasure. *Search for the Snow Leopard* tells of an internationally successful female anthropologist who leaves her partner—who is constricting both her career and her sexuality—and travels the world, rediscovering sexual pleasure. *Masseuse 3* is a surprisingly complex story about the nature of love, where the central male character is unable to love women who love him (including a prostitute who gives up sex work for him) and always returns to a woman who treats him badly. *Blue Movie* centres on a male porn director who is trying to work out the nature of his own sexual attractions. Other examples in the bestseller list were *Ancient Secrets of the Kama Sutra, Bonnie and Clyde: Outlaws of Love, Euphoria, Jinx, Rocco Never Dies, Seven Deadly Sins* and *Sorority Sex Kittens 1 & 2*.

What caught our eye was how many of the violent scenes are actually contained in these couples videos. Of the sixteen violent scenes, nine occur in videos that are explicitly marketed to women. And it's interesting that Rocco Siffredi, who provides three of the seven examples of physical aggression, is one of the most popular male porn stars with female consumers of pornography, who enjoy his form of sexual performance. Perhaps the issue of violence in pornography is no longer, as it was in the 1970s, about men's pleasure. Perhaps now it is about women's pleasure.

The Objectification of Women in Pornography

Violence is one of the major concerns about pornography in Australia. But people are also concerned more generally about whether pornography 'objectifies' women. Some people use slightly different words to discuss the issue of objectification— they may talk about 'demeaning' women, or 'degrading' them—but the general concern is the same, and there is general agreement that objectification is a bad thing.

Ask people what they mean by objectification, however, and you find out that we can't even agree on the basics.

For some people, having casual sex with somebody counts as objectifying them. If you don't truly love the person that you're with, then you're not really engaging with them as a person. You are only engaging with their body; that is, treating them as an object. Other people say that if you show women engaging in particular sexual acts, such as giving blow jobs or having anal sex, then you are objectifying them because those are demeaning acts.

For other people, pornography is objectifying if it is all about the man's pleasure. If the woman is literally passive, lying there for the man's pleasure and just doing what she's told, then that's objectification. For still others, if women are shown to be sexually active, then they are being treated as men's fantasy objects because women in real life aren't sexually active in that way—so showing women as sexually active is a form of objectification.

For still other people, it is demeaning or objectifying to show sex between people who don't have equal social status; for example, sex between an older and younger person; a boss and an employee; somebody who is clothed and somebody naked. This implies domination—that the more powerful person is in charge, while the less powerful one is subordinate, or treated like an object.

For other people, all photographs and videos—all representations—are literally objects. Whenever you take a photo of
somebody, you turn them into an object, replacing a human relationship with a relationship with an object. So all representation
is objectification.

There is simply no agreement on what 'objectification' means.
And so, in investigating whether the bestselling pornographic
videos in Australia objectified women, we once again followed
common sense. The common argument is that pornography turns
women into sexual objects, but shows men as sexual *subjects*—the
ones in charge, the ones who decide what to do and whose pleasure is important. So we asked the coders to look at the different
ways in which men and women were represented in the videos.
Who was in charge in each scene? Were they presented as characters, with names and voices, that we could identify with? Or were
they literally just silent, nameless bodies? And whose pleasure was
important? In bestselling pornography in Australia these days, is it
still the case that it's all about showing men's pleasure? Or are the
women in pornography getting some pleasure too?

You could argue, with some justification, that you can't count
something as vague as 'objectification'. How could you measure
such a thing? Numbers are blunt instruments, allowing no room
for subtlety or nuance. But that hasn't stopped social scientists
from counting objectification and demeaning representations in
pornography for decades now. In fact, social science, by definition, involves counting things that you can't really count—love,
hate, health, happiness, sexual pleasure, relationships, political
ideologies. There's an advantage to doing this, in that numbers
allow us to see the big picture. Detailed descriptions in words that
tell us about individual lives, or scenes in pornographic films, can
give us a poetic insight into the complexity of human beings. But
you can't do that with a population of 20 million people, or with
838 scenes from pornographic films.

So we tried to list some of the different ways in which you can
treat somebody as a sexual object, and then had the coders look at
how those were played out in mainstream videos.

One key issue was physical stereotypes. There's a common
concern that women in pornography are not shown as real people:

'practically all women' in porn, some claim, 'are blond, bubble-breasted and perpetually, insatiably eager for sex'.

Is it true? Do pornographic videos rely on stereotypical phys-ical views of women? And what about men—are they physically stereotyped?

Our coders counted 1494 characters in the fifty most popular videos—52 per cent were female, 47 per cent were male, 1 per cent were hermaphrodites or transsexual and 0.3 per cent were drag queens. We first looked at the issue of age.

Sixty-seven per cent of characters appeared to be aged between seventeen and thirty (given the necessarily subjective nature of these judgements, it was not possible to be more precise in developing the age categories). Most of the bestselling videos were American and a small number were European; none were produced in Australia. Given the American production context, the videos followed American law—actors must be at least eigh-teen years old, records proving their age must be kept on file, and every video must show the address where the files for each actor are kept. Given this, the litigious nature of American society and the strength of right-wing religious anti-pornography groups in the United States, it is very unlikely that any mainstream porn producer would dare to break that aspect of the law. So it seems safe to assume that none of the actors in these tapes is under eighteen.

Twenty-four per cent of the characters appeared to be aged between thirty-one and forty, 5 per cent appeared to be aged between forty-one and fifty, and 1 per cent appeared to be aged over fifty-one. Our coders judged that 0.4 per cent (six instances) looked as though they were under sixteen years of age (although, as we've already noted, it's highly likely that they were at least eighteen). The majority of these characters were Asian or Latino, which raises a question about the judgement of the age of non-white characters by white viewers. (In 2.6 per cent of cases, coders were unable to confidently assign a character to an age group.)

Gender was definitely an issue here: 83 per cent of the female characters appeared to be aged between seventeen and thirty, compared to 49 per cent of the male characters. By contrast, only 13 per cent of the female characters appeared to be aged thirty-one to forty, compared to 35 per cent of the men. And 2 per cent of the female characters appeared to be aged forty-one to fifty, compared to 9 per cent of the men. There were apparently only nine female (1 per cent) and eleven male characters (2 per cent) over the age of fifty-one. We can thus say that both male and female porn stars tend to be significantly younger than the general population, and that female porn stars tend to be significantly younger than male porn stars.

Our coders also assessed character body types using five categories: 'skinny', 'slim', 'average' (an Australian size 12—either 'toned' or 'untoned'), 'bulked up' and 'overweight'. Only 0.1 per cent of bodies in these videos (two cases) were rated by coders as being skinny, where that was taken to mean being unhealthily underweight, while 37 per cent were rated slim and 45 per cent were rated average (27 per cent untoned, 18 per cent toned). Ten per cent of characters were bulked up, 5 per cent were overweight and 3 per cent couldn't be coded because we didn't see them unclothed or see their full bodies.

But again, gender is an important variable here, with 65 per cent of the female characters rated slim, but only 5 per cent of the men. Meanwhile, 24 per cent of the female characters were average (untoned), compared with 30 per cent of the male characters, and only 7 per cent of the women were average (toned), compared with 31 per cent of the men. Only one female character was bulked up, or muscular, compared to 21 per cent of the male characters. Two per cent of women and 7 per cent of men were overweight. The rest were unclear.

So women in pornography tend to be slimmer than the men, and male characters are more likely to be muscular. It's worth noting, with current fears concerning anorexia and thin models in fashion magazines, that very few female porn models were actually skinny—half of them were of average size (toned or untoned). You certainly wouldn't get that result if you analysed the women in fashion parades.

We also looked at breast size. Does mainstream pornography reduce women to giant silicone breasts on legs? The researchers noted whether characters had 'small', 'average' or 'large' breasts. In the films analysed, 725 characters showed their breasts. Of these,

19 per cent had small breasts, 39 per cent had average breasts and 42 per cent had large breasts. The researchers also noted whether actresses in the videos had obviously had cosmetic surgery on their breasts ('boob jobs'). They concluded that 29 per cent had obviously had breast surgery and 60 per cent had obviously not had breast surgery; in 11 per cent of cases they were unsure.

Clearly, these figures are way above the average for the general population—porn models are not representative of the average person. But at the same time, the 29 per cent figure (for boob jobs) is far from a majority, and 58 per cent of the women in these bestselling videos were able to become porn stars without having large breasts. We suspect that there is a much larger range of attractive body types shown in porn than there is in other media genres, such as advertising and fashion and women's magazines. To sum up our findings, it's not that the male consumers of pornography particularly like large tits, or small tits, natural tits or fake tits. They just like tits.

Despite the widespread concern that all pornographic videos and DVDs show women as big-breasted, small-waisted, blonde bimbos, there are in fact two quite different kinds of pornography within the mainstream, each showing different body types.

The first kind we might call 'fantasy' porn. This tends to be the more expensive, upmarket, couples porn that is aimed at women and men and presents 'fantasy' bodies. Both the men and the women in these videos have idealised body types. The men are handsome and muscular, with broad shoulders and slim hips. The women are stereotypically beautiful, with small waists, large breasts and rounded buttocks. They all have lovely skin. It's completely unrealistic.

But another, equally popular kind is the 'naturalistic' genre. This is down-and-dirty porn, cheap and nasty, and aimed largely at men. It's often shot in people's lounge rooms or in motel rooms, with poor lighting and bad camera work. The men and women in these videos are often flabby—the women don't have the classic *Playboy* body type and the men don't have muscles. The women have hairy armpits; the men have hairy backs and shoulders. These videos don't fit the stereotype at all. They show real-looking women and men, and they insist that they are sexually attractive too.

It's impossible to generalise about the kinds of bodies that appear in mainstream porn because the two aforementioned types of porn are opposites, yet they're both bestsellers. Some people like fantasy bodies—they want to see idealised beauty. Other people find that type of beauty looks plastic and fake—they are turned on by seeing real people having sex. Both of these genres can be found in mainstream pornography.

Finally, penis size does matter in porn, even if breast size is less important. Of the 587 male or transgender characters who showed their penises, only 3 per cent had small penises, while 42 per cent were average and 55 per cent had penises that were appreciably longer and/or thicker than the average penis.

How else could you tell if women were being objectified in films? We looked at whose point of view the films were told from. On the question of whether the central character was a man or a woman, we found that 54 per cent of the videos had no central character and were not told from a specific viewpoint; 20 per cent were presented from the point of view of a central male character; 20 per cent were presented from the point of view of a central female character; and 6 per cent were structured around two central characters—one male and one female.

We also looked at who actually spoke in the videos. This is important because it lets the characters show that they are people, with inner lives and thoughts—not just pieces of furniture. The researchers counted proper conversations between the characters—not just when someone said 'Yes, yes, fuck me' during sex—and found that 53 per cent of the characters took part in conversations: 51 per cent of female characters spoke in this way, and 56 per cent of male characters. The average amount of speaking time for female characters was two minutes, twenty-two seconds. The average amount of speaking time for male characters was two minutes, nine seconds. So women and men both spoke for roughly the same amount of time in these videos.

We counted how much the characters spoke directly to the camera, because in television, the person who gets to speak directly to the camera is usually the person in charge—the newsreader, the presenter, the game show host. The contestants or guests never speak directly to the camera. In these films, 179 characters spoke directly to the camera for an average time of only twenty-three seconds; this included 137 female characters (17.6 per cent of female characters) and thirty-eight male characters (5.5 per cent of male characters). The mean amount of time spent talking to the camera by those female characters was twenty-nine seconds, while the mean amount of time spent talking to the camera by male characters was five seconds. So the women in mainstream pornographic videos in Australia are not silent objects who just do what men say. Women are in charge. (Compare this with the numbers of male and female game show hosts on Australian television!)

Again, we face the curse of the numbers—when you're trying to give an overview of the mainstream, you can't go into detail about everything that was said. And some of the instances of conversation were particularly interesting. For example, the final scene of *Awesome Asians* sees well known porn personality Shaun Michaels interviewing two female porn stars, 'Kameesha' and 'Leanne'. When Michaels asks the girls why they do pornography, they answer that basically they do it because they enjoy it. They talk about their favourite kinds of sex and explain how they started in the industry. Porn stars are not generally great actors, and 'Kameesha' and 'Leanne' appear to be quite genuine in these conversations. They aren't performing sexual titillation—they're just describing their own careers.

Who was in charge in the sex? Who initiated it? Commentators who are worried that in pornography women 'are uniformly portrayed as the passive objects of men's sexual urges' will be reassured to know that women in pornography are anything but passive. Sex was initiated by women in 24 per cent of these videos, while 13 per cent had sex initiated by men, 6 per cent had sex initiated by both/all participants equally, and 34 per cent opened in media res, so nobody was seen to initiate sex (the other scenes didn't have sex in them). So more women initiated sex (including 'both/ all'; 29 per cent of scenes) than men (19 per cent). Far from being passive, the women in pornography are active sexual participants.

Whose pleasure is being paid attention to? Are the kinds of sex shown in pornography all about men's pleasure? Can you even count sexual pleasure in pornography? We decided to take the orgasm as the basic unit of pleasure, though this is admittedly simplistic and maybe even male-centred. The results revealed that at least one aspect of mainstream pornography is still strongly and clearly sexist.

Our researchers found that in 12 per cent of sex scenes, both genders had orgasms. In 4 per cent of scenes, only women had orgasms. But in a whopping 68 per cent of scenes, only male characters had orgasms. It's clear that women in mainstream pornography aren't having enough orgasms—and, perhaps, are still not having enough sexual pleasure, for all of the sex that they are actively initiating.

Most Popular Sex Acts in Top 50 X-rated Videos/DVDs in Australia in 2003

Sex Act	Time in Sample
Vaginal penetration by man, with penis ('other', including woman on side with one leg in the air, scissors, woman's legs on man's shoulders)	18h 33m 25s
Oral sex on man by woman	15h 26m 07s
Anal penetration of woman, by man (penis)	7h 35m 30s
Exhibitionism	5h 53m 47s
Vaginal penetration, by man, with penis (doggy style)	5h 40m 46s
Vaginal penetration, by man, with penis (woman on top)	5h 01m 33s
Oral sex on woman by man	4h 45m 27s
Dildo use, handheld	3h 49m 56s
Masturbation (male)	3h 28m 51s
Masturbation (female)	3h 18m 48s
Oral sex on woman by woman	2h 54m 03s
Talking dirty	2h 28m 49s
Intersexed lovemaking	2h 00m 20s
Nipple stimulation	1h 50m 50s
Kissing, man and woman	1h 16m 32s
Hand job by a woman	1h 16m 29s
Breast rubbing	1h 13m 37s
Rubbing of area around vagina without penetration	1h 07m 17s
Vaginal penetration, by man, with penis (missionary position)	1h 05m 49s
Rubbing of body other than those areas specified elsewhere	1h 04m 32s

On the other hand, at least they are experiencing a wide and interesting variety of sexual acts. Some people worry that sex is all about vaginal penetration—men's favoured mode of sexual practice. As Andrea Dworkin puts it, in pornography, 'Sex, a word potentially so inclusive and evocative, is whittled down ... so that in fact, it means penile intromission'. And, as 1970s feminism argued, penis-in-vagina sex often isn't the best kind for giving women orgasms.

If pornography only showed that kind of sex, then we could say that it was focused more on male pleasure than female pleasure. But it turns out that there is quite a range of sexual acts in pornography. The researchers counted how long the actors did each of them in every video, and then we added up everything that went on for a total of more than one hour over the fifty best-selling videos (see previous page).

So there is, indeed, plenty of 'penile intromission' in the vagina. We divided this up into a number of different categories because different positions are generally regarded as giving more or less pleasure to women. The missionary position—woman on her back, man lying on top—is generally believed to give the least clitoral stimulation and thus the least direct sexual pleasure to women. The doggy style (women on all fours, man entering from behind) and the woman on top are generally regarded as giving much more direct sexual pleasure to women.

The variations on the 'penis in vagina' theme make up three of the top ten most popular sexual acts. The top act, far and away the most popular with a staggering eighteen hours in the fifty videos, is the 'other' category. This includes the innovative and exciting sexual positions that pornography seems to be so good at, and that would break your back if you tried them in real life: the woman's legs on the man's shoulders, the woman on the side with one leg in the air, and so on. The second most popular variant is doggy style, and the third is the woman on top. The missionary position, which offers women the least sexual pleasure, ends up right down the list at number nineteen.

It's encouraging to see that the amount of time devoted to male and female masturbation in these videos is roughly equal, with only ten minutes between them. Feminists have long encouraged women to masturbate as a way of learning to enjoy their own sexuality, and it's good to see pornography joining in this campaign. It's also good to see the range of non-penetrative behaviours that pornography portrays, including nipple stimulation and kissing.

On the other hand, we note that when it comes to oral sex, things are much less fair. Women spend more than fifteen hours giving oral pleasure to men; in return, men give only four and three-quarter hours of oral pleasure to women.

Finally, we looked at whether pornography was giving a realistic picture of what kinds of sex acts might actually lead to orgasms. Female characters had 142 orgasms in the sample of videos. The top cause of orgasms was penis penetration of the vagina (28 per cent of orgasms); most of these were in the category of 'other' positions (11 per cent), then doggy style (9 per cent) and woman on top (6 per cent). Only 2 per cent of female orgasms in mainstream pornography were caused by missionary position sex. Far more common were female orgasms caused by masturbation (23 per cent) and oral sex (16 per cent). Also popular was anal penetration (8 per cent).

Do masturbation and oral sex cause more female orgasms than the missionary position? You can judge for yourself if porn videos are accurately representing female pleasure.

Male characters had 635 orgasms in the films analysed. The top cause here was masturbation (38 per cent), and there's a reason for this. Porn videos are traditionally very keen on the 'money shot', where you actually see the man coming. This guarantees that you are watching real, not simulated, sex. So even when men are having penetrative sex, they will usually pull out for the final orgasm. Knowing that this was the case, we specifically told the researchers that if the man pulled out and then quickly 'finished himself off', that should not be counted as masturbation. But if the men pulled out and then masturbated before they finally came, masturbation it is. Vaginal penetration caused 33 per cent of male orgasms—23 per cent in 'other' positions, 6 per cent doggy style, 2 per cent with the woman on top and 2 per cent in the missionary position. The other popular causes of male orgasms are the anal penetration of women (12 per cent), blow jobs by women (8 per cent) and hand jobs by women (7 per cent).

What does all this research and number-crunching tell us?

First, that pornography pays more attention to women's pleasure than some people think. It's far from perfect, but it does show women as active sexual agents, not just as passive sexual objects. They initiate sex and talk to other characters and the camera. Mainstream pornography in Australia also includes female sexual pleasure, such as female orgasms and sexual acts designed to give women pleasure. There just aren't enough female orgasms, and there isn't enough oral sex performed on women by men.

Based on our research, pornography does not really objectify women more than men. Physically, there was a tendency towards younger, slimmer women. There was also a tendency for men to be muscular, but it wasn't as strong. However, when it came to other sexual characteristics, it was definitely the other way around—women can have small breasts, but men are definitely not allowed to have small penises. Videos were equally narrated from the points of view of female and male characters, who got to talk in the videos at roughly equal rates. However, in terms of taking on the 'hosting' role and talking to the camera, women did this much more. Women also initiated sex more than men. There was even a much wider range of sexual acts than some writers have anticipated, many of them designed to give women pleasure; it wasn't all 'penile intromission'. However, women are still getting far fewer orgasms than men—and a lot less oral sex.

Overall, it's about half and half. On some measures, men are the more active sexual subjects in pornography; on others, it's the women.

The Internet

The main focus of our research was on mainstream pornographic videos because that is what the majority of consumers still use. But the internet is also important, and it's the medium that many people are worried about.

Videos and DVDs in Australia have a classification system, but the internet isn't censored in the same way. The *Broadcasting Services Amendment (Online Services) Act 1999* came into force on 1 January 2000, making it illegal for any Australian server to carry any X-rated material. But this system is more of a public relations exercise than anything else. It isn't proactive. The OFLC only acts when a complaint is made by a member of the public, and there aren't that many complaints about X-rated material on Australian servers—in the whole of 2005, for example, only seventeen complaints about this were made. Secondly, the internet is a global system. If a company does have their Australian webpage closed down, they can just move all of the material to a server in a different country.

So what kind of material is available on the internet?

One key concern in public debate is child pornography. This is a big issue, one that is separate from that of mainstream pornography consumption, and so we've devoted a chapter to the issue of children and pornography in this book (see Chapter 7). Child pornography isn't what most Australian consumers are looking at, so what kinds of mainstream images are available on the internet? What kinds of sexually explicit images are people consuming online?

Sextracker.com is a popular adult links site, with more than 46 million unique visitors every day. It provides links to tens of thousands of pornographic websites around the world, all rated and sorted into categories—'Asian', 'Amateur', 'Fetish', 'Free', 'Gay', 'Hardcore', 'Hetero', 'Lesbian', 'Other', 'Softcore' and 'Teen'. It has a 'Top Sites' function that lets you see the most popular sites. This is the mainstream of internet pornography, the sites that people are choosing to visit.

The top five links are to similar links websites (which in turn link you to other links websites; which link you to other …). But in terms of sites with actual content, the most popular pornographic pages on the internet are those belonging to amateur sites—four out of the top twenty, the largest single category of content. Number six in the top twenty is Southern Charms, the 'largest amateur site in the world' (www.southern-charms.com/sc-main.html), which gets more than 16 million page views per day. The site's introduction is, indeed, charming:

> Southern Charms provides amateur girls from all around the world the opportunity to have their own website … Southern Charms

prides itself on being a very clean site. We do not lie, cheat or steal from our customers. We do not provide images that are illegal. You will not find any obscene material at all on Southern Charms. You will only find clean adult amateur fun.

Mainstream pornography on the internet reflects mainstream values:

> All of our models are licensed and we have model releases on file for each and every one. You will not find any underage models at Southern Charms. Please rest assured that if someone communicates to us that they are interested in underage pictures of models, we will report it to the appropriate authorities immediately.

And the site's owners are keen to emphasise the amateur nature of their models: 'The collection of ladies we have are of all ages, and are from all parts of the World. Each girl on SC is REAL, and has been verified as being a real person'.

When you visit the page showing all of the women who have posted their pictures on the site (www.southern-charms.com/ALL-mainfull.html), you are immediately struck by the sheer range of women represented. The main photo of 'AbbeyLynn' shows her bending over, her generous buttocks ripe with cellulite. Her main page says:

> Over the past three and a half years, I have had the experience of many emails from my members and fans and meeting a few of you!! Thank you all for sticking by me and encouraging me to express myself while having lots of fun!! Without all of you, I wouldn't be here!

'Heidi' is more traditionally pretty, slim, with long blonde hair. But on her home page she writes: 'I never thought I was pretty enough to be seen as a model. I hope you love the photos as much as I loved having them done'. By contrast, 'Libby UK' looks like a grandmother, and writes: 'Welcome to my web-site. My name is Libby and I am a cuddly 69 year old who, with your help, is growing old disgracefully'.

As a completely mainstream internet pornography site, this is perhaps not what you might expect: a range of body types, women speaking for themselves, and a strong emphasis on amateurs exposing themselves for their own pleasure. The other amateur sites in the top twenty are Your Amateur Porn (number eleven), Amateur's Homepage (fifteen), and Amateur Movies (twenty).

The other kind of content sites that appear in the Sextracker .com top twenty are age-specific. There are three of these, and we found it interesting that two focus on young women and one focuses on 'mature' women.

Youngleaf's Gallery (www.youngleafs.com/index.shtml) is number thirteen in the top twenty. It offers the 'latest and greatest teen pics daily'. Teeniefiles (www.teeniefiles.com/main.htm) is number seventeen: 'Your home for the hottest 18+ chicks on the net'. But above the latter, at number sixteen, is Mia Matures (www.miamatures.com). This site focuses on older women, with photo captions such as 'Cock sucking mom to be takes a full length!' and 'Mature woman fucks her daughters [sic] hot boyfriend in her room'.

In the sites specialising both in younger and older women, there is a different attitude towards the material from that found in the amateur sites. The language is noticeably less respectful. Youngleaf's Gallery claims that the women on it are 'banged to the very limits of what [they] could take'. On Mia Matures there are 'positive' captions such as 'Gorgeous mom fucking' and neutral ones such as 'Older lady fucked by horny young guy', but there are also captions that use unpleasant language: 'Older blonde whore doing younger guy'; 'Mature plumper poked by sons [sic] friend'. The recurring themes of the site, however, are 'Some things get better with age' and 'Experience matters'. Even here, the images show women enthusiastically taking part in sexual acts. There is no sign of coercion or passivity and the women are not represented as objects.

We did manage to find some horrible and very upsetting stuff. It certainly does exist and we condemn it outright. But it is very far from being mainstream or dominant.

It takes a bit of work to find the worst material. You can't just Google 'rape pornography'. If you do, you'll be offered antipornography sites that discuss 'Pornography as a cause of rape' (www.dianarussell.com/porntoc.html) and 'The documented effects of pornography' (http://forerunner.com/forerunner/X0388_Effects _of_Pornograp.html). In the end, we typed 'rape' into the Sextracker .com search function. Nine websites came up after a search of several tens of thousands of listings.

It's worth saying that despite extensive efforts, we didn't manage to find any photographs of real rapes on pornographic sites on the internet—literally, none at all, though there is some horrible faked stuff. Most of the websites we found make it explicit that they are offering 'fantasy' rape situations, with captions telling you that you're looking at actors performing these scenes. But we did find one genuinely disturbing site, which pretended to be showing real rapes. It's clear when you look at the photos that these scenes are faked. But there are none of the disclaimers about 'fantasy' that are offered on other sites, the closest thing to this being the small print at the bottom of the home page stating that 'All models are over 18 years of age'. There is a commitment to naturalism here that is really disturbing. Some of the photographs are hideous, even showing what appears to be blood as women are raped. Even if the rapes are not real, the pleasure that is offered to the viewers is—they are invited to take pleasure in imagining that the rapes are real.

This material clearly exists. But it's not the mainstream; it is not what the vast majority of consumers of pornography access on the internet. We managed to find nine sites with faked rapes, and not a single pornographic site showing real photographs of rapes. By contrast, there are hundreds of thousands of sites on the internet that show people enjoying sex. And the most popular of those are amateur sites, whose very ethos is that the people involved appear on them because they enjoy it.

What Consumers Like

Contrary to the popular conception of mainstream porn in Australia, it does not comprise rapes, other sexual violence, or child abuse material. Yes, it's possible to find these things if you look really hard—although we found no evidence of real rape pornography on the internet, and no child pornography on the popular websites. But for Australians who consume some form of sexually explicit material, that's not what they're looking at. In the best-selling porn videos that represent the mainstream of the genre, more than 98 per cent of the material is clearly free from any kind of violence. We've come a long way from the 1970s, when critics claimed that pornography could be defined as a genre that showed rapes and other violence against women. On the internet, the most popular mainstream sites are amateur sites that show average women as being sexually attractive, and where viewers are meant to be turned on by the fact that these women are not only consenting but are doing it for their own pleasure.

If you haven't consumed much pornography yourself, this might be a bit surprising to you. Given that this is the mainstream, why have so many commentators been so unhappy about pornography over the years?

So that's what's in porn. But what effect is pornography having on consumers? Are the women consuming pornography, for example, likely to develop negative attitudes towards other women because of the sexually explicit material they're consuming? This question of effect is one we examine in the next chapter.

4

Does Pornography Cause Masturbation?
The Effects of Exposure to Porn

We can all reel off the negative effects that porn might—or might not—have. It might turn men into rapists, it might destroy relationships, lead to addiction, it might make people objectify women ...

But what are some of the possible positive effects?

Are there none?

And if you think that there aren't any, how do you know that? Is there some research that's explored possible positive effects and found they don't exist?

We know for a fact that there isn't any research like that because researchers have never even bothered asking. Researchers have always started from the assumption that pornography has no positive effects—without evidence for that assumption—and then based their research on that.

When we surveyed more than 1000 Australian consumers of pornography, we asked them, 'What effect has pornography had on your attitudes towards sexuality?' Only 7 per cent said it had a negative effect, while 59 per cent said it had a positive effect. (The rest said it had no effect.)

The knee-jerk response is to say that porn consumers would say that. But does this tally with what smokers say about smoking (most want to quit) or what fast-food consumers (the great majority of us) think about the nutritional benefits of fast food? Most of the time, most people know when something is bad for them, even if they keep going back for more. To put this another way, if we routinely trust empirical studies on what other consumers say about their consumption habits, then it makes sense to think that pornography consumers, who represent one-third of all Australians, have at least the same degree of insight into theirs.

What 'Studies Have Shown'

If you read or listen to the media, you'll know some of the negative effects that commentators claim are caused by exposure to pornography:

- Pornography turns people into rapists.
- Pornography makes people believe that women should be treated as sex objects.
- Pornography turns people into paedophiles and even child murderers.
- Pornography creates unrealistic expectations of sex and thus puts people off having real relationships.
- Pornography makes people commit non-sexual violent crimes.
- Pornography gets people addicted and destroys their lives.

So is it true that 'studies have shown' that pornography has these negative effects? The simple answer is 'no'—but things are never that simple.

Since the 1970s, social scientists have been interested in the possible negative effects of pornography, particularly whether pornography causes rape, or causes its users to have negative attitudes towards women. They have used four main kinds of studies to try to find out how powerful these negative effects are (though never even considering the possibility that there might be any positive effects from exposure to pornography):

- aggregate studies
- laboratory experiments

- sex offender studies
- surveys.

In aggregate studies, researchers compare how much pornography is sold in any given society with its reported levels of sex crimes, particularly rape, to see if there is any correlation. Most social scientists have now given up doing these kinds of studies because of confusion over what they do or don't prove. They never really gave us much useful information anyway. Some aggregate studies suggest that in societies where pornographic material is more readily available, rates of reported rape drop, or rise less quickly than other forms of crime. But other studies suggest that there is a correlation between the availability of pornography and rape rates. Not only are the results contradictory, but there are problems with the basic assumptions of this research. It assumes that the people consuming pornography are the same people who are committing sex crimes. But this assumption is never proved.

Laboratory experiments are the most interesting ones for these public debates because some social scientists have managed to produce negative effects from exposure to violent pornography in laboratories. In these experimental studies, researchers expose subjects to violent pornography and then measure changes in their aggressiveness and attitudes towards women. The results of this research are also contradictory.

We should note that most researchers agree that viewing non-violent pornography does not produce negative effects, although a couple disagree on this. So when people claim that 'studies' have shown negative effects of exposure to pornography, they're talking very specifically about violent pornography—the kind that's illegal in Australia, and which accounts for only a tiny minority of the material that people are viewing on the internet (see Chapter 3), and which the consumers of pornography overwhelmingly say that they don't like anyway (see Chapter 2).

But even in regard to violent pornography, the results are confusing. Some researchers have managed to produce negative effects in consumers from viewing violent pornography in laboratory experiments. These include increased tendencies to aggression against women; an increased acceptance of violence against women in general and rape in particular; an acceptance of rape myths; the production of rape fantasies; an increase in the self-nominated likelihood to commit rape; and decreased support for women's rights.

But it's not that simple. Other researchers have been unable to replicate these results, finding that when they show the same kinds of pornography to the same kinds of people, they haven't produced the same negative effects.

And to confuse things even more, the results of the other kinds of studies suggest the opposite—that consumers of pornography do not have worse attitudes towards women.

For example, in the third kind of study—the sex offender study—researchers interview subjects who have committed sex crimes (including, though not always limited to, rape) to find out about the offenders' exposure to pornographic materials. These studies have consistently shown that rapists tend to use less pornography than control groups and that, on average, they come from more sexually repressed backgrounds and are exposed to pornography at a later age. It's the opposite of what you'd expect if the consumption of pornography caused rape. It looks more like sexually repressed backgrounds cause rape.

When we look at the fourth kind of study, the survey, we find different information again. There is agreement among researchers that surveys of actual consumers of pornography prove that these consumers have attitudes towards women that are the same as, or often better than, the population generally.

How do we explain this? If the sex offender studies and the surveys show that pornography doesn't cause negative attitudes towards women in the real world, then how is it that scientists can sometimes produce such negative effects in the laboratory?

One possible explanation, to use social science jargon, is that there may be 'mediating factors' that haven't yet been identified. For example, it might be that there are only particular kinds of violent pornography that cause aggression, or it might be an effect of the amount of pornography shown, or be dependent on whether there is a story-line or not, and so on. We're not convinced by this argument, though, as nobody's provided any proof. So it's best to use the principle of Occam's razor—choose the simplest possible explanation that fits the facts.

In this case, we think that the simplest possible explanation involves the way that the laboratory experiments are conducted. In these experiments, the people who are shown pornography are not consumers of pornography; or rather, they may be, but they're not asked, so many of them probably aren't. They are usually college students, who don't know what the experiments are about. Some of them may like pornography. Others might hate it. Others might never have seen it before.

By contrast, in the real world, the vast majority of people who consume pornography do it because they want to. They enjoy it and it gives them pleasure. Obviously people who see it by accident, or who are forced to watch it in abusive situations, are going to have very different reactions to it. The 'subjects' who are exposed to pornography in laboratories are not watching it, as people do in the real world, for pleasure.

In laboratory experiments, the viewers are shown, without knowing what they're going to see, material that many of them find upsetting or distressing, including violent pornography.

In the real world, consumers choose what kinds of pornography they are going to watch. If they like seeing idealised bodies having loving sex in candlelit scenes, then they will choose a couples porn video that suits that. If they want to see rough sex in a dark alley, then they will choose that.

These are key points because even the scientists who have managed to produce negative effects from exposure to pornography admit that it only works on people who don't usually watch pornography. The scientists have found that people who are familiar with and enjoy pornography don't get upset or aggressive when they are exposed to it.

There are other differences as well. In laboratories, the subjects are shown pornography in public. They are usually in university settings, surrounded by other test subjects and social scientists.

In the real world, when people watch pornography they tend to do it in situations where they are either alone or with people they feel sexually comfortable with (as we saw in Chapter 2). Imagine watching pornography with your mother sitting beside you and think about how anxious that might make you feel. It's not how it happens in the real world.

In the experiments, the people exposed to pornography have to watch it for extended periods, sometimes for up to an hour.

In the real world, it is not uncommon for people to fast-forward to the bits they like, and only watch short segments. A full hour watching a porn video would be a marathon for many people.

In the experiments, the people watching the porn are not allowed to masturbate.

This is somewhat different from the real world, where pornography and masturbation go together like a BBQ and a beer—you can't have one without the other. In fact, there's a case for arguing that, in the real world, the main effect of exposure to pornography is masturbation. In which case, can you imagine sitting for an hour watching pornography, in a room full of potentially intimidating strangers, in a situation where you are not meant to get sexually aroused? It's not as though pornography is renowned for its story-lines, acting, cinematography or music. There's not much there to distract you. If you're not getting any sexual pleasure out of it, you'd get pretty bored apart from anything else.

The reason that laboratory experiments can sometimes produce negative effects, while sex offender studies and surveys show that these effects don't happen in the real world, is because the experiments miss the basic purpose of pornography for consumers—it's used for pleasure. In the real world, people watch pornography that they like, they masturbate, they have an orgasm. In laboratory experiments, the subjects are exposed to material that they don't necessarily like, for an hour, in a room full of strangers, with their hands firmly on the table where everyone can see them. It's a common belief that after having an orgasm, men fall asleep. In most cases, they don't get hyper and excited; quite the opposite, in fact. But we would imagine that after an hour of mixing boredom with sexual tension in a room full of test subjects and social scientists, with no release at the end, it's possible that the subjects would become quite stressed.

Australian Survey Results

So what's the situation in Australia? In our survey of more than 1000 consumers of pornography, as well as all of the personal information we discussed in Chapter 2, we also asked the consumers a series of questions designed to test their attitudes towards women.

Once again, the question of how to use numbers comes up. If you want to measure attitudes towards women, how do you decide what to count? There's a very real sense that by the time you've decided what to count, you've already decided what results you're going to get—you've already imposed your own prejudices. For example, one of the most respected researchers of the negative effects of pornography, Professor Dolf Zillmann, claims that pornography increases men's 'sexual callousness' towards women. But when you look at what his experiments measured, the definition of 'sexual callousness' included the belief that casual sex is OK. For example, if a man agreed with the statement, 'That old saying "variety is the spice of life" is particularly true when it comes to sex', then he was counted as having a negative attitude towards women. The same thing happened if agreement was given to the statement: 'You never know when you are going to meet a strange woman who will want to get laid'. This is because Zillmann believes that men should have 'respect' for women, and that pornography 'deglorifies women in the eyes of men'—he calls this a negative effect.

This is obviously a subjective judgement of what is positive and what is negative in gender relations. Many feminists would argue that men shouldn't be putting women on pedestals or 'glorifying' them, and that it's quite OK for women to enjoy casual sex. We discussed this in Chapter 2, where several of the women we interviewed made this point explicitly, saying that they believed that it was sexist when men said that women were not interested in casual sex.

We tried to have our questions cover as wide a range of issues as possible in order to be as objective as possible. We looked at a number of topics that feminism has identified as important: equal pay, women holding positions of authority, women's right to sexual pleasure, access to abortions, the acceptability of rape and the right to a career. We also tried to word our questions in ways that weren't too politically correct—for example, you could never ask people if they agreed with the statement, 'It's OK to rape women'. Very few men would dare to publicly agree with that, no matter what they might personally feel. So we asked instead whether the consumers agreed with the more neutral statement: 'It is acceptable for a woman to stop a sexual encounter at any point, no matter how keen she may have been initially'. The five other statements we asked them about were: 'Women should get equal pay for equal work'; 'Women should have access to abortion on demand'; 'It is acceptable for women to continue to work outside the home after they have children, if they want to'; 'It is acceptable for a woman to be sexually assertive'; and 'I would not mind working with a female boss'. We then used their responses to give each consumer an 'Attitude towards women' score—the higher the score, the better their attitude. Once again, we know that this is simplistic, and that you can't really measure the subtleties of attitudes towards women. This is a limitation of the social science genre, but we have to accept it in order to get a sense of the big picture.

We took the scores and compared them with various pieces of information about the consumers. First, we compared their attitude towards women with the amount of pornography they consumed. If exposure to pornography did create negative attitudes towards women, you would expect to see a relationship—the more pornography consumed, the worse the attitudes towards women.

But this wasn't the case. Statistically speaking, watching more porn doesn't correlate with worse attitudes towards women, according to our comprehensive survey. This isn't a surprise—as we have already discussed, most surveys of porn users in the real world have found the same thing.

However, when we ran some other numbers, we did find some positive correlations. Pornography doesn't cause negative attitudes towards women. But religion does. Atheists had significantly better 'Attitudes towards women' scores (27.3) than Protestant Christians (24.2). Catholics are in the middle, which is surprising given the question about abortion (25.4). Buddhists are almost as positive as atheists (27.1).

So does that mean that exposure to religion causes negative attitudes? Or is there some other relationship? It's funny how even asking the question sounds stupid—how can you reduce the complexity of somebody's religious beliefs and practices to a simple equation? But that's what 'studies' of pornography and attitudes towards women do all the time. However, we won't do that. We wouldn't say that exposure to religion 'causes' negative attitudes towards women. But there is a correlation there. We will leave it up to other researchers to explore what that relationship might be and how we might combat any possible negative effects of religion on attitudes to women.

Remember—although this sounds odd, these are genuine results. There is a statistically significant correlation between having religious beliefs and having a negative attitude towards women.

Other correlations we found included that men as a group had worse attitudes towards women than women had towards each other (26.1 to 27.6).

Age had a bearing too. The older the person was, the worse their attitudes towards women (23.8 for the oldest group, aged sixty-six and over; 27.1 for those under eighteen). The younger generation has better attitudes towards women than their elders.

People with less formal education had significantly worse attitudes towards women. People who had completed only primary education had the worst score as a group (22.5), while those with postgraduate degrees had among the best (27.1).

The place that you live has an effect too. People living in rural areas had worse attitudes towards women (25.3) and those living in inner urban areas had the best (27.1). The further away from the city centre that you live, the worse your attitudes towards women (except for people in remote areas, who actually had better scores than anybody except those living in the inner cities).

Political inclinations made a significant statistical difference. One Nation voters had the worst attitudes towards women, then Coalition voters, then Labor voters, then Democrats voters. People who voted for the Greens had the most positive attitudes towards women. There's a correlation between voting for a right-wing party and having a bad attitude towards women.

Our studies show that although it is possible in laboratory experiments to use pornography to create negative attitudes towards women (that is, using people who don't as a rule use porn), in the real world there are no such effects. But our own research has also suggested that there are some very real culprits out there, correlated with bad attitudes. We wouldn't be so simplistic as to claim that exposure to right-wing political parties causes negative attitudes towards women. But there is some kind of link there and it would certainly be worth exploring.

The Positive Effects of Pornography

One of the interesting things about 'studies' is that they have never asked the consumers of pornography what they thought the effects on them have been. It seemed to us that even if we don't take everything that people say on face value, it would still be interesting to find out from consumers what their experiences have been with pornography.

As we discussed at the start of this chapter, we asked the 1023 consumers that we surveyed, 'What effect has pornography had on your attitudes towards sexuality?'. We asked them to tick one box for either 'A large negative effect', 'A small negative effect', 'No effect at all', 'A small positive effect' or 'A large positive effect'. If they said it had an effect, we asked them to 'provide brief details'. The results were that 1 per cent of respondents felt that pornography had a large negative effect on their attitudes towards sexuality; 6 per cent thought it had a small negative effect; 35 per cent thought it had no effect; 31 per cent thought it had a small positive effect; and 26 per cent thought it had a large positive effect.

It's worth taking a moment just to think about this. How spectacularly wrong have researchers got this issue?

The entire tradition of research into pornography has investigated possible negative effects. The results account for the experiences of 7 per cent of consumers of pornography.

The other 93 per cent of consumers of pornography don't feel that they've experienced any negative effects.

Some critics of our project have said that we can't trust these numbers, because people who have really negative experiences with pornography would be less likely to complete our survey. We're not entirely sure about the logic of that argument but we're happy to consider their percentages—what percentage of porn users do *they* think have positive experiences from using it? If they don't have any figures, we'd expect them to do some research and come up with some before claiming that ours are wrong.

We mentioned above that researchers have shown very little interest in researching the actual consumers of pornography, but have tended to do laboratory experiments on non-consumers. Now we can begin to understand why this has been the case. If they ever did ask consumers about the place of pornography in their lives, they would find that the entire research tradition has been looking in the wrong place.

It also explains why some media commentators who have discussed the research we've made public in earlier stages of this project have responded by claiming that pornography consumers clearly don't understand their own minds or that our sample is unrepresentative. The problem for commentators who believe that the subject of pornography is cut and dried and that no more correspondence needs to be entered into, is that if we actually researched porn consumers in a scientific manner, we'd be forced to re-open the debate. We'd be forced to ask, 'What *are* all of the possible effects of exposure to pornography?' Then we would have to test them all—the positive as well as the negative. That would be a rather different approach to what allegedly has been a closed issue.

So what are some of the possible effects? There's been no systematic research into the possible positive effects of pornography. The closest we could find were a few throwaway comments in studies into other issues: pornography might provide gay men and lesbians with the only representations they see of other people like themselves, and the only validation of their sexual urges; it might challenge restrictive gender roles; and it might provide therapeutic benefits in overcoming shame about sex.

What do the consumers themselves say are the effects that pornography has had on them?

If you look at the table on the next page, you'll see that nine out of the top ten effects reported by the consumers themselves were positive. Only one, at number ten, is a negative effect.

Top Ten Effects of Pornography

Rank	Effect	Percentage of Consumers
1	Makes them more relaxed and comfortable about sex	14%
2	Makes them more open-minded and willing to experiment	10%
3	Makes them more tolerant of other people's sexual pleasures	7%
4	Causes sexual arousal and pleasure	6%
5	Educates them about the mechanics of sex	6%
6	Helps in maintaining a sex life in a long-term relationship	5%
7	Makes them more attentive to partner's pleasure	3%
8	Forms identity and offers reassurance for marginalised sexual groups such as gay men	2%
9	Helps them to talk about sex with partner	2%
10	Causes them to objectify people	2%

By far the most common effect described was that of becoming less repressed and more comfortable about sex. Consumers used expressions like 'relaxed' and being less 'inhibited'. This is one of the possible positive effects that has been mentioned in passing by previous researchers. Second is being more 'open-minded'; consumers also used terms like 'adventurous', in that they were willing to try new things. At number three was an increased tolerance of other people's sexual pleasures; that is, things that they wouldn't enjoy doing themselves but had learned to accept other people doing. The consumers commonly added a phrase like 'so long as no-one gets hurt' to this. At number four we have what seems like an obvious effect of pornography—it causes sexual pleasure. Given that other researchers have found that viewing pornography is commonly accompanied by masturbation, we suspect that the reason this didn't rank higher was simply that people didn't really think of this as an 'effect' of pornography.

At number five, talking about 'education' and 'learning', consumers mentioned basic biological information, such as what a woman looks like naked, as well as techniques and ideas. Number six is an interesting one. Some of our respondents in long-term relationships mentioned how they used pornography for 'spicing up' or introducing 'variety' into their sex lives with their partners. Number seven also goes against some of the stereotypes, with consumers saying that pornography had made them think more about their partner's pleasure, what they could do for them. Number eight was from gay men, lesbians or people who were into bondage or sadomasochism, who said that pornography had shown them that they were not the only people who felt like they did. The genre had helped them to find an identity and a community. Number nine was another example of a social use of pornography, helping consumers to open discussions with their partners about sex.

On this point, it's interesting to see how many of the effects of pornography turn out to be social. The stereotype of pornography is that it isolates people. Mike, sitting alone in his cubicle (see the beginning of Chapter 2), is the stereotype of the man who uses pornography to replace real relationships, who becomes so obsessed or addicted to it that he can no longer deal with real people. But in the real world, it seems that pornography, for many consumers, is part of real relationships—not an alternative to them. Indeed, for many of them, it improves their real relationships.

It is only when we get to number ten in the list of effects that we encounter the first possible negative effect: eighteen people (2 per cent) said that pornography led them to objectify people (using the words 'objects' or 'objectify'). Lower down the list, a tiny number of people also identified other negative effects: sixteen people (2 per cent) said that porn caused them to have 'unrealistic' expectations, both about themselves and about other people's bodies and pleasures; five people (0.5 per cent) said that pornography had caused problems in a relationship; four people (0.5 per cent) found it had led to a loss of interest in real sexual contact; and four others (0.5 per cent) had problems with addiction to pornography.

Of course, we must pay attention to the full range of possible effects—the negative as well as the positive. Just because the number of people who experience negative effects is so much smaller than the number who experience positive effects doesn't mean that those negative effects are unimportant. We take this so seriously that in Chapter 8 we offer practical advice to consumers experiencing such negative effects. But at the same time, we mustn't lose focus. Yes, we mustn't ignore possible negative effects, but we shouldn't over-emphasise them either. When 57 per cent of consumers say that the effects have been positive and only 7 per cent say it has been negative, it makes sense that the major focus of our research should be on the possible positive effects.

We'd like to make one final point about possible negative effects. All three of us teach students about the effects of the media, and there's always one student in the class who says, 'But if even one person could turn into a murderer because of a violent film or turn into a rapist because of pornography, then that's one too many. We can't take that risk'.

The problem is, how reasonable is it in our society to ban everything that could potentially have a negative effect? If even one person might turn into a murderer because of a text, for example, then should we ban it?

On Friday, 29 July 1994, Paul Hill walked up to an abortion clinic in Pensacola, Florida with a shotgun. An elderly doctor, 69-year-old John Britton, had just arrived at work with his wife, June, a retired nurse, and a friend, a 74-year-old man called James Barrett. Hill pulled out his 12-gauge and shot John and James in the head, killing them instantly. June was wounded in the attack.

Hill was not at all repentant for the murders. The Bible made it clear that he was doing the right thing. He had long advocated violence against abortion providers, quoting from the Bible when doing so. 'The Christian principle is to do unto others as you would have them do unto you', he had claimed publicly. 'Whoever shed unborn man's blood by man shall his blood be shed.' (This is derived from Genesis 9:6.) He also said, 'If an abortionist is about to violently take an innocent person's life, you are entirely morally justified in trying to prevent him from taking that life'.

And it's not just a single example we're talking about here. The group Religious Tolerance estimates that since 1989 there have been twenty-four murders or attempted murders of doctors who have provided abortions in the United States, all inspired by the Bible. There have also been 179 bombings or arson attacks on abortion clinics, and several thousand instances of physical attacks, invasions of clinics and vandalism.

That's a lot of violent effects from one book. You might think that we would do well to ban the Bible to avoid these kinds of possible negative effects.

But of course that wouldn't be reasonable. Exposure to the Bible has caused these very negative effects, but the book has positive effects on the overwhelming majority of its users. They find hope and religious comfort in the Bible, and it inspires them to great works of charity and kindness. It helps to build communities.

So we can't argue that just because there is a possible negative effect from something, we should automatically ban it. Maybe you disagree with us and you would like to ban the Bible along with every other text that might possibly have a negative effect on anybody. In this case, we respect your opinions and we agree to disagree. But there's not going to be much left to read in the library.

Consumer Comments on the Effects of Pornography

The consumers that we interviewed for this project had a lot to say about the possible effects of pornography. This was one of the issues that really concerned them.

We were impressed by the sheer variety of responses. Nobody believed that pornography would turn men into rapists: 'The bloody Catholic Church ... reckon, you watch some porno film then you'll go out and rape some girl ... It's bullshit all that. Bullshit'. Some people believed the opposite, that pornography provided sexual release and so made sexual assault less likely: 'Thing is, if you're not getting any, you ain't got a girlfriend, you've got some sort of sexual hang-up with buying a hooker, then you're gonna start exploding if you don't get something'. However, not everyone agreed with that: 'I don't know if it's a valve to let off the pressure. Fine, what pressure? You know, it sounds like we're all a bunch of sexually frustrated people running around who are going to do stupid things if we don't get a root ... Whereas I don't think that's the way it is'.

Several consumers thought that pornography might lead users to see human sexuality in particular ways, but there wasn't agreement on what those ways might be. One consumer suggested that pornography is phallocentric (obsessed with penises): 'Guys just think the cock is the focus, well, intercourse is the focus ... well not all women come that way, so, I wonder whether the porn industry has contributed to those ideas?' Another suggested that pornography might create the 'expectation' that 'men want sex all the time'. She said this wasn't true and that, in fact, 'It's more the other way around [that women want sex all the time]'. A third suggested that pornography creates a misleading view of sex because it doesn't show how difficult, complicated and messy the negotiations involved in the sex act actually are—it makes it look too easy: 'Sometimes it gives me a false notion of people ... my expectation and what other people want are two different things. People say "no" or "piss off" or something like that'. One woman recalled how the sex she saw in pornography while at school failed to represent young men accurately: 'I thought it was really unrealistic and silly ... the way men behave [in porn]. They're so ... commanding and passionate and, especially in high school ... the boys are so not like that. They haven't got a clue what they're doing, so I was looking around the room thinking, "Oh he's impressed. He's never actually had sex"'.

A lot of the consumers we interviewed spoke about pornography being 'educational', showing viewers how to have good sex. One woman, for example, said that pornography correctly 'reinforce[s]' the idea that sex is 'fun and silly'. This was particularly true for marginal sexual identities. One gay man used pornography as a 're-affirmation of my sexual identity ... you don't get in the mainstream media images of blokes sort of getting off, except in *Queer as Folk*, and so we—gay, poof people—are largely invisible in terms of being sexual organisms and sexual identities outside that which is considered aberrant. So porn sort of gives you this erotic charge but also reaffirms you've got this sexual identity involved with another bloke—there's this sexual action you can do'.

One point that we found interesting was that several of the consumers said it doesn't make sense to talk about the 'effect' that pornography has on ideas about sexuality without looking at the wider cultural context, on the effect that other media and institutions such as church, family and education have on attitudes towards sexuality. One woman argued: 'I don't know about the porn so much … I think what is much more influential and much more pervasive is the movies and the television shows … I think that that whole thing where women are supposed to be passive, guys are the ones who are supposed to initiate things, guys are the ones who are supposed to ask you out, and the whole thing of if you're forward sexually then you're a slut … being an aggressive woman isn't a good thing [in film and television]'. One woman who first saw pornography in her teens said: 'I think at that stage there were too many other negative social impacts happening regarding self-image, image of females, what the worth of a girl was, peer pressure about boyfriends, all that crap, for the pornography to make a huge difference to it'. Others noted that they were getting negative effects from other institutional contexts: 'I was going to Sunday school and they were saying, you know, sex is bad and stained, and don't do anything'. For several consumers, encountering pornography had the positive effect of reassuring them that there wasn't something wrong with them because they were interested in sex: 'I think it did give me exploration of, hey, I'm having these feelings, I'm interested in sex, I don't know what's out there, and seeing these images and going, "Oh, this is how people get off!"'

Perhaps the most idiosyncratic effect of pornography in our group of consumers was that one older gentlemen learned to read French: 'I got a copy of the *Kama Sutra*. It was in French and it was in the State Library … but I had no knowledge of French so I taught myself French and in three months I translated the book; that was why I learnt French in the first place, and subsequently I translated several other books from French into English'.

Several researchers have pointed out that in debates about the effects of media, people who worry about media violence and so on are usually worried that it will have an effect on *somebody else*, never on themselves. This was also true with our interviewees. None of them felt they personally had experienced a negative effect from consuming pornography, but some thought that pornography could have a negative effect on other people. Three of the women we spoke to, who were comfortable about the place of pornography in their own lives, worried about the effects it might have on men—that it might 'stir up' men or give them unrealistic expectations. A few of the consumers worried that pornography might have a negative effect on mentally ill people who are 'confused between the barriers of fantasy and reality', or on virgins who didn't have any real experiences to compare it with, or on people with addictive personalities, or on people with conservative social views who 'think that a woman's place is in the kitchen'.

But they didn't think that the possibility of these people being negatively affected justified banning all pornography: '0.1 per cent of people in the country … may respond to that, but the other 99.9 per cent of us have to deal with [the resulting censorship] … just on the off chance that, you know, someone may react badly to it'.

Having said that, none of the consumers that we interviewed believed in 'anything goes'. They all had views on the importance of classification and controlling the circulation of pornography. When we asked consumers the questions 'Do you think that pornography is a problem in our society?' and 'Do you think that it should be restricted?', many of them spontaneously made a distinction between good pornography and harmful pornography. The key word that kept coming up—ten of the people we spoke to used it—was 'consent'. As we noted in Chapter 2, consumers identified consent as an important part of what they enjoyed in pornography, and here they also argued that it was important in terms of pornography's effects.

Thirteen interviewees specifically said that pornography shouldn't show 'rape' or 'violence', and many of the consumers spontaneously identified other kinds of pornography that they thought were unacceptable and should be censored. Although we didn't ask specifically about child pornography, fifteen of the interviewees spontaneously brought this up and said it should be illegal.

They discussed these things as political issues, rather than from their own personal experiences: 'I guess … violence would be a problem [in pornography] but I have never seen any ... you see some spanking videos, but nothing, you know, with a lot of force. But that's about as close to the violence that I've seen on video ... wowsers and the Christian types, they say it's [violent pornography] out there, so I guess it's out there somewhere. But I've never seen it or come across it, and I've seen a lot of videos'. No interviewee had seen child pornography.

We were interested to see that the consumers weren't just being politically correct and saying the right thing. One woman told us how she had actually acted on her beliefs: 'I had a challenge when I worked at [a company], someone in IT there was downloading child pornography movies onto one of our servers ... and they were caught and they managed to talk their way out of it to senior management. I would have thought that was not something you could talk your way out of, saying, "I didn't know what I was doing". And I just thought, "I can't talk to that person, they're a sick bastard and I'm going to make their life a misery". So I went to friends in the police who were in the child protection squad, and thought if management won't do something about it I will'.

Generally, consumers were liberal in their arguments about censorship, saying that apart from rape and child pornography, 'consenting adults' should have the right to view what they wanted in the privacy of 'my own home'. They railed against the nanny state: 'I think that the government has too much say in what I want to see ... I don't need to be spoon-fed or babysat and if I want to see it then that's my decision'. As another consumer put it, 'Get the fuck out of our bedrooms'.

There was a general distrust of public officials and 'bloody politicians'. One consumer argued: 'There are not people on the censorship board looking at adult material who are either young or sexually diverse or involved in the adult industry, in the sex industry ... it's not a realistic cross-section of Australian society at all and so you've got conservative kinds of people who are always going to object, trying to tell people who are not like that what they want to watch; it's ridiculous'. Another said: 'You do get sort of offended by the fact that these people are making judgements

... I mean, why don't they ring me up? I'll go up there and be a censor. It wouldn't worry me ... it's like I said to my wife, where do these people get these qualifications from? What do I have to do to get that? Shouldn't I, as an avid watcher of DVDs and VCRs, be as qualified as what they are? There are movies that I will not watch. I'll put them on, I'll just look at the quality, look at *one* scene and I'll be like, "That's not good enough"'.

As we have noted, these consumers insisted that we need some form of censorship: 'You've got to have a censorship system there ... we need laws and regulations [or] people out there would be beating each other up, killing each other, doing whatever they want. There's got to be some restriction there to keep society in place'. And they were not anarchists: 'We need the police. The police are our saviour in Australia'. One consumer said: 'I'm not saying there should be a free love, "Let's talk about everything" sort of mentality, but there ... should be ... a middle ground'. There was agreement among consumers that restrictions should apply to rape materials and child pornography.

In discussing the effects of pornography and the need for censorship, consumers were well aware that the media tend to focus on the negative side of pornography. One woman noted: 'I think there is too much focus on the *ab*normal person who takes pornography use too far and ... uses pornography to shield their own violence or abnormal sexual behaviours. And I don't think the media focuses on ... the fact that there are a *lot* of people who ... *don't* take it to that degree and use porn as a regular, normal and healthy part of their own sex lives'. Another noted that the media focus on 'pedophilia—I don't know of anyone I've associated with who's ever been into that. And I don't know of anyone who has any time for or derives enjoyment from watching torture'. Another noted: 'The only time I hear it or see it in the newspaper they take the extreme, like trannie sex or bondage stuff. They just head straight to the extreme stuff and then say that because of that they should ban everything'. One man noted: 'I do think that it's put up as the scapegoat for a lot of problems ... you'll see how men get arrested for other things and it's like, "Well, he had a room full of pornography", and I think that's completely irrelevant. You know, if he had a room full of butterfly collections it wouldn't get mentioned because they don't think it's relevant'.

The consumers suggested that unrepresentative minority groups tend to drive the media debate: 'I think small but vocal minority groups jump up and down and go, "It's wrong, this is nasty, this is naughty", and get an awful lot of airplay and get an awful lot of media time and people get influenced by them, then you get stuff being censored that wouldn't normally be censored … They say that they are representing Australian families but you don't represent me, thank you very much'. In particular, they noted that religious groups tend to drive this debate, which is ironic given, as we saw in Chapter 2, how many consumers of pornography are religious. As one religious porn user said, 'God gave us glorious gorgeous bodies and we should enjoy them. The pornography part probably doesn't relate too well with the whole religion thing but sometimes one just goes, "Okay, yeah, that's part of my life that doesn't really fit in with the whole religious part"'.

Several of the consumers we spoke to also noted that because of the media focus on the negative aspects of pornography, and the fact that you never hear users of pornography quoted in the media, they had to live 'in the closet' about the fact that they used sexually explicit material. One said that it was hard 'to come out and say, "Yes, I advocate pornography", because that would make people think, "eeeu, you're dirty"'. Perhaps because of this, many porn consumers mentioned that they had formed social groups with like-minded people. Again, this social aspect of pornography doesn't fit in with the stereotype of it destroying real relationships and isolating people.

We will now turn our attention to what is perhaps the key argument about pornography in contemporary Australia.

As we noted in Chapter 1, arguments about pornography tend to change over time. In pre-modern Europe, material was censored because it offended God. In the nineteenth century the key worry was that it could corrupt the working classes. In the latter part of the twentieth century, it was the potential for causing violence against women that most concerned people. In twenty-first century Australia, we think that the most important debate is about the potentially negative effects that pornography might have on children. (We have devoted Chapter 7 to the discussion of this danger.)

This was an issue that the consumers of pornography that we interviewed felt very strongly about. There was absolute agreement among consumers that, 'obviously, it should be restricted for children, that's a given'. They thought that younger people 'might get the wrong idea and use it out of context … they might not know how to handle it'. One interviewee condemned companies who use pornographic pop-ups on computers: 'The problems I do have with pornography is when companies peddling it on the Web have it set up in such a way so that once, shall we say, a father, aged over eighteen, mature and responsible, makes his own decision and looked at pornography … the next thing you know anyone who opens the computer gets pornographic pop-ups left right and centre. That's not good'.

Several consumers were also concerned about what they saw as a double standard in Australian censorship, where people, including children, are allowed to see violence but not sex. As one person put it, 'I think … [the higher] the amount of violence and blood and gore and anti-social behaviour, the higher the rating … I would much rather my children saw naked people than dead people'. Several of the consumers we spoke to were mums and dads, and they talked about how they protect their own children from pornography. They said that it should be the parents' responsibility: 'Parents are the ones who have to do the censoring. And by doing that they have to educate their children before they hit that stage, on what's right and what's wrong'. One woman, who said that she made sure her daughter didn't find explicit material on the internet, said: 'No-one wants to take responsibility for themselves, everybody wants to blame someone else … if your child accesses pornography, it's not the internet's fault, or pornography's fault, I think it's your fault. You should make sure that you take the steps so that doesn't happen'.

These mums and dads all had strategies in place to make sure that their children didn't find their pornography. One woman explained: 'We have a rule where there is a time and place … If it's [pornography] going to be put on, it's going to be put on after they've gone to bed, and they don't get up. If my daughter gets up to go to the toilet, it's "Goodnight Elizabeth, go back to bed" …. Or else the TV gets turned off. You know, we can always rewind the video'. Another male interviewee described a similar strategy: 'I've got two sons … they are in and out of the room all the time. But we've got other TV rooms so they don't come into my room when they know there is a law. After eight o'clock, that's mum and dad's room and we sit there and relax … we've hidden them [pornographic tapes] and … they're all under lock and key and the kids have got no access because they don't know where the key is'. One consumer said that he has Net Nanny on his computer and he doesn't view internet pornography: 'Because of my kids'. Another went so far as to say: 'I won't let them [my kids] go on the internet … I'm just too scared that it's [pornography] going to come up'. Taking an alternative approach, one woman explained that there was material she didn't want her daughter to see, and she discussed this with her: 'There are certain things I prefer her not to look at and I've said that to her and I've said … "I'd just rather you didn't look at this particular area yet" … And I haven't said she can't, I've said, "I'd prefer you not to", and we talk about it on that level'.

These consumers are typical—they are very much concerned about the dangers that pornography might pose to children.

An Alternative Approach to the Effects of Porn

The main possible effect of exposure to pornography, everybody would agree, is masturbation. Beyond that, researchers often seem to end up asking the wrong questions. In the real world, consumers of pornography have attitudes towards women that are at least as good as, and maybe better than, the attitudes of the general population. There are other aspects of social life—religion, politics, education—that seem to have a stronger correlation with negative attitudes towards women. Additionally, 93 per cent of consumers of pornography report no negative effects.

Yet the entire tradition of social science research into pornography has started from the assumption that porn is a major cause of negative attitudes towards women, and has then set out to prove this. In laboratories, by showing pornography to people who don't normally watch it, and by ignoring the fact that pornography in the real world is used for pleasure, some scientists have managed to produce negative results from exposure to pornography.

Meanwhile, in the real world, consumers tell us that pornography has made them more relaxed and comfortable, more tolerant and open-minded. It has given them pleasure and improved their relationships. And they are not hopeless dupes who are thoughtlessly pro-pornography. They are very clear. Rape pornography is unacceptable to them. Child pornography is unacceptable to them. And pornography shouldn't be available to children.

This raises an interesting point that hasn't been much considered in public debate: is there a difference between good pornography and bad pornography? Is it possible, for example, to have feminist pornography? We consider this question in the next chapter.

PART II

Current Issues and Debates

5

On Our Backs
Feminist Pornography
Then and Now

In 2005, New York journalist Ariel Levy received considerable attention for her book *Female Chauvinist Pigs: Women and the Rise of Raunch Culture*. In it, Levy describes what she terms 'the female chauvinist pig' who is, according to the back cover blurb, 'the new "empowered woman" who wears the Playboy bunny as a talisman, pursues casual sex as if it were a sport, and takes off her bra to win favour from the boys'.

On the one hand, Levy acknowledged that feminists have actively participated in the sex industry for many years not only as performers, but also as producers. On the other, she condemned the 'porno-chic' culture of sexual exhibitionism as an artificial, inauthentic form of sexual expression for women. Her opening case study, the reality soft-porn series *Girls Gone Wild*, certainly seems to be an example of unethical media production (for an explanation of *why* we say this, see the discussion of ethics in Chapter 8). The series producers travel to resort bars and beaches, inviting young women to flash and/or simulate solo or group sex for their cameras. The participants are unpaid but are rewarded with branded clothing, and, as Levy admits, while some participants seem to be subject to 'peer pressure', there's no shortage of young women volunteers. Certainly, in Levy's description, the *Girls Gone Wild* producers come across as exploiters. One tells Levy that the aim is to attract not 'girls-next-door' but 'tens', who are described as '100–110 pounds, big boobs, blonde, blue eyes, ideally no piercing or tattoos'.

In the face of what seems to be nothing more than a repackaging of good old-fashioned commodification of female sexuality, it would seem unlikely to claim that feminism has had a real impact on the way porn is made, distributed and used. But that is what we want to explore in this chapter. Picking up on the case of the *Debbies* that we discussed in Chapter 3, is it possible that feminism has actually had some impact on pornography? Could *Girls Gone Wild* actually be evidence of the *success* of feminism, rather than its failure?

We—Alan, Catharine and Kath—all consider ourselves to be entirely pro-feminist. And certainly none of us would argue, as Levy puts it, that 'the feminist project [has] already been achieved', or that misogyny, discrimination and violence are no longer real constraints in women's everyday lives. We know that these are still real problems for women. But we would also argue that pornochic, or raunch culture, is in fact a product of feminism. It sounds counterintuitive but we think that without feminist politics, we would not be looking at *Girls Gone Wild*.

In this chapter we explore the history of women and pornography, and look at the ways in which feminism has changed the kinds of pornography that get made. And we are not simply claiming that women are, as Levy puts it, '*empowered* enough to get Brazilian waxes … and join the frat party of pop culture'. When we say that contemporary pornography (and attitudes to porn) has been affected by feminism, we are looking at it as the clearest, most graphic representation of cultural attitudes to sexuality. In addition, we're looking at these attitudes in a historical context. While it's true that some feminists have strongly opposed pornography, it is not the case that all feminists have done so. In fact, even in the late 1960s and early 1970s, there were feminists who believed that the answer to bad porn was not no porn … it was better porn.

Who Said Porn Was Feminist?

As we discussed in Chapter 3, one of the main objections to pornography in media articles is that it is bad for women. We often hear the claim that 'feminists' are opposed to pornography. This isn't entirely true. Some feminists oppose all pornography—but others do not. We mapped out the anti-pornography feminist discourses in Chapter 1, but there is also another history—of feminist attempts to engage with and change pornography.

Feminist attitudes to pornography are intrinsically linked to attitudes to other forms of sexuality, particularly commercial sex work. While it is true that many second-wave feminists opposed the sex industry and regarded female sex workers with pity or scorn even in the 1970s, there were many who did not draw such clear distinctions.

Feminists as diverse as Amber Hollibaugh and Pat Califia have observed that many feminist activists were themselves sex workers in one capacity or another (albeit often closeted). Others, such as Susie Bright, took up the critiques of radical feminists such as Andrea Dworkin and interpreted them as a challenge to create new representations and stories of female (and feminist) sexuality. If pornography (and, indeed, any public expression of sex or sexuality) was seen as a site of male privilege, these women reasoned, then it was time for women to claim these privileges for themselves. As Bright put it:

> Here's the irony ... every single woman who pioneered the sexual revolution, every erotic-feminist-bad-girl-and-proud-of-it-stiletto-shitkicker, was once a fan of Andrea Dworkin. Until 1984, we all were. She was the one who got us looking at porn with a critical eye, she made you feel like you could just stomp into the adult bookstore and seize everything for inspection and a bonfire ... We saw the sexism of the porn business ... but we also saw some intriguing possibilities and amazing maverick spirit. We said, 'What if we made something that reflected our politics and values, but was just as sexually bold?'

The 'politics and values' Bright refers to were those of the women's health and self-help movements, in which women sought to create new theoretical and practical models of female health and sexuality that were not based in medicalised or male-dominated traditions. As porn star turned feminist porn producer Candida Royalle put it:

> We were reclaiming who we were as women, our true essence, what we deserved as human beings. We were shedding our political preconceptions. These efforts [running a women's café and free clinic] highlighted a wonderful sisterhood, and the right to sexual pleasure.

As we discussed in Chapter 1, the early 1970s were the height of the post-pill era known as the 'sexual revolution'. Not only was there a burgeoning counterculture embracing 'free love', but easy access to reliable contraception meant that women were able to experiment sexually without fear of unwanted pregnancy. Broader popular culture became increasingly tolerant of explicit sexual imagery, with the 1972 release of the iconic film *Deep Throat* marking what came to be known as the 'golden age' of cinematic porn. At the same time, researchers Masters and Johnson released their studies of human sexual response, which foregrounded the importance of clitoral stimulation to women's sexual pleasure.

The early 1970s also saw a proliferation of popular feminist non-fiction texts that aimed to 'de-mystify' female sexuality and promote female autonomy in reproductive and sexual health, including sexual independence in the form of fantasy material that promoted masturbation. These texts, which included the Boston Women's Health Book Collective's *Our Bodies, Ourselves* (1973), Lonnie Barbach's *For Yourself* (1975), Nancy Friday's *My Secret Garden* (1974) and Shere Hite's *The Hite Report* (1976), drew on Masters and Johnson's sex research to promote masturbation and sexual fantasy as a prime source for women's sexual independence. Betty Dodson's *Liberating Masturbation* (published in 1974 and still in print as *Sex for One*) promoted masturbation as an antidote to what many feminists saw as a dead-end investment in heterosexual romance *and* a cure for individual neuroses. Dodson was influential in promoting vibrators as reliable devices for self-pleasuring and, while these were available in some department stores, in the main they were sold in male-oriented sex shops. Consequently, when feminist health worker Joani Blank started the first 'feminist sex shop', Good Vibrations, as a mail-order company in 1977, vibrators and erotic fiction formed a major part of her stock. As academic Meiya Loe puts it in her study of the history of Good Vibrations as a form of 'feminist capitalism', the 'ideology of sexual empowerment' was an implicit aspect of Good Vibrations' branding and marketing strategy. As we argued in Chapter 1, censors had been trying to stop women having access to information about their sexuality—sexual pleasure as well as birth control—for many decades, claiming that it would corrupt them. In this context, the fact that women were finally getting access to information about sex was clearly a feminist breakthrough.

As in the United States, the Australian women's health movement from the 1970s onwards explicitly encouraged sexual exploration in a feminist context. As writer and activist Kimberly O'Sullivan explained in a 1997 article, the Leichhardt Women's Health Centre (a feminist inner-city clinic) ran evening courses on women's bodies and sexuality that:

> consisted of intense discussions of bodies and sexual self-images and always included a genital self-examination … The Centre also promoted a leaflet on tips for reducing painful periods, one of which was to have an orgasm. It cheerfully advised that if you don't feel like sex with a partner, use a vibrator, which was strongly recommended for the sexually self-sufficient woman.

Although feminists had been producing and consuming sexually explicit writing and imagery since the 1970s, it wasn't until 1984 that feminists began to produce and distribute sexually explicit imagery in the traditionally 'masculine' domains of magazine and video pornography. It could be argued that these productions were a direct response both to feminist challenges to the broader commercial sex industry, and to the 'lesbian sex wars', in which some lesbians opposed butch/femme and BDSM sexual play because, they claimed, they were a form of 'violence against women'. Lesbian partners Nan Kinney and Debi Sundahl met at a Women Against Violence Against Women meeting, but believed that feminist targeting of the sex industry as a prime site of protest against male oppression was based on class prejudice. As Sundahl put it, 'Why, when abuse happens across class and race lines did we choose to march in poorer sections where the sex theatres were, and where poorer women made a living?' The pair used Sundahl's earnings as a stripper to fund the lesbian sex magazine *On Our Backs*, whose title was a direct challenge to the anti-porn tendencies in the feminist magazine *off our backs*.

Their company, Blush Entertainment, also included the Fatale video production and distribution companies. Fatale films featured mainstream porn performers like Nina Hartley and Sharon Mitchell alongside lesbians who hadn't previously performed in pornography. The films were designed not only to be erotic, but to instruct lesbian and bisexual women in the diverse pleasures of women's sexuality by offering examples of alternative sexual practices (such as female ejaculation). In a 1997 interview, Sundahl said she started the company:

> because both gay and straight men had tons of sexually explicit material, and lesbians had *zero* ... Fatale created the genre of authentic lesbian erotic videos, directly challenging the ruling stereotypes of lesbians created by men for men through their girl-on-girl videos.

Both *On Our Backs* and Fatale videos achieved limited distribution in Australia in the 1980s, and are credited by Kimberly O'Sullivan as a catalyst for the formation of various underground lesbian sex publications and parties in Australia in the 1990s, notably the *Wicked Women* magazine and parties, which ran from 1988 to 1996 (O'Sullivan frequently contributed to the magazine and was its editor from 1994 to 1996). As O'Sullivan explained in her 2001 interview for The Understanding Pornography in Australia project:

> *On Our Backs* was a bit of a grandmother of lesbian porn ... it was a great magazine. The Book Shop [a queer bookshop] at Darlinghurst was the only place that would import it and distribute it. With the Australian dollar, which was still bad back then, it was phenomenal.

You were paying $20 for a magazine! It was sort of over-the-top, and so there was some resistance to buying it.

Consequently, *Wicked Women*'s founding editors, Lisa Salmon and Jasper Laybutt (then Francine), were, as O'Sullivan puts it, 'inspired to start a home-grown version' using a dodgy second-hand typewriter and their workplace photocopier. Although the first edition only had a print run of ninety copies, it was successful enough to expand its circulation (and its contributor base) throughout Australia. Like *On Our Backs*, *Wicked Women* caused considerable debate within the lesbian feminist community, and this led to serious distribution problems at times. As O'Sullivan put it in her 1993 'retrospective', gay men's businesses supported the magazine long before lesbian businesses did. In both Sydney and Melbourne women's bookshops, *Wicked Women* was hidden under the counter, in stockrooms or behind other magazines. According to O'Sullivan, shop owners were wary of offending lesbian customers, or making lesbian porn visible where men might see it. Of course, 'without a sign in the shop saying it was for sale … it also meant that women could not look at it'. While lesbian businesses became more supportive as the publishers began to promote *Wicked Women* parties, performance evenings and other community events, the magazine continued to weather controversies and conflicts, including censorship by printers, 'girl-cotts' over the publication of a press release from a man–boy love group, protests over the publication of articles from male writers, and opposition to Jasper Laybutt's gender transition. Although the magazine eventually became financially unsustainable and ceased publication in 1996, it was a labour of love for its producers and is still cited as an inspiration for young feminist porn producers in Australia. As O'Sullivan said in her 2001 interview:

> Particularly in the early days, we were living what the magazine was representing. It was an extension of what you were doing in life anyway. If the magazine was pushing the boundaries, it was reflecting the fact that you yourself … [were] pushing the boundaries, and living amongst all of this sex radical atmosphere in that particular era.

Feminist Pornographers Go Mainstream

While lesbians were beginning to make their own pornography, heterosexual women were also challenging the idea that porn was only for men. Having worked as a performer in porn's 'golden age' from 1975 to 1981, Candida Royalle reflected on her life, rethinking her involvement in the industry:

> I decided there was nothing wrong with the *concept* of sexual entertainment, but most of the actual films reflected a sexually shame-based society and its negative attitude toward women ... I decided that the answer was to create materials that bespoke a more loving and healthy attitude to sex and women. Were women exploited? Yes, because while we were essential to the production of porn and, in fact, what drove the sales of pornography, our sexual needs were not addressed: we might as well have been blow-up dolls.

Royalle was part of Club 90, a New York–based feminist peer-support group for sex workers, including strippers, prostitutes and other golden age porn performers such as Annie Sprinkle and Gloria Leonard. Although some of these performers had previously written and directed their own films—*Deep Inside Annie Sprinkle* was one of the bestselling videos of 1985—the women of Club 90 decided to create a new genre of video pornography. It would not only be written and produced by women, but would be specifically designed to answer feminist critiques of porn and to appeal to (largely heterosexual) female audiences. The result was Royalle's company Femme Productions, which made videos drawing on aesthetics designed to appeal not only to women, but also to 'couples, the educated man, and maybe even the raincoat crowd'. Femme videos featured 'classy' production values, had story-lines that emphasised relationships and emotion, and focused on cunnilingus rather than fellatio. Notably, they did not feature external cum shots, also known as the 'money shot' of conventional pornography.

Although Royalle's videos for Femme Productions are widely credited with pioneering the now mainstream (and commercially successful) genre of 'couples porn', neither Royalle's heterosexual videos nor Sundahl's lesbian films were seen as marketable in the mainstream porn industry until they had established their own independent distribution networks. Feminist magazines refused Femme's advertising on political grounds and conventional, male-focused porn magazines couldn't see the appeal. Royalle's breakthrough came in 1985, when the mainstream US women's magazine *Glamour* ran a positive feature. Women's magazines such as *Cosmopolitan* were also instrumental in popularising women's erotic media, which included not only films and videos but also erotic short stories and novels.

Erotica—By Women, for Women

In the 1980s, Good Vibrations' parent company, Open Enterprises, branched out into publishing. Like Good Vibrations, Down There Press espoused an overtly feminist ethos, specialising in sexuality and self-help books. In 1988, Susie Bright, an editor of *On Our Backs* and staff member at Good Vibrations, approached the store's owner, Joani Blank, with an idea. Bright and Blank began soliciting contributions for the first issue of *Herotica*, an anthology of women's erotica. According to Bright, *Herotica* was specifically designed to be attractive to middle-class women who might be deterred by more explicit writing and images. Nancy Friday's *My Secret Garden*, a very explicit collection of women's sexual fantasies, which included many things that would be automatically banned in most jurisdictions were someone to make a movie about them, was an international bestseller. But Bright says that 'lesbian fiction was easier to find than straight women's erotica. We didn't want anything apologetic or deferential; it had to have some imagination, some verve, some confidence. That confidence didn't really exist in a widespread way. We tried to cultivate it as we acquired the work'.

Like many other feminists of their time, Bright and her colleagues at Down There Press were attempting to develop a new genre of sexual imagery for women, one that was unthreatening, erotic and not a direct copy of images that could be considered 'male'. This was not an easy task. In her recollection of the earliest covers for the *Herotica* collections, Bright writes, 'I'm embarrassed to describe these attempts, but the effect we were aiming for was something that would symbolise female genitalia but wouldn't frighten anyone with an outright beaver shot. We also didn't want to put an actual woman on the cover, because we didn't want a single figure to define what female eroticism was'. As feminist academic Jane Juffer notes, despite sharing an editor (and some contributors), *Herotica* was a very different aesthetic and political project to *On Our Backs*. From the very first issue, Bright carefully differentiated *Herotica* from less politicised women's erotica that could be seen as 'a commercial term for vapid femininity, a Harlequin romance in a G-string'.

The collection was successful enough that the second anthology (and each subsequent anthology) was distributed internationally by Penguin books, in mainstream bookshop chains. Other anthologies followed and by the 1990s, as Juffer notes, 'Erotica' had become a major category in mainstream book distribution chains such as Borders, Dymocks and WH Smith. In 1994, Virgin Publishing launched the Black Lace series of erotic novels, which contained surveys inviting readers to comment on their favourite plot lines and sexual themes. These ranged from fetishes that might be prohibited under some Western classification regimes (particularly dominance and submission, which links to the contents of the couples videos, as we discussed in Chapter 3), to classic romance narratives. Virgin's 'Nexus' line of novels was described by an Australian reviewer as 'perverse Mills and Boon', although 'certainly not high brow cliterature'. It is not specifically marketed as 'by women, for women', but, like Black Lace, is promoted as 'erotica' rather than pornography. Like much 'erotica', it contains explicit descriptions of sexual behaviour that would very likely be prohibited by Australian classifiers, including golden showers and bondage and discipline.

Escapist, arousing and responsive to its readers' needs and desires, erotica was a post-feminist fusion of pornography and the romance novel. As Juffer put it, 'one of the conditions of everyday life that women's erotica must deal with is the desire for yet the scepticism of romantic love'. Like fans of romance novels, erotica's fans were eager to contribute to their favourite genre. By the 1990s, glossy magazines like *Playgirl* and *Australian Women's*

Forum solicited erotic recollections and fantasies from their readers by inviting them to reflect on what turned them on. Some, like Australian writer and journalist Linda Jaivin, were able to convert short stories written for glossy women's magazines into a serious enterprise. Jaivin's 1997 novel *Eat Me* was an international best-seller and launched her into a high-profile (if short-term) career as a 'sexpert'. It also provoked a minor scandal in the United States when some bookshops refused to stock it, due to its 'provocative' (and award-winning) cover art, featuring suggestive arrangements of melons, bananas and other fruit.

The increasing explicitness of women's erotica in popular women's magazines met with resistance from the Australian Office of Film and Literature Classification. An issue of *Cleo* magazine (a local version of *Cosmopolitan* that promoted, in researcher Meg Le Masurier's terms, a populist form of 'fair go' feminism) was recalled when it published an extract from one of Anais Nin's classic 1940s erotic short stories. The only women's magazine devoted entirely to female sexuality, *Australian Women's Forum*, found itself increasingly subject to censorship, with editor Helen Vnuk forced to cut any story that featured hints of 'sexual violence', such as spanking or 'forced' sex, both popular themes in women's erotica. She also was forced to cut any story that featured men and women under the age of eighteen. This meant that 'sexual awakening' stories had to be edited so that all participants were clearly over eighteen. In her book *Snatched*, Vnuk credits this increased censorship with *Forum*'s 2001 demise, although, to be fair, this may also have resulted from increased competition from online erotica and pornography. As we will discuss in Chapters 6 and 8, the unregulated space of the internet allowed for a much more diverse range of sexual genres to proliferate. In the case of women's erotica, online forums have allowed more freedom for the readers and writers of female-dominated genres such as slash fiction, where non-pornographic pop culture narratives such as *Harry Potter* and *Star Trek* are rewritten with explicit sexual scenes.

Cheesecake and Zines: Third-wave Feminist Erotica

The internet played a powerful role in popularising aspects of the third-wave forms of feminism, exemplified by the Riot Grrl movement. Although 'pure' Riot Grrl culture was fairly short-lived, it was highly influential in reshaping the feminist aesthetics of sexuality in the late 1990s and into the twenty-first century. Originally it was US-based and loosely comprised of bands and fanzines, or zines, which deployed the values and rhetoric of punk in the name of feminism or, as the slogan put it, 'revolution girl-style now'. However, with the parallel rise of online networks, it quickly became a global movement. For example, Rosie Cross, the creator of the online zine *GeekGrrl*, was based in Sydney, yet her zine had readers around the world.

In addition to adopting a 'do-it-yourself' attitude towards cultural production and distribution, young women who organised around, or identified with, the Riot Grrl ethos adapted the punk subcultural strategies of parody and appropriation. Riot Grrl zines borrowed or stole 'conservative' images from retro porn, home economy textbooks and children's picture books to simultaneously mock and pay loving tribute to the very forms of feminised expression that had been rejected as 'demeaning' by the women's movement of the 1970s and 1980s. As feminist researcher Martina Ladendorf has observed, the young feminist producers of zines like *BUST*, *Bitch*, *Disgruntled Housewife* and *Smile and Act Nice* favoured the ironic juxtaposition of retro cheesecake pin-ups with 'cute' graphic images such as 'Hello Kitty' to illustrate their discussions of body image, employment opportunities, bands and other traditionally feminist topics. The use of cute, fluffy, pink or 'feminine' images was, argues Ladendorf, a similar strategy to the reappropriation of the term 'girl' (as opposed to 'woman') within Riot Grrl texts. Tiaras, slip-dresses, high heels and make-up were adapted by straight and queer women in a kind of 'high-femme' feminism, as described by *BUST* editor Debbie Stoller:

> Unlike our feminist foremothers, who claimed that makeup was the opiate of the misses, we're positively prochoice when it comes to matters of feminine display ... We're well aware, thank you very

much, of the beauty myth that's working to keep women obscene and not heard, but we just don't think that transvestites should have all the fun. We love our lipstick, have a passion for polish, and, basically, adore this armour that we call 'fashion.' To us, it's fun, it's feminine, and, in the particular way we flaunt it, it's *definitely* feminist.

This combination of language and imagery was designed to address young women who were, at this point, feeling alienated from the second-wave feminists who were appearing more and more like authoritarian mother figures, and less like sisters or peers. Sexuality, gender and representation were core issues within Riot Grrl culture. Performers like Bikini Kill's Kathleen Hanna appeared on stage with the words CUNT, SLUT and RAPE written on their bodies, in a provocation designed to confront issues of constraints placed on women's sexuality. The sex industry, including porn and stripping, was discussed extensively, particularly in the writing and music of young women who worked within the industry itself. Sexuality was represented within these texts both as a site of risk or fear and a site of sexual power. Feminist sex radicals and pornographers like Betty Dodson, Annie Sprinkle and Susie Bright were represented as 'she-roes' and teachers within feminist subcultures, by the same young women who attended 'Reclaim the Night' rallies. Journalist Michelle Goldberg described them as follows: 'Full of images of campy 50s pin-up girls and downtown rocker chicks and stories about strong, brilliant women alongside first-person narratives both humorous and heart-rending, [girlzines felt] like the coolest slumber party in the world'.

Chick Porn as Community Outreach

Life partners Shar Rednour and Jackie Strano 'trained' at Fatale Media and Good Vibrations respectively. In 1998 the couple established SIR (Sex Indulgence and Rock'n'Roll) Video, an alternative porn production company. Their first videos, *Bend Over Boyfriend* and *Bend Over Boyfriend 2*, were aimed at consumers of 'couples' porn and featured Good Vibrations staffer Carol Queen and her partner Robert Lawrence (and a cast of amateurs and porn professionals) consciously and graphically instructing male/female couples on the art of male-receptive anal sex. The BOB films were described by one feminist reviewer as 'a new generation of sexy sex ed, an eye-opening foray into the taboo region of straight, male, virgin ass'. In the films, feminist sex worker and qualified sexologist Carol Queen, whose publications include *Exhibitionism for the Shy*, comments that:

> being communicative might be a 'new thing' for the 'ladies', who are probably 'not used to' communicating what they want/don't want from their men, but can, and must listen, while their men voice what *they* want, for anal sex obviously warrants more communication than ordinary hetero sex. Queen even expresses hope that this communicative effort might have some influence on one's regular, noncommunicative sex life.

Both the BOB videos and SIR Video's later films, *Hard Love and How to Fuck in High Heels* (a portmanteau film consisting of two separate titles), include explicit or implicit instruction on the use of 'dirty talk' as eroticised sexual negotiation. As producer and performer Shar Rednour puts it:

> What we do, we do because we don't get excited by the porn that's out there. Also, we know as sex educators that there's not enough dirty talking out there, and we feel like communication transforms people's sex lives. It can transform regular people into sex stars.

Like the zine scene, SIR Videos reflects the third-wave DIY feminist ethos:

> 'We're like the punk rock company', says Jackie. They made both *Hard Love* (in which Jackie stars) and *How to Fuck in High Heels* (Shar's star vehicle) in four days—and had time to shoot a music video for one of The Hail Marys' songs and throw themselves a benefit so they could pay for renting the cameras, to boot.

Although *Hard Love and How to Fuck in High Heels* was the uncompromising product of San Francisco lesbian butch/femme subculture, it had surprising cross-over appeal. In 2001, the video was awarded the prize for 'Best Girl-on-Girl' sex at the Adult Video News awards (the equivalent of the porn Oscars). And not all cross-over feminist 'edu-porn' is the product of a DIY culture. Third-wave feminist pornographer and sexuality educator Tristan Taormino's first video—an adaptation of her sex-manual *The Ultimate Guide to Anal Sex for Women*—was produced in collaboration with John 'Buttman' Stagliano's production house, Evil Angel. Like many US chick pornographers, Taormino was an editor of *On Our Backs* and her approach reflects the feminist pro-porn tradition. In her memoir of the film's production, Taormino writes, 'I think the problem with most sex education videos is that they teach you how to do something, but they don't inspire you to run out and do it. I wanted to make a video that would be educational as well as hot and sexy'. The collaboration with Stagliano involved a great deal of compromise since, unlike SIR's 'dyke community' porn, Taormino was working with one of the most established producers of heterosexual pornography. She was able to negotiate several elements that were important to her personal and political philosophies into the film, including the use of condoms in all scenes performed by actors who were not already an established couple, latex gloves for some digital penetration scenes, and a veto on facial cum shots (which are frequently mentioned as a turn-off for female viewers). The film culminated with director Tristan being anally penetrated by all ten of her co-stars in what she described as 'the ultimate feminist gang bang'.

In her study of lesbian porn, and of the lesbian-produced BOB series, US academic Heather Butler states that 'if lesbians attempt to educate … the hetero mass, they not only contribute something authentic to this world that would completely exclude them otherwise but they make their *own* desire visible as well'. While the owners of feminist bookshops in the 1980s sought to hide explicit lesbian images from men, for many third-wave feminist pornographers (and for the publishers of *Wicked Women* for that matter), being seen by male audiences seems to be either a non-issue or a positive side-effect of their erotic exhibitionism. For example, Melbourne performer/producer Bumpy drew a distinction between performing for heterosexual males in the mainstream sex industry, which she found uncomfortable, and performing in front of straight men who might enter into the lesbian performance scene or purchase lesbian-produced porn. For her, 'this is the freedom to do all the things and wear sexy clothes, or get naked or be exhibitionist … where *our* sexual preferences lie'.

Susie Bright, Annie Sprinkle, Carol Queen and other US-based feminist porn pioneers, as well as SIR Video's Shar and Jackie, and Australia's *Wicked Women*, were frequently mentioned as inspirations or reference points for interviewees in The Understanding Pornography in Australia project. There was no universal consensus as to what constituted 'best practice' feminist porn and SIR Video, in particular, provoked considerable debate, particularly among lesbians. One interviewee, Julie, who identifies as a 'pleasure-activist', recalled inviting some lesbian friends to a screening of SIR Video's *Sugar High Glitter City* at Sydney's Gay and Lesbian Mardi Gras. Offended by the depictions of butch/femme strap-on sex, the friends walked out. Domino, the editor of Sydney dyke sex magazine *Slit*, recalls a similar reaction at a fundraising screening of the film, where audience members were concerned by a 'lack of context' in a scene where a police officer pressured a prostitute for sex, while others were offended by the use of dildos. SIR Video's *Hard Love and How to Fuck in High Heels* received a similar response in France at the 2000 *Cineffable* lesbian film festival. The following year, French lesbians boycotted a panel on women pornographers (which included French director Catherine Breillat) at the Creteil International Women's Film Festival, arguing that women's porn was the product of a backlash against feminism. Bumpy felt that *Sugar High Glitter City* was just not quite sexy enough for her tastes, though she appreciated the effort involved in making lesbian porn, since the only video she had performed in, *King Vic*, also resulted in what she felt was an insufficiently hard-core product.

Why Do Australian Women Make Porn?

There is a common view that the only reason anybody would produce pornography is for the purposes of making money. But that just isn't true in Australia. There is a massive market for pornography here, but almost everything that is sold in Australia's commercial mainstream is produced overseas (either in America

What Do Women Like?

This is a complex question. It's easier, in fact, to determine what women **don't** like:

- **Ugly men**—for example, *Adult Video News* staff writer Heidi Pike-Johnson has justly observed that many women are turned off by videos where unattractive men are teamed with super-attractive women. This may account for the popularity of gay and bi videos among both straight and queer women.
- **Facial cum shots**—many of those interviewed for the Understanding Pornography project reported being turned off by facial cum shots, particularly when an actress clearly dislikes the experience.
- **An obsession with cum shots generally**—some women dislike all cum shots or money shots, which they claim emphasise male orgasms at the expense of female pleasure.

Where Can Women Find Porn They Do Like?

For those who want a classic introduction to heterosexual women's porn, with none of the turn-offs listed above, Candida Royalle's **Femme Productions** seems to be a natural start.

Those who like harder edged, nastier heterosexually oriented porn should check out the films featuring handsome Italian porn star **Rocco Siffredi**. Rocco has many female fans and is widely admired for what appears to be consistently genuine sexual enthusiasm. It should be noted, though, that while Rocco has made a *lot* of videos, some might be too edgy or aggressive for porn novices.

Women who prefer porn that emphasises emotional relationships may enjoy videos by **Comstock Productions**. Its documentary/porn films feature real-life couples discussing their relationships reality-TV style, and engaging in explicit (but intimate) sex.

There is a comparatively narrow range of lesbian-made films available, notably those by **Fatale Video** and **SIR Video**. Those who prefer educational porn may enjoy Annie Sprinkle's 'post-porn' videos (details available on her website), Nina Hartley's series of 'How To' videos, or Betty Dodson's video masturbation workshop.

Women's sex shops like **Good Vibrations**, **Toys in Babeland**, **Grand Opening** (all in the United States), **The Pleasure Spot** and **Bliss4Women** (both in Australia) usually provide recommendations and reviews, and even sell women's field guides to porn and erotica on their websites.

Of course, many of the images produced 'by men, for men' appeal to women, too.

or Europe) and imported. There are very few Australians actually making money out of producing sexually explicit images. Only one or two Australian porn videos are made each year, compared to the thousands that are imported. Of the well known porn magazines—*Playboy, Penthouse, Hustler*—only *Penthouse* produces an Australian edition; only some softcore, downmarket men's magazines such as *People* and *Picture* are produced locally. And there are only a few websites that produce original content for money, such as Seducedstraightguys.com.

Rather, what we found through our research is that the production of pornography in Australia is, for the participants, quite literally a labour of love. They make it for their own pleasure. The answer to the question 'Who's making pornography in Australia?' isn't 'large corporations'. It's ordinary Australian individuals and couples, doing it for no money or running, at best, cottage industries.

We discuss the production of pornography in Australia in more detail in Chapter 6, but it seems relevant, in this discussion of women and pornography, to mention at this point the reasons that some Australian women—and Australian feminists and lesbians— are involved in the production of sexually explicit material. In fact, when we set out to interview Australian porn producers as a complement to our survey of consumers, we discovered the majority of 'cottage industry' producers were women.

Since even cross-over feminist pornography has a relatively small market appeal, most porn produced by Australian women falls into the self-funded, DIY 'community media' category. The glossiest Australian feminist/queer-inspired porn magazine, *Slit*, is produced entirely by volunteers, has a $15 cover price and runs at a loss. Since 2002, it has increased its print run from 700 to a 'couple of thousand' issues, which are distributed in Australia and overseas. In the editorial for the first issue, Domino and her fellow editor Stealth wrote:

> we made this mag because we are smutty dirty grrls who like to talk about sex, read about it, see it, feel it, pretend it, dream it … because we are voyeurs and because we like to stick our noses in other people's fantasies before sticking various domestic objects

into each others orifices ... and well, being the editor of a dyke sex mag makes checking your email a tad more exciting ... and we are interested in considering the possibilities of creating a dialogue of sex and sexuality which is non commodified and which takes back control over our bodies and desires rather than proscribing them, 'cause we are trying to figure out how to find axis of liberation, cracks in the structure of capital, autonomous enclaves where we practice an economy of desire rather than capital.

Like its forerunner, *Wicked Women*, *Slit* is part of a broader Sydney queer and feminist community network, linked by performance events such as *Gurlesque*; the 'Lezzo Strip Joint' run by ex–*Wicked Women* performers Glita Supernova and Sex Intents; the women's punk night, Scooter; and the *Sheila Autonomista* DIY women's festival. *Slit*'s editors attract contributions from models, writers, performers, strippers and photographers in this local scene, and have the added advantage of an online presence that allows them to solicit contributions (and advertisers) from outside Sydney's relatively small alternative queer scene. While *Slit* promotes itself as a 'dyke sex mag', Domino believes that it has a broader appeal. She says that 'a lot of straight women enjoy it as well just because it's got unconventional images of women and strong images of women, and so you don't have to be a dyke yourself to appreciate it'. She also receives positive feedback from the Sydney BDSM scene, the alternative punk scene and 'freaky people'. Much of this feedback comes, she says, from people who remember *Wicked Women* and see *Slit* as a means of documenting the current underground lesbian and queer scenes.

Although her own tastes have changed over time, Domino's favourite sexually explicit media are alternative zines. Both *Wife* and *Skint 2: King Porn Mag* explored gender and sexuality through sexually explicit stories and images, rather than offering conventional pornography. As she put it:

In terms of imagery I've become more interested in the range of women's expression of their sexuality and I guess that comes from seeking out those images, but I guess that's kind of relating to porn in a different way as well. I now relate to it as not just imagery that looks sexy, but actually imagery that's interesting or beautiful or that's communicating something. So I think the way I look at it has changed and I think that's also about making it, that ... rather than looking at it from that consumption base, saying 'ah yes,' in a more analytical way.

Just as *Wicked Women* attracted controversy from inside and outside the community, *Slit*'s editors have also had to deal with conflicts. There have been few issues with distribution in local bookshops and sex shops, although one store owner insisted women didn't buy porn. But some women have told the editors that the magazine is 'too rude', and there was a major problem with the printing of the first issue:

DOMINO: That would have been early 2002 and right up to when we were getting the quote from the print shop we explained to the printer that it was a dyke sex magazine, you know dyke, dyke, dyke, lesbian, sex, sex, sex, sex, sex, magazine, you know, rude pictures, rude writing, photos. And they went 'yeah, yeah', then when it came to printing it they said it was illegal. They said, 'We can't print this, it's illegal, it'll have to go to Canberra'. So the OFLC were helpful in explaining and confirmed our understanding that nothing we were doing was illegal; there were no animals or underage people or anything.

INTERVIEWER: So what happened then?

DOMINO: They refused ... I wrote a letter to them basically explaining the situation and the legal situation and that they'd made a prior promise to print our magazine and accepted the artwork on that basis. We'd provided a deposit; it had even got to the stage where we provided a 10 per cent deposit. They wouldn't return our calls or have any other contact with us. I think they were at that stage worried about allegations of homophobia, so we left it and found another printer.

INTERVIEWER: Did you get your deposit back?

DOMINO: Yeah. I had to go and pick it up.

INTERVIEWER: So they didn't say what particularly they found illegal about it, because presumably if some mainstream lesbian porn magazine had gone to them ... do you think they had a problem because of your particular kind of images?

DOMINO: Well, that's the thing. We had a think about it and then I realised that there was one image there that I guess was more controversial than the others and it's where Glita Supernova in a nun's habit with a nun's neck thing, a cross around her neck in various poses ... and then one of them with the cross up her cunt.

Interestingly, a similar incident occurred over an issue of *Wicked Women* that featured a sexually explicit image of the Virgin Mary, by Sydney artist Linda Dement.

Australian porn zines are, like almost all Australian feminist/ queer porn, a profit-free zone. Domino's favourites, *Wife* and *Skint*, were produced by Sydney artist and activist Nicole Barakat and Melbourne writer Aizura Hankin (now Aren Aizura). *Wife* was a classically lo-fi photocopied zine combining writing, nude photographs, and cartoon illustrations and instructions from home-making manuals. Barakat created the zine to draw links between the femme, dyke and Lebanese aspects of her identity. Unlike some of the interviewees for the project, Barakat performed, and distributed her zines very specifically within the Sydney queer community at events like *Gurlesque* and Scooter.

Aizura produced *Skint 2: King Porn Mag* in 2000 as 'erotica and pornography about female masculinity, and particularly kind of dyke sex, sort of moving into gay sex and kind [of] trans-sexual stuff, transgender stuff ...' It combines photo portraits of Melbourne drag kings with articles and explicit fiction contributed by Melbourne writers. The story 'Boys Like Us' features sex between a lesbian 'boy' and her male 'daddy'. Funded by an $800 tax return, the production is more professional than the average photocopied zine. Aizura distributed the zine at local events and through online zine forums, charging $5 (or the equivalent in local currency) a copy, which, she admits, 'is steep for a zine'. Although *Skint* was produced specifically for the Melbourne drag king community, it had surprising popularity outside lesbian and queer communities:

AIZURA: I went to the National Young Writers Festival and I found all these like straight boys just coming up and asking me for copies. And so I, you know, I'd just give them one ...

as a kind of experiment you know, to see what would happen, and people were very into it ... [Buyers were] mostly queer people I reckon, but there's certainly a big contingent of straight people who either liked it, or were really really really into it. And one boy who I met at Newcastle ... a year after I'd done it, we were introduced, and he was like, 'Oh, you're Aizura, you're that chick who did *Skint*! Yeah, I've got a copy of your zine sitting on my bedside table at home', and I just was like (laughing), 'Oh, ok, that's really good ... cool', and then we sort of continued talking and you know, I think he's completely straight.

INTERVIEWER: Does the idea that straight men would masturbate over that kind of stuff surprise you?

AIZURA: It doesn't surprise me that straight men would masturbate over lesbian stuff, but I think that ... what I wanted to do was really detach masculinity from being about men, or being solely about men, and so a lot of the stories kind of really do cut men out of the equation [of] sort of masculinity/femininity, or you know, sort of sexual dynamics in general ... And so that in a queer way ... and it's also about fucking with masculinity in terms of there's lots of, you know, anal sex going on, and really not very ordinary heterosexual straight sex. So, it did surprise me a little bit, I mean, you know, but at the same time, I guess who am I to say? There must be lots of straight boys who get off on the idea of being fucked in the ass, by you know, sort of a woman, or a you know, a boyish girl and that is cool ... yeah, that's great.

Aizura had inquired at Melbourne's feminist sex shop, the Good Vibrations–inspired Bliss for Women, but the owner, Maureen Matthews, was concerned that some stories involving age-play and blood-play might breach classification laws, and suggested the zine should be sent to the OFLC. This was a reasonable response, considering Leah Baroque's zine *Eroticus* had previously been seized in a raid of Melbourne alternative bookshop Polyester Books, and become something of a test case for alternative porn producers (it costs several hundred dollars to classify a magazine). In a 2002 interview for the Understanding Pornography project,

Matthews regretted the impact the classification guidelines had on her business, since they severely limited the amount of woman-produced porn she could provide her customers.

While she did stock two locally made videos that had been classified by the OFLC, they were 'educational' materials, classified R and M respectively. The R-rated video *Sugar and Spikes* was a true example of community porn. It had been produced by a Melbourne BDSM party promoter, Mistress Tan, as a response to frequently asked questions on her website, and featured local BDSM community members demonstrating 'safe, sane and consensual' play, including instruction on introducing a partner to one's fantasy life. In her interview for the Understanding Pornography project, Tan explained that she had funded the video with the $20,000 savings from her day job as an office administrator, but recouped the money by selling the video from her website (lowering the cost after she broke even).

Leah Baroque's 'banned' zine *Eroticus* was almost out of production when she was interviewed for the project in 2002. Baroque began producing the zine as a 17-year-old schoolgirl in regional Victoria. A fan of *Australian Women's Forum*, she had several of her own erotic stories published and wanted to continue writing and circulating them after the magazine folded. Her first issues were very much within the 'grrl' aesthetic, with glitter and pink ribbon on the outside, and explicit sexual stories on the inside. After moving to Melbourne, Baroque and her editorial partner, Amy, continued to produce and distribute the increasingly popular zine, recruiting male and female contributors from international e-lists and through the local erotic spoken-word events they promoted, where content ranged from heterosexual romance to queer kink. Ironically, the 'banning' of *Eroticus* had increased its audience to the extent that Leah and Amy expanded the publication beyond their means and were then forced to discontinue production.

The only Australian women seriously considering the expense and inconvenience of producing video porn were Sydney-based Aer Agrey and Melbourne filmmaker Anna Brownfield. Both Agrey and Brownfield were influenced by feminist politics and by their appreciation of 'golden age', narrative-driven porn films.

Agrey said, 'I've worked in an adult shop and I don't particularly like the products they put out, the porn ... I mean, I say I love porn, but when I think about the porn I love, it's more the old-school porn ... I could only find about two [modern] films that I really liked, that I thought were good for women'. After forming her production company, Macrobiotic Erotic, with a specific emphasis on promoting sexual pleasure and safer sex, Agrey met Brownfield, who had similar goals for her company, Poison Apple Productions. Brownfield's low-budget film *The Money Shot* was the semi-biographical story of an unemployed film-school graduate who makes a porn movie. Casting for the male roles in their first combined production, *The Band*, took place in 2006, attracting a certain amount of amused coverage from the mainstream media.

Like many of the women interviewed, including those who worked for commercial porn companies, Agrey and Brownfield had strong views on what constituted a feminist influence in pornography. Karen Jackson, web mistress of forthegirls.com and an ex-contributor to *Australian Women's Forum*, described her entry into online porn in her 2003 interview for the project as follows:

> I was writing for *Australian Women's Forum* on what porn there was on the internet for women—this was about 1999 or 2000—and I couldn't find anything except this one site called Perve.com, which was also run by an Australian woman called Carol Patterson. I got into contact with her and she said, 'Why don't you get into the business?' So I did. I started just making free sites and I've mainly been doing stuff for women because it was what I was interested in. I really like the idea of offering porn for women because so much of the stuff on the Internet is so anti-women ... The way I'm operating is that my porn for women is trying to reflect women's sexual experience as opposed to men's, because I've had all these people saying, 'What is porn for women? Is it just pictures of naked men?' And I say, 'No, it's not really because for a start a lot of women aren't turned on by naked men—what they want to see is couples photos'. But so many photos in porn are all from the man's point of view and the man's pleasure and the man's fantasy so you can get entire sets of photos where you don't even see the man's face and the woman's constantly looking at the camera and it always has to

end in the money shot. And it's the same with porn videos; it's not about the woman.

Jackson doesn't commission her own photos but purchases photo sets from professional distributors, which she posts on the multiple sites she administers:

> KAREN: I run a site called Pure Cunnilingus and it does super well (laughs). It took me forever to get the content for that; it's got about 1100 photos on it.
>
> INTERVIEWER: Oh wow!
>
> KAREN: And I had to plunder ... you've know I've got about 10,000 photos on my hard drive and I had to plunder every single set that I own if I want[ed] to get enough photos to put on this cunnilingus site. And that's one of the other things: in every single photo set you get or every movie it's blow job, blow job, blow job.

Jackson and her business partner prefer to emphasise the heterosexual, emotional narratives that fit the non-threatening tradition of 'women's erotica', despite their graphic images:

> INTERVIEWER: What about the fetish section? I had a look at that and it seemed a little mild ... you know, I've seen a lot more hardcore. So how do you cope with that area?
>
> KAREN: I think what happened there was we had a ... couple of fetish pictures and we thought, 'Ah well'. I guess the main thing is they are all [about] female domination one ... I don't think we've got any male domination. In terms of other fetishes, it's really more a matter of this is just a taste and I guess if you want to go down the fetish path, then there are other sites available.
>
> INTERVIEWER: So you are giving more of a taster on your site? It's not something you'd go into more deeply?
>
> KAREN: No, I mean, it's not that we aren't into that ... (laughs) Both of us are happily monogamous people. We're not off doing all that swinger stuff and ... it's not a matter of whether it turns us on or not, it's that we had those photos and we thought, 'Oh well, they're interesting, we'll just put them there'. And

they were female domination and they looked a bit fun so off they go. But there's also the thing that if women are heavily into the fetish scene, they're not going to join our site—they will be off to the designated fetish sites. If you're going to look at that then I guess we are marketing to heterosexual women who are *Cleo/Cosmo* women who are fairly vanilla I think.

Empowerment or Conformity?

Although she inspired the birth of feminist porn, Andrea Dworkin never accepted its legitimacy. In her autobiography, *Heartbreak*, she wrote: 'Feminist porn is irrelevant. What women need to do is break out of male control, and porn is an act of conformity'. It's clear that, like their overseas counterparts, Australian women make all kinds of pornography, for all kinds of reasons. It's also clear that for these feminist porn producers, making porn is not simply a matter of joining 'raunch culture' as a 'female chauvinist pig'. While there are, no doubt, many women who seek 'empowerment' in fairly superficial or misguided ways, we would argue that, on balance, this shouldn't be read as a sign that popular culture (and for that matter pornography) and feminism are incompatible.

Like Ariel Levy and others, Dworkin argues that 'One of the things pornography has done is that it's changed the way women experience their bodies so that sex is what you look like, not what you touch or what you feel and do'. Yet there are other feminists, including all three authors of this book, who argue that pornography is one of the few media forms where a diverse range of bodies and sexual styles are deemed attractive and sexy, and the rise of amateur and DIY porn can be seen as an example of this tendency.

So far we've looked at the content of mainstream pornography in Australia and the main arguments about pornography—the central debates and issues. As we noted at the start of this book, anti-porn feminism has been one of the strongest and most visible public forces speaking out against feminism. And, as we said, it is vitally important that we listen to the arguments of these anti-porn feminists and not simply dismiss them. They are talking about very real issues, and women are still facing many kinds of discrimination and oppression in Australian society. But it's also important to note that these feminists do not speak for all women. There are many women in Australia, including feminists and lesbians, who think that the problem isn't pornography itself—it's bad pornography that doesn't pay enough attention to women's pleasure or indeed to the diversity of sexual interests that define our society.

This is one of the reasons that Australians have become involved in the production of pornography. As we noted above, Australia isn't a large enough market to sustain a fully commercial pornography production industry. The people who do get involved in production in this country do so for reasons other than making money. One reason is that some lesbian and heterosexual women don't see their pleasure being represented in mainstream commercial pornography and want to remedy that situation. But there are other reasons for getting involved in porn production in Australia, and in the next chapter we look at the broader impact DIY, amateur and cottage industry porn have had in Australia over the past decade.

6

DIY Porn
Fans, Amateurs and Cottage Industries

WANTED! LADIES FOR PLAY. Hi, we are a hot young horny couple who are looking for ladies who would like to watch us have sex and who would like to play with my wife while we fuck. We are very horny so sex is practiced quite often. We are new to the porn industry and hope that one day we can actually star in one or a magazine or video would be nice. Please feel free to send a pic with your reply, the sooner you reply the sooner the hot sex can start. We hope to hear from you soon, hope you like the pics. We want to do more so if you like them we'll send more, ok seeya. Love and kisses D&J. All replies answered.

Five colour photos, clearly taken at home with a tripod, accompany this ad in *Australasian Vixen*. Four out of the five show conventional, close-up 'porn' shots; for example, vaginal penetration from behind, vaginal penetration with woman on top, and fellatio. In most sexy personal ads participants are either nude or dressed in lingerie, but in D and J's photos, she wears a striped, sleeveless casual dress; he wears a tracksuit and T-shirt (and running shoes in one photo). His fly is undone, so that his erect penis is visible, and her dress is pushed up to reveal her buttocks and pubic hair, but almost no genital detail. Hands with wedding rings (his

and hers) are visible in two of the pictures, but the most interesting overlap of porn and domesticity occurs in the only full body
shot. The couple is posed in profile, in 'doggie' position (both still
clothed as described), both smiling. She looks slightly downward
and ahead; he turns his head to smile at the camera. Both have
what could be described as 'average' looks: he has a bit of a belly;
she has stretch marks on her thighs and buttocks.

This photo is clearly taken in the couple's lounge room—
a chair, a flower arrangement, a telephone table with heart-shaped
cutouts, and an entertainment unit are visible in the background.
It is not a 'good' picture; the edge of her head is slightly out of
frame on the left, while on the right something that appears to be
an open door with a towel draped over it juts in. Not only is the
photo very clearly the work of a home photographer using the
timer on his/her camera, but the wall above them is covered in
framed family photos. Although very little detail can be made out
in the magazine reproduction, it is clear that some of the family
photos are studio portraits of a family group, while others are
mother and baby pictures, and others are snapshots of children.
Others show adults alone or in affectionate group poses.

D and J are indeed 'new to the porn industry'. Like many amateurs they are able to 'play' at being porn stars by photographing
themselves having sex, by advertising for new partners and, most
importantly, by appearing in a full-page ad in a swingers magazine, which includes not only other amateur photos but photo
spreads by professional porn models. D and J seek 'exposure' in
an environment that invites both contributors and readers to blur
the boundaries of 'amateurism' with those of professionalism, for
their own sexual pleasure. Many advertisers in *Australasian Vixen*,
as in other swingers magazines, seek actual contact with potential
sexual partners, and indicate their tastes and level of experience—
phrases like 'bi-curious', 'first-timer' and 'limits respected' are
common. Others, however, advertise as 'collectors', who merely
seek to exchange photographs or invite fantasy-driven written
and/or telephone correspondence with other amateurs. It is clear,
also, that there are readers who respond to ads without actually
intending to make contact—these are the 'time-wasters' that
'genuine' advertisers advise should not reply.

In the 1970s and 1980s, the majority of opposition to pornography focused on several key issues. Radical feminists and political and religious conservatives argued that pornography demeaned the women it depicted. Some agreed with US academic Catharine MacKinnon that pornography constituted a form of hate speech and incited violence against women. Others, like Andrea Dworkin, argued that pornography was a kind of propaganda tool that framed 'good sex' as sex that celebrated male erections and orgasms above and beyond all other forms of sexual expression. Australian academic Sheila Jeffreys also claimed that heterosexual pornography was designed to teach both men and women to eroticise women's oppression. All of these theorists linked their opposition to porn with their broader opposition to the commercial sex industry. For those who draw radical feminist (and conservative) frameworks, sex workers in prostitution and pornography are understood as dupes or victims who have allowed their bodies to be exploited. As criminologist John Scott puts it:

> By the middle decades of the twentieth century it was commonly claimed that the majority of prostitutes [and porn performers] were coerced, forced and ensnared into a trade which, it was popularly understood, could only be entered into for financial reasons, reducing the most intimate of human relations to a cash nexus. Prostitution [and pornography] was seen as diametrically opposed to 'loving' relationships, which were regarded as providing the basis of a healthy and well-functioning society.

This model of understanding pornography and prostitution has been opposed by many women within the sex industry, on the basis that it disrespects the rights of women to make choices about their own bodies and sexualities. As Chapter 5 illustrated, many feminists have argued that explicit sexual images do not necessarily demean or degrade women and, in fact, can offer them new opportunities to express themselves sexually. And, as D and J's ad illustrates, the growth of amateur, DIY (do-it-yourself) and cottage industry porn has made it very clear that public or commercial sex can take place within domestic spaces, and can even form part of loving relationships. It is true that the reference to 'my wife' in D and J's ad suggests that the male partner was the author. Classical radical feminist analyses of pornography would suggest that even if the female partner has actively participated in the production of the images, it was only as the result of coercion by, or collusion with, the patriarchal male (as represented by her husband). Yet the (growing) field of academic research into amateur porn suggests that even though women who make porn are still more likely to be stigmatised than their male counterparts, they are often very highly motivated to do it. As one Australian amateur puts it, 'It's just a hobby for me [but] it's not really a great industry—I plan on having kids one day and I don't want to have to explain [myself] if [my] photos ever pop up somewhere'.

This was one of the most interesting findings of the Understanding Pornography project. Many amateurs and DIY pornographers seem to see themselves as part of a community of fans and connoisseurs, made up of exhibitionists and voyeurs. They are not only the producers of pornography, they are their own 'ideal spectators'. Amateurs like D and J especially seem to take pleasure in the knowledge that they are both the objects and subjects of their own pornographic fantasies. For many DIY porn enthusiasts, online amateur sites offer spaces where those with common interests can interact. As Helen, a Brisbane-based DIY fetish porn producer, explains: 'I guess I wanted to give back to the community ... It's a very centralised little community—there are not that many of us in the world. I just started with some photos and it just grew from there after some positive responses'.

Just as reality television and 'factual entertainment' programs from talk shows to docu-soaps (such as *Australian Idol*) have blurred the boundary between 'celebrities' and 'ordinary people', so amateur porn has blurred the boundary between 'porn stardom' and 'ordinary heterosexuality', between 'kink' and 'domesticity', between 'public' and 'private' sex. Since even the most glossy Hollywood pornography by definition offers the representation of 'real bodies' (even if they're not typical, they're certainly not animations) having 'real' sex as opposed to simulated sex, amateur filmmakers and performers have a better chance of reproducing 'celebrity' or 'stardom' in porn than they might in other genres.

After all, the generic term for any pornographic performer is porn *star*, not 'porn actor'.

Paradoxically, when researcher Ruth Barcan interviewed 'Keith', a director of amateur porn, he put forth the view that the audience for amateur porn has grown as viewers have become increasingly sophisticated and developed a desire 'to relate' to the performers having sex on film. In Keith's view, amateurs are performing their ordinariness, rather than their 'stardom'. They are trying to produce performances that ordinary people can 'relate' to, and this is what makes them attractive. But while the desire to 'relate' to, the image may partly explain why people make porn for themselves, it doesn't explain why so many people choose to swap, sell or otherwise publicly circulate the pictures and videos they create at home.

At the same time, the relative accessibility of the technologies that allow 'publication' on the Net, and the popularity of webcasting and blogging, have revealed that porn consumers are eager to look at and fantasise about 'imperfect' bodies. As we discussed in Chapter 3, amateur sites are the most popular porn sites on the internet. As our interviewee, Victorian webmaster and publisher 'Craig' explains, it is the very ordinariness of Web amateurs that makes home-made porn so appealing:

> A lot of internet webcam sites have become very popular, because people like the factor of seeing someone who is not a paid porn star getting their gear off or having sex with somebody ... I think it's kind of like the next door neighbour factor—they don't really know who it is, but they like the fact that it could be someone they walk past in the supermarket or someone who lives down the street ... The biggest growth in porn in the last ten years has been in the amateur area; the other areas are pretty much maxed out.

Online amateur sites and webcam groups have opened up a realm of 'domesticated' pornography that is simultaneously public and private. In his ethnographic study of a 'sex-pic' trading community, British sociologist Don Slater found that his interviewees enjoyed participating in what they saw as a pleasurable alternative to everyday life, especially when:

> the chat [on the sex-pic site] ... can itself become eroticised as
> representations, flirting, heated and pleasurable sex talk, cybersex,
> in which the actual encounter between participants becomes, as
> the typical comment goes, 'like being inside a piece of interactive
> pornography'.

This desire to voluntarily immerse oneself in 'interactive pornography' is not exclusively the province of male porn fans. In
his study, Slater found that female participants particularly appreciated the internet as a place where they could 'explore desires
which are too taboo, embarrassing or dangerous for off-line life:
mainly bisexuality, exhibitionism, group sex and promiscuity'. This
finding was supported by a study done by Australian researchers
Marj Kibby and Bronwyn Costello of a heterosexual webcam
exhibitionist site which, they argue, allowed not only a space for
female sexual experimentation and exhibitionism, but formed a
community that supported women's voyeuristic desire to be sexually entertained by men. In addition, it offered a space for men to
perform as eroticised objects of female desire.

Our own interviews supported these findings—there are
plenty of women who want to make their own porn. Indeed, as
Kibby and Costello observe, it can be easier for amateur women to
'perform' porn than it is for men. As they succinctly put it, 'there
is no sock equivalent to the fishnet stocking', and many elements
of eroticised masculine costuming, such as cock rings or uniforms,
are commonly understood as being homoerotic rather than being
appealing to women. Kibby and Costello note that members of
the webcam community are critical of male participants who limit
their interaction to what is termed 'crotch-cam', or the close-up
framing of their genitals, excluding the rest of their bodies from
the frame. This is considered by community members to be a poor
excuse for 'doing a show' and female community members frequently refuse to interact with such men, who are seen as 'selfish'.

As well as producing pictures and using webcams, members
of this pornographic online community also use the internet to
chat with each other. In Chapter 7 we'll discuss concerns about
children's involvement in internet chat, but in this context it's
clear that for these amateurs it's a positive thing. It is difficult in

this context to determine whether online sex is public or private, and whether it is real or fake. As Rival, Slater and Miller have observed, online sexual 'pleasures and transgressions' evidently depend on a clear separation of sexuality from 'real life'. At the same time, the separation of sex and 'real life' is not always clear-cut. Slater observed that 'many logged conversations [in his study] move within minutes from tastes in porn to the problems of single-parenthood, money problems, dead-end jobs'.

Similarly, Kibby and Costello's sex chat is often grounded in the ordinariness of everyday life as people discuss where they're from, their age, their marital status, their jobs, their computer problems and the weather, all the while displaying erotic images of their naked bodies.

Clearly, 'internet porn' does serve as a pleasurable space where sexual fantasy offers an 'escape' from the everyday. At the same time, amateur porn and X-rated swap sites seem to demonstrate that sex, even pornographic or taboo sex, is *interconnected* with everyday life. Not only are everyday domestic issues discussed on a pic trading site, the space of the site itself is 'domesticated' in participant's discussions; for example, these may include the formulation of guidelines for online sexual etiquette and the

---

Great Moments in Amateur Porn

- **Jennicam & the webcam phenomenon:** Once again, pornography leads the way in the domestication of a new communications technology. Just as it was porn that drove the take-up of amateur photographic equipment, the VCR and the internet, so once again it showed the world what could be done by an enterprising individual with a webcam.
- **Pammy and Tommy:** Pamela Anderson (Lee), often voted as the woman that men would most like to sleep with (even if not to marry), a post-feminist icon, businesswoman and beloved by gay men everywhere, shows the world that she doesn't only have sex for money.
- **One Night in Paris:** Paris Hilton, famous for being famous, is now also famous for inspiring perhaps the best title ever of a porn movie against stiff competition that includes *Edward Penishands* and *Buttbanged Naughty Nurses*.

negotiation of jealousy and competition between online and 'real-life' sex partners. As Slater and his fellow researchers describe it, the study of their particular web community 'shows that the objectification of sexuality on-line appears to be fuelled at least as often by the urge to order sexuality (and [online] relationships and practices themselves) along ethical lines as it is to gratify it transgressively'. In other words, these porn fans do not view their own enjoyment of pornographic representations of sexuality as 'de-humanising' or 'objectifying' themselves or others. Instead, sex pic trading is seen as part of everyday sexuality: pleasurable, but not without its problems and ethical challenges. As Slater has put it, it is this acknowledgement that the world of porn and amateur exhibitionism is *not* divorced from everyday life that makes the experience 'real' for participants.

Technologies of Sex

The situation that we found in our research is that contemporary Australian DIY pornographers are using domestic technologies—the camera used for family photos, the home computer—to create what could be considered a cottage industry for porn.

But is this sexualised use of household entertainment and media technologies new? And is the blurring of respectable house-holders and pornographers a twenty-first-century phenomena? A look at the history of porn indicates that while very strong lines were drawn in the past between 'good' wives and mothers and 'bad' porn performers, the role of the hobbyist performer or pro-ducer of porn is as old as porn itself. This isn't just a result of new technologies—people have always being making porn for pleasure.

In her influential book *Hard Core*, US researcher Linda Williams looks at the origins of film and video pornography in the context of other media forms. She examines the content of photographer Eadweard Muybridge's stop-motion studies of naked men and women in his 1887 *Animal Locomotion* series, which fascinated both scientists and the public of the day. As photographic tech-nologies advanced, they allowed the human body to be examined in close detail. Accounts of early still photography and cinema, she argues, are full of expressions of a desire to know, and more importantly, *see* the truth of sexual difference, of bodily movement and bodily pleasures. As we discussed in Chapter 1, sexually explicit images are not a new thing—we can find them throughout history (including in Pompeii). But given the ease and realistic nature of producing photographic images compared with detailed drawn or painted images, it's not surprising that the twentieth-century growth of visual pornography developed hand in hand with early photography and filmmaking. And because photographic images clearly showed the identity of the real person in pornography, it caused new problems for the actors who might be stigmatised by their appearance in it.

The earliest primitive form of cinematic porn was the stag or 'smoker' film which, Williams and others have argued, served not only to entertain and arouse, but also to drum up business for sex workers in the brothels where the illicit films were screened. Some of these films took the form of what Williams terms a 'genital show', with women stripping, bending over or spreading their legs for the camera. Others offered a series of randomly connected 'genital events' or disjointed girl/girl or boy/girl sex scenes.

While contemporary audiences draw a distinction between sex workers and 'legitimate' actresses, in the nineteenth century the border was not so clear-cut. Performing in public was not a respectable occupation for women of the day, and many actresses, dancers and music-hall performers supplemented their incomes with part-time prostitution. Even if they never posed for pornography, the women who appeared in early photographs and early cinema would have been considered very much outsiders by the 'decent' families of their time. At the same time, their images quickly became part of everyday family entertainment.

It is interesting to consider the differences between the women who appeared in early pornography and the photographers and filmmakers who produced it. Commercial photography studios were usually male-owned and operated and were considered perfectly acceptable businesses. But as historian Thomas Waugh argues in his exhaustive history of gay pornography, *Hard to Imagine* (1996), from the eighteenth century 'respectable' photographic studios and photographic 'artists' produced volumes of sexually explicit material, either for their own private use or for commercial distribution. Their situation was similar to that of contemporary Californian film crews, who are able to work on an ad for breakfast cereal one day and porn shoots the next. Since they did not appear in the image, their social mobility was greater than that of the men and women who appeared onscreen.

Unlike early photographs and 'dirty postcards', the screening of cinematic porn created an opportunity for a public, if illicit, shared experience for male porn viewers. Men's clubs or groups of male friends could bond over depictions of 'real' sex. At first this occurred almost exclusively in clubhouses, brothels or private homes. By the 1960s and 1970s, however, the increasing social acceptance of sexual expression meant that porn was becoming more public. The 1972 film *Deep Throat* has been mentioned several times in our work, simply because it signalled such an important turning point. It was the first porn film to become a mainstream media phenomenon. Porn (and porn performers) was no longer secret men's business. Women began to visit porn theatres with their friends or partners, and the line between slutty porn performers and the respectable wives and mothers who must be protected from exposure to porn became blurred. And, as indicated in Chapter 5, the women's movement had increased the acceptability of sexually explicit materials as an aspect of women's everyday lives.

By the 1980s, porn could easily be integrated into the domestic scene. Affordable VCRs meant that men and women no longer needed to visit sex cinemas in order to watch pornography. Home porn viewers were no longer reliant on the decisions made by professional directors and editors. By using their remotes to skip boring dialogue or loop exciting scenes, porn fans effectively became amateur editors, able to impose the narrative of their own sexual tension and resolution over that of the director and onscreen actors. The era of DIY porn had begun.

While some porn fans had previously produced their own home movie-style porn on Super 8, these films needed to be commercially processed. Many respectable wannabe porn stars were unwilling to risk exposure and so were forced to rely on the more discreet technology of the Polaroid camera to produce still images. The advent of the handycam allowed porn amateurs to create their own mini-movie, which could be kept as a memento or swapped with fellow enthusiasts. By the mid-1990s, the new technologies of home computing and webcams had become affordable for would-be pornographers.

Labours of Love: Fanzines and Other Forms of DIY

Amateur or DIY porn doesn't always involve original photographs or video. Sometimes amateur porn can be recycled from very inoffensive mainstream media texts; for example, a foot fetishist could 'borrow' images of barefoot celebrities and compile them with home-scripted fantasy plot lines. It is also clear from specialist websites that fetishists form fan cultures with specialised sexual tastes and search for references to their favourite pastimes in popular media. For example, many BDSM websites contain lists that faithfully cite even the faintest hints or allusions to BDSM sexuality in pop songs, films or television shows, such the comic spanking sequences in *Ally McBeal* and *Sex and the City*, or references to 'safewords' in *Buffy the Vampire Slayer*. Others go further than simply collating lists and edit together highlights from their personal collections for commercial redistribution. In his historical study of gay men's porn, Thomas Waugh describes a still of Alan Ladd being flogged in the 1946 film *Two Years Before the Mast* as 'the prize of one S/M aficionado's collection'.

According to journalist Laurence O'Toole:

> In the porn shops of North Beach, San Francisco, you can find shelves of video compilations ... recovered from the mainstream and remade as porn. There's Eugene Bernard's series of classic corporal punishment clips from cinema and television, full of scenes of cowgirls being spanked by cowboys and of tanned, muscular male leads being strung up and whipped in biblical epics, on the high seas, or in the Sheriff of Nottingham's dungeon.

The DIY porn zine *BP* (*Betty Paginated*) is almost impossible to classify. On one hand it's classic recycled fan porn, filled

with pirated images from video freeze-frames and old pornographic magazines and wrestling programs. But *BP* is an amateur
zine produced by (softcore) porn professionals: Dann Leonard, a
former *People* magazine editor, and Helen Vnuk, the former editor
of *Australian Women's Forum*, who has also worked for *Picture*
magazine.

In classic zine style, *BP* is highly personal, containing interviews with porn producers and professional wrestlers, diary entries
by the publishers, letters and fiction contributed by readers, and
reviews of books, zines, videos and wrestling matches. Although
the written text is largely produced by professional journalists, the
zine represents amateurism through its celebration of the many
loves of its producers. According to Dann Leonard, most of the
content is produced by Helen and himself:

> Occasionally someone has submitted something to me, and I've felt
> kind of vaguely obligated to run it ... but that's pretty rare and I
> can't even think of an example off the top of my head. Basically
> most of it is stuff that I want to run, and really I don't give a shit if
> people aren't interested in it.

Each issue combines pornographic pictures with discussions
of celebrity wrestlers, reviews of other zines and tributes to particular porn stars ('I coughed my filthy trouser yogurt heaps of times
over this chick'). The 'Born for Porn' edition (no. 22) also contains erotic semi-nude pictures of Helen Vnuk, shot by Australian
glamour photographer Bambi. The photoshoot was a gift from
Dann for Helen's thirtieth birthday and sits at the 'tasteful' end of
the classic genre of the 'naughty wife' home-porn shot. The pictures aren't happy snaps by hubby or even a boudoir makeover in a
suburban photo studio. They are both amateur and professional.

In his interview for the Understanding Pornography project,
Dann explained that although he was a professional journalist, it
was his 'hobbyist' writing for *Betty Paginated* that first got him the
job at *People*:

> The first issue [in 1992] was just a six page, photocopied, extended
> letter that I sent to like six people that I knew, and I got ... good
> feedback on it, so I put out another one a couple of months later,

and it was about ten pages, and then got more positive feedback and I was sending it to more people, and by the end of the year, I'd put out like five issues … [Then] Helen saw this ad for *People* magazine in the *Weekend Australian* and … suggested [that] instead of sending my boring stories that I did about grape prices and you know … storm damage to cereal crops and stuff like that, that I should send articles that I've done in *BP*. So basically through *BP* I got the job and we went over there and really didn't think about the zine … I thought, 'Well, shit, I'm doing this as a day job now, why should I do a zine anymore?' So I didn't really touch it for like a year or so, and then, I just started thinking, 'No, there's things I want to write about that I can't really write about at work'.

Although Dann and Helen estimated they lost up to $3000 on some issues, after factoring in printing and postage costs, at the time of their 2002 interview they were continuing to produce issues once or twice a year. As Dann put it:

BP's been so good to me, and to Helen, because we both got our jobs through it, in Sydney. I feel like it's something that I should keep going … because it's basically a very important part of my life, so, in a sense I don't do it as a chore. If I don't feel like doing it, I won't put out one for, I think the longest I've gone without doing one, was like eighteen months when I first got here. And now I just did one and got going again, so as long as I keep enjoying doing it … I'll keep doing it. It's purely a labour of love.

Dann and Helen emphasised that *BP* was not designed as a masturbatory aid—'I feel sorry for anyone who actually uses it to wank over!'—but was designed to provide glimpses of the porn world and 'the inside of Dann's brain'.

Giving Back to the Community—Cottage Industry Porn

As with the lesbian pornographers we discussed in Chapter 5, some people simply aren't represented in mainstream pornography and so have to produce porn for themselves. While some amateur pornographers and porn fans produce their own writing, photos and videos in order to complement the more 'mainstream' aspects of the industry, a significant minority of Australian pornographers that we spoke to saw themselves as representing forms of sexuality that were excluded by conventional porn. Many of the producers of, and performers in, this kind of porn were only part-time media producers but were involved full-time in the sexual subcultures they represented. A number of small BDSM and fetish-themed websites in Australia functioned to promote community events, showcase the work of local photographers and models, advertise the commercial services of professional dominants and submissives, and in some cases run kink-oriented dating or personal ads. They targeted a subculture with diverse tastes and preferences and, although they were developed in the interests of promoting community unity, their life spans were fairly short. The publications *Melbourne KinkScene* and *Sydney KinkScene* and the online site ScreamZine all began and then ceased publication during our three-year project. All three were produced by one or two people and burnout seemed to play a significant factor in their demise.

A key issue, too, was the limitations placed on content by Australia's classification laws. As we discussed in Chapter 3, the classification laws in Australia explicitly exclude anything that might be considered 'violence'. This brings us back to the thorny issue of how to define violence. As we said in our content analysis, we didn't count consensual sadomasochism—such as spanking—as violence. It didn't fit into the social science definition of violence that we chose: 'Any form of behaviour directed toward the goal of harm; or injuring another living being who is motivated to avoid such treatment'. If you are going to count any kind of physical contact as violence, even if it's not trying to hurt people, and they don't mind it, then every contact sport would have to be coded as violence under media rules, which obviously doesn't make sense.

However, the classification laws take a different approach. Under current legislation, consensual sadomasochistic acts between adults—including spanking, dripping wax onto someone's body, body piercing for sexual pleasure, bondage, golden showers and fisting—are all classified as 'sexual violence' and are therefore illegal.

This makes things difficult for those Australians who enjoy such sexual practices. As the ex-editor of *Fetish Australia* magazine described it in an interview for our project: '[We] went bust after two issues ... because of what they couldn't show in a fetish magazine here. You could show somebody being whipped, but you couldn't show red marks ... so you tell me how you whip someone without reddening their skin!' Consequently, most BDSM-themed images are effectively banned in Australian videos and publications, unless they are very obviously represented for educational purposes only (as with Mistress Tan's video *Sugar and Spikes*). It's a funny situation because none of these practices are actually illegal in Australia. So you can do them—but you can't photograph yourself doing them.

This places BDSM practitioners in the unique position of being unable to legally purchase locally produced images of legal practices. As Jackie, the editor of Australian 'golden showers' magazine *WetSet*, put it when we interviewed her: 'We seem to have a little bit of a problem in this country with fetish porn ... the girl can have a very large smile on her face, she can be going, "Yeah, yeah, piss in my mouth please", but the OFLC thinks it's humiliation'.

In addition, the guidelines forbid 'consensual depictions that purposefully demean anyone involved in that activity for the enjoyment of viewers' within the X classification for films, videos and DVDs, and within even Category 2 (restricted) magazines (which are only permitted to be sold in sex shops). Consequently, even activities which are clearly defined as consensual cannot be legally included in porn sold or distributed within Australia. Additionally, it is illegal to advertise a Category 2 publication in any publication that is not itself Category 2. This means that small fetish magazines cannot advertise their existence to consumers who do not already consume pornography.

This had an impact on one our interviewees, who, prior to these laws being introduced in the late 1990s, had marketed his niche spanking magazine, *Paddles*, successfully to women through advertising in *Vogue*, *Cleo* and *Cosmopolitan*. As he put it:

> The coupons used to come in by the dozen [from] female after
> female after female. [But] they changed all this and they stopped all

that, because I can only advertise *Paddles* magazine now in another Category 2 magazine, of which there's only a handful in Australia … how the hell do you find out about it if it's only sold in an adult shop?

Like *WetSet*, *Paddles* relies primarily on international sales made through its website, which is hosted offshore to bypass Australian classification rules. And once again, we found that the pornographers involved in the production of these magazines were doing it for their own pleasure rather than for money. Both *WetSet* and *Paddles* commissioned work from professional writers, illustrators or photographers—*Paddles* primarily featured erotic stories, line drawings and black and white photography. *WetSet* also sought reader-generated contributions through a series of websites, providing small modelling fees for 'featured' amateurs (in one case 'discovering' the hobbyist amateur video producer of the *Pissgirl* series). Readers also provided the bulk of the content for the Australian glossy swingers contact magazines *Vixen* and *Rosie*, with *Rosie* also producing a series of amateur porn videos, shot largely in hotel rooms. Swingers have been credited as pioneers of the now mainstreamed amateur trend. According to US porn industry magazine *Adult Video News*, the first all-amateur video production house, HomeGrown Video, was launched 'in the Betamax era' by a Californian swinger, George Swain, who videotaped his lovers and friends. The company's current owners, brothers Farrel and Moffitt Timlake, believe that their company was innovative in that it never put restrictions on the upper age (it was, of course, over-eighteens only), weight or ethnicity of its porn performers, nor did it specify that particular kinds of sex should be included in a home-made performance. Consequently, they say HomeGrown was an innovator in producing the kinds of niche or specialty porn (featuring performers over forty, internal cum shots etc) that now form part of the general porn market.

Given that so much of the hobbyist porn produced in Australia is sourced from fairly small subculture communities, such as the lesbian underground party scene or the BDSM community, it is not surprising that a number of small-scale porn producers experienced problems in making porn so close to home. The lesbian porn producers we discussed in Chapter 5 fit into this category. *Wicked Women* editor Kimberly O'Sullivan found that meeting her readers' demands for authentic hardcore lesbian sex photos was particularly difficult:

> KIMBERLY: We wanted to produce explicit material, but we were drawing our models from within the lesbian community. There was no money to pay professional models or actresses where they were going to be believable. The minute ... anything they did was slightly unbelievable, people were going to pounce on it in a second.
>
> INTERVIEWER: So did you end up, like, just running out of people to ...
>
> KIMBERLY: Absolutely! I really ran out of people and I didn't want just the same people over and over again. Because there was the same three people that were repeatedly photographed and that became problematic ... or where I got new people, what they were prepared to do was fairly limited. [They] wanted soft, nice, beautiful erotic shots of themselves. People would buy [the magazine] and go, 'It's a bit too soft'. That was really going to become a problem towards the end. I mean, there were other reasons [but] that was one of the reasons that the magazine closed. I could see that this was a big ... editorial problem and I didn't really have a way around it.

One way to avoid this problem was to recruit couples for photoshoots. 'They saw it as a sexy thing that they did together which was really good, natural eroticism and energy. They were really comfortable with each other and they know their little things that they liked doing. They saw it as an escapade', said Kimberly. But this tactic had limitations:

> At one stage I did this fantastic photoshoot in a kitchen [with a couple] doing like ... this domestic thing. Having sex on the table and all that sort of stuff. It was all great, [the] photos were done, I thought it looked really good; we're going to be able to use this really well ... It was fine, it's getting ready ... to be designed. [Then] one of the parties rings me, hysterical. They'd broken up; they don't want the photos run, that sort of thing. So that was a bit annoying,

but I decided that I had to do the right thing by them and actually not run the photos … I've got to live in this town too.

Melbourne writer and performer Bumpy ran into similar difficulties when she and a group of friends decided to make their own porn video with visiting US drag king Mo B Dick:

> When we planned it we were all single. We had our first meeting; it was more [of a] sexy, 'Yeah, we can all have sex with each other!' And then, in the meantime, two of us had got into relationships just within the last week or two … And it's very difficult, if you're really hot for someone, to have sex with someone else; whether they're your friends, or it's just for film or not.

In her study of participants in the popular Australian softcore *Home Girls* 'girl-next-door' porn magazine produced by ACP press, academic Ruth Barcan observes that amateur porn stars can also be stigmatised in small heterosexual communities. While Barcan focuses particularly on the stigma women have suffered, men can also be stigmatised for expressing their sexualities in unconventional ways, including pornographic display. For example, web photos or profiles on a swingers website could be used as evidence in a custody case and, although this has not been tested, possession of 'refused classification' BDSM-themed pornography could also be seen as evidence of poor character.

The same technologies that allow members of sexual communities to create their own porn can also be used to circulate material that documents abusive or non-consensual sexual situations. We would be wary of being read as promoting amateur porn as a 'better' form of pornography than commercial porn. Many amateur or cottage industry sites are ethically produced, however, by people who genuinely enjoy participating in a feedback loop of exhibitionism and voyeurism. While SuicideGirls is perhaps the best known indie porn site, there are many others that seek to represent real alternatives to stereotypical media standards of sexuality and beauty. For instance, US site Vegporn.com is run by a cottage industry model, FurryGirl, who launched it in 2003 as 'the first and only site made by plant-eaters'. There are no restrictions on the models' upper age, gender or sexuality, but they must be vegetarian or vegan. In addition to the private member's area that houses explicit photosets and a message board, there are also interviews with animal–rights activists and articles on veganism and sexuality. FurryGirl also runs an online sex shop that specialises in animal-free and environmentally friendly sex products, including a vibrator powered by solar energy. Vegporn.com links to the website of Fuckforforest.com, a fundraising porn site run by Norwegian environmentalists Leona Johansson and Tommy Hol Ellingsen. It also links to 'alternaporn' site NoFauxxx.com, which promotes itself as 'porn that doesn't fake it', featuring:

> Cute pin-up girls, hot boys, chubby chicks, gorgeous BBW babes, steaming hot couples, punk, goth, hippy, natural, pierced, tattooed, shaved and unshaven models, sexy trans-gender/transsexual models (FTM & MTF), erotica, straight, gay, lesbian, and bi-sexual models, black models, asian models, soft-core, hard-core, and realistic SM and bondage. We only publish exclusive, original, smart, and artistic content, and there's something for everybody.

The site's approach is quite a contrast to the commercial porn policy of separating different sexual styles in niche or 'specialty' categories, as reflected in the casting call for the site's first DVD in collaboration with US sex shop Blowfish:

> There are no specific scenes to audition for—scenes will be designed via collaboration between the director … and the actors. The theme of the DVD will be hedonist/party scene/carnivalesque/burlesque … Heterosexuals are encouraged to apply, as long as the theme/ sexual acts performed maintain a strict distance from 'mainstream' or 'straight' sexual activity.

Recognising that even performers in community-produced 'alternaporn' can live to regret their decision to model, FurryGirl posts the following on her site, in answer to the frequently asked question, 'If I change my mind, will you take down my photo?': 'The short (preventative) answer is that if you're already very concerned about what your parents/coworkers/conservative friends would think if they ever found nudie pictures of you on the internet, you probably shouldn't be doing porn anywhere, even on nice indie sites run by nice people'.

This is good advice. True, celebrities like Pamela Anderson and Paris Hilton have had their privately made home porn videos made public without suffering serious negative consequences. For others, the blurring of the line between domesticated sexuality and public sex can have nasty and very unjust repercussions. All of the interviewees on the Understanding Pornography project had to deal in one way or another with their own decisions to manufacture, perform in or distribute porn. None expressed serious regrets, but neither had anyone experienced porn as a utopian world of free sexual expression.

There are many feminists who would argue that any form of sexual exhibitionism perpetuates the cultural myth that women's primary function is the sexual and emotional service of men. There are many religious and political conservatives who would claim that all sex that takes place beyond the confines of coupled romantic love and the marital bed (lights out, no camera) is deviant, dangerous or sinful. For these critics, the reasons amateurs offer for their choices to make porn are really not relevant. It is true, too, that once an image is made public, its producer has absolutely no control over the way in which it is received by audiences. No matter how ethically produced the pornography is, there's nothing to stop a consumer from simply interpreting it as, say, 'a bunch of stupid bitches getting fucked'. Likewise, amateur porn pictures posted on a swinger's site can take on a very different meaning when they appear on the cover of, for example, a newspaper.

In Chapter 3 we examined the mainstream of pornography in Australia—the kinds of videos and internet sites that porn consumers choose to watch. As we said, porn is a huge business. You can make a lot of money distributing pornography in Australia.

But if we're concerned about the people who actually make porn—how they are treated, why they do it—then the picture in Australia is very different. There isn't that much production of pornography in this country, and what there is, from our research, is overwhelmingly produced as a labour of love. People—women as well as men—do it for sexual pleasure, because they have an exhibitionist streak and like the idea of doing it in public. Or they do it for community reasons, perhaps because the sexual group that they belong to has been outlawed from pornography by current classification legislation and so, if they want to see sexually explicit images that turn them on, they have to make them for themselves.

In contemporary media culture, the boundaries between 'real' and 'fake' experiences, and 'public' and 'private' experiences are shifting dramatically. Anyone who moves into this new territory, whether they appear on *Big Brother* or on an amateur porn site, risks a backlash from those who would prefer clear distinctions to be made between performers and audiences, or exhibitionists and voyeurs. It is evident from our research that most of those participating in DIY porn production have their own reasons for doing so and are willing to accept the risk.

The production and consumption of pornography within the domestic space is not unproblematic, however. Even those adults who are relatively unconcerned by explicit material may have very real and valid concerns around young people's access to pornography. The same technological changes that ushered in a new era of DIY porn also allow minors unprecedented access to previously restricted material. Additionally, new file-sharing software has allowed graphic images of child abuse and child sexual assault to be solicited and circulated online. These issues are explored in depth in the following chapter.

7

The Pursuit of Innocents
Children and Pornography

An internationally famous pop star stares blankly at you from out of the newspaper, his picture snapped as he's taken into custody. The police have found thousands of pictures of children forced into having sex with adults on his laptop.

An 8-year-old girl is raped and murdered in a shopping centre toilet while her older brother waits outside.

A mother is arrested for making pornographic videos of herself, her children and her husband and distributing them on the internet.

What the hell is wrong with people? What kind of world do we live in when children are being sexualised and physically harmed by adults? How did we come to this?

These were certainly some of questions that confronted us as we wrote this chapter. Childhood should be a time when children feel safe, loved and nurtured. Yet it is disturbingly clear that children around the world, including children who live in relatively affluent homes, are sometimes physically and sexually abused. Their trust in the people who care for them is violated in the worst possible way. Even more astonishing is the fact that the perpetrators of these crimes sometimes record them and that other adults take pleasure in witnessing the abuse of these children. And there is no doubt that while this abuse is not new, the internet has provided a new forum for distributing such images.

It's hard to know where to start with a subject as distressing as child pornography. In fact, it's a subject that is so emotive that we think it's important to begin by separating out the different issues that often get conflated in media coverage.

A lot of media reports confuse three different and equally important issues when it comes to protecting children online. They confuse child pornography (which depicts children in sexually explicit poses), cyberstalkers (adults who try to make sexual contact with children via email and in chat rooms) and cyberporn (adult pornographic material that children and teens may accidentally or intentionally access). All three are issues that demand serious attention. Yet they pose very different threats to our children and they each require very different solutions. We're going to begin with one of the most serious crimes: the production, dissemination and possession of child pornography.

Child Pornography

It's very unlikely that anyone you know or are likely to know has seen or tried to find child pornography. The most comprehensive studies have found that the great majority of producers and consumers of child pornography are members of an entrenched and deeply secret subculture.

Making or using child pornography is rightly considered one of the worst crimes. Child pornography shows children—legally defined in most Western countries as people under the age of sixteen—in sexual poses and sexual activity. There is, however, a lot of material traded as child pornography that also shows children engaged in everyday activities such as swimming, bathing or dressing, and which has been put to use in a sinister context.

While we are constantly bombarded with distressing media stories suggesting that paedophile rings are growing, we are rarely given any hard facts. One of the biggest problems in gauging the size of the trade in child pornography is that the laws proscribing any contact with such material are so broad that it's barely possible to do any research in the area without winding up in prison.

For legal and ethical reasons, the authors of this book agreed to make no attempt to access any sites that claimed to feature people who looked to be or were under the age of eighteen. However, we did interview somebody who knows a lot about the subject and we looked at the best available research into the subject.

Taskforce Argos is a Queensland state police body chartered to investigate sexual crimes against children. Part of that charter involves investigating child pornography on the internet. In 2005 we spoke to Inspector John Rouse, then head of Taskforce Argos, and asked him about the availability of child pornography on the internet.

The first point he made was that police don't like to use the term 'child pornography'—they prefer the term 'child abuse material'. He went on to say that child abuse material is not part of commercial pornography distribution on the internet.

'My impression from the Web-based distributors of pornography', he told us, 'is that they're not real keen on child abuse pornography at all. They're probably like you and me—they find it appalling'. He said that the chances of stumbling across this material on the internet are minimal as it isn't really distributed on web pages. Paedophiles use the internet as a form of communication, posting images to each other electronically through 'peer-to-peer communication software'. So you can't really find child abuse images just by surfing the Web—no abuser would risk posting them where the police might come across them. What you have to do is join an online community and ask to get images sent to you.

Inspector Rouse told us that child abuse material is largely produced commercially in poor or developing countries, including former Soviet bloc nations. In Australia, however, 'there is no evidence of commercial production to date'. What child abuse material is produced in Australia is made 'not for a commercial purpose, more for self-gratification, or distribution among ... paedophile networks'.

Inspector Rouse told us about one case where:

We are alleging that the photographer [of a shot of a man having sex with a 5-year-old girl] is the father of the 5-year-old girl ... the

father shared the 5-year-old girl and took the pictures ... there's
numerous stories like that that I could tell you ... a lot of it is going
to be intra-familial offences of photographing their own children ...
About 35 to 40 per cent of the male offenders that were arrested
out of Operation Auxin [which targeted child abuse material] were
parents, in family situations ... a lot of married men with children.

Inspector Rouse's comments about the situation in Australia fit
in with international research on the same issue. One of the few
credible scholars who has done recent and detailed work on the
content and consumption of child pornography is Philip Jenkins,
a distinguished Professor of History and Religious Studies at
Pennsylvania State University. Professor Jenkins decided to take
on this harrowing task because he was concerned that the barriers
to researching child abuse material meant that the public was not
getting good information about how much of it there was online
and how many people used it. He worked methodically for three
years to locate well-hidden bulletin boards and other sites where
people swapped and discussed child abuse materials. To avoid
viewing the images, he disabled the 'autoload image' function of his
Web browser. When he visited bulletin boards and other sites where
child abuse images were exchanged, he only saw written text and
generic icons indicating that photographic material was available.

Despite not having actually viewed images of child abuse material, Professor Jenkins was still able to gather a lot of very detailed
and disturbing information about the underworld that uses this
material. Enthusiasts of child abuse materials talked in great detail
about the content of videos and photographs on the bulletin
boards he visited and they regularly reviewed material for each
other. According to the discussions, the material included images
of preschoolers being molested and older children being raped.

Jenkins begins his book *Beyond Tolerance: Child Pornography
on the Internet* by warning that we need to keep the problem in
perspective, 'since the actual number of traffickers are not vast'.
He estimates that people involved in the hardcore child porn
subculture number in the tens of thousands globally, certainly a
disturbing number but one that represents only a tiny fraction
of online material. He also notes, reassuringly, that the bulletin

boards and newsgroups he used for his research are 'exceedingly difficult to find' and cannot be located by using an ordinary search engine. Easily accessed websites that claimed to show young teens, he found, almost always showed adult women and men claiming to be younger than they were. Genuine child pornography, Jenkins concludes, is made, shared and consumed by a very small underground circle of people who are almost all male.

To give another example of the scale of the problem, in 2004 the biggest police operation ever mounted in Australia to target consumers of child pornography netted 194 men out of a population of 20 million. The chief of operations in the state of NSW, Detective Superintendent Kim McKay, made similar comments to Inspector Rouse when he told the media that Australia did not have large rings of child pornographers, that the internet had made distributors and consumers easier to catch, and that the real problem lay with the failure of some governments in developing and poorer countries to protect children from abuse.

But even though the trade in child abuse materials comprises a tiny part of the traffic on the internet, Professor Jenkins observes that the 'scale of the enterprise they support is depressing, as is the constant infusion of new materials'.

So who are these men? And what drives them?

The common picture of a paedophile is of an anti-social and pathologically inadequate drifter who lives on the very fringes of society. In fact, based on his years of visiting bulletin boards, Jenkins concludes that a significant proportion of these men are tertiary educated professionals. Certainly they are people who need to have a very sophisticated grasp of the computer technology they use to access and share material. Another study into child abuse materials noted that 'the range of people involved in child pornography offences seems to cross boundaries of class, income and profession. Doctors, technicians, businessmen, teachers, media personalities, policemen: these are just a few of the kinds of people who have been found guilty in recent criminal proceedings of possessing child pornography'.

The bulletin board conversations Jenkins recorded certainly show that many enthusiasts of child pornography are capable of trying to rationalise their abhorrent behaviour. A good example of this is provided by a British collector, Adrian Thompson, who was convicted in 2000. He adopted as a motto the acronym VEDNE, which stands for 'View Evil, Do No Evil'. Jenkins comments that:

> The phrase neatly encapsulates the attitudes of many board participants, or at least their public personas ... Throughout the correspondence on the boards, numerous contributors emphasise the innocence of their interest, their hobby. They are 'just looking'; they would not enact their fantasies in a real-world context; and they express vigorous hostility towards anyone who genuinely has sex with a child—though Thompson's motto concedes that the material he was collecting was 'evil'.

This justification is nonsense of course. Child porn enthusiasts are just as implicated in the abuse of the children as the real-life abusers. By creating a demand for these images they are potentially encouraging the abuse of children and, by taking pleasure from them, they are compounding the damage done to the victims. While it may well be true that many who view child abuse materials draw the line at offending against a child in real life, it's no comfort to the children whose abuse they take pleasure in.

The users of this material, then, are not likely to be living in your street, only because they form such a minority of the population. But by the same token, he or even she may be someone who seems entirely aboveboard. Most worryingly, he or she is probably a family member or somebody already known to the child. Sadly, the great majority of sexual abuse of children is perpetrated by a family member or by someone known to the family.

Even if the child abuser is not somebody in the family of the victim, they will probably be someone who is seen to be trustworthy. They may be a politician, a journalist, a religious leader, a judge or a teacher. Paedophiles, whether active or merely voyeuristic, do not appear in the monster costume you'd expect, given their media image. All of the evidence suggests that they are often very good at gaining the trust of parents and children and that they may gravitate to positions of authority where they have access to children.

So what should we do to protect our children?

It's clear that we need to teach our children that you can't judge an adult by his or her job, by their kind smile or even by their connection to a family. The single most important thing children need to know is that they have a right to say 'no' if an adult tries to touch them inappropriately or does something that makes them feel uncomfortable, and that they should tell an adult they trust about what happened right away. Sexual abusers of children rely on the fact that most children have been taught to obey adults and that some will do so unquestioningly. Children need boundaries, of course, but they also need to be told when it's OK to disobey a grown-up and why. One of the strongest arguments for age-appropriate sex education in our schools is that it lifts the taboo on discussing bodies and sexual feelings, makes children more comfortable about disclosing any abuse to parents or others, and gives children a healthy sense that they have a say in who touches them and who doesn't.

When it comes to the much bigger question of how we eradicate the trade in child abuse materials, the picture is much bleaker, according to Professor Jenkins and other experts. The main ways in which its consumers and producers are caught, on the basis of police data, are entrapment in chat rooms by police officers posing as children or young teenagers, discovery of child abuse materials when they put their computers in to be repaired or, very rarely, discovery by internet service providers who alert law enforcement agencies. As Jenkins found, however, the great majority of hardcore enthusiasts of child pornography are experts at evading detection. They never visit chat rooms, they use bogus email addresses and identities, they upload material and distribute a password decoding the downloaded images days later on a separate bulletin board, and they are very careful about where they store their collections. For all of these reasons, it's far more likely that newcomers to the subculture, not the hardcore members of it, will be caught.

That said, we should resource and support all possible initiatives to target the trade in child abuse materials and to encourage child protection laws in countries where the sex trafficking of children and young teenagers is endemic. Professor Jenkins also strongly believes that there needs to be a concerted international effort to suppress the newsgroups and bulletin boards that provide a forum for fans of child abuse materials.

There is, unfortunately, no magic bullet that will rid us of child pornography or child sexual abuse. But if we want to confront the problem, we need to do it rationally and resource solutions which are evidence-based. We also need to give the children in our own communities the confidence to talk to trusted adults about anything bad that happens to them.

Cyberstalkers

Australian photographer Russ Grayson came home one evening to find a man standing on the footpath in front of his house taking photographs of frangipani flowers lit by the late-afternoon sun. Frangipani trees grow all over Sydney, the city he lives in, and the air in many streets is fragrant with the perfume of their white blossoms all through summer.

Grayson writes that on his approach, the man asked if he minded him taking the photographs. 'We started talking. He had recently developed an interest in photography and practiced by taking images around the neighbourhood. Glancing to the young woman accompanying him, he said, "I bring my wife with me … I don't want to be mistaken for a paedophile". A strange statement, I thought. What could taking photographs on a public street have to do with sex crimes against children?'.

The amateur photographer's apprehension, as Grayson goes on to note, was not as strange as it first seems. That summer had seen a number of attempts by local mayors in Sydney's beachside suburbs to ban the photography of children in public places. The trigger for the proposed bans was the conviction of a man for nuisance after he was observed taking repeated covert photographs of topless women sunbathers with his mobile phone. But it wasn't topless women who were the subject of the intense public debate that followed. It was children who were deemed most at risk.

In the Anglo-Australian cultural imagination, the beach is a central marker of national identity. It's a place that symbolises the allegedly easygoing, egalitarian and unpretentious Australian character. Many Australian children spend half their lives at the beach in summer and, until an awareness of skin cancer prompted more attention to covering up in the sun, most of them spent their summer half-naked. When the shadow of the paedophile falls across this iconic and idealised space, we can be sure that something very deep-rooted is troubling parents and others who care about children.

The figure of the cyberstalker is ubiquitous in many alarmist media stories, despite scant evidence that children and young teenagers are actually being routinely seduced or abducted by these shadowy figures. Here's a classic introduction to this kind of story: 'Imagine a stranger sneaking into your home, seducing your son or daughter while you watch TV in the lounge-room. That is just what is happening every day … as paedophiles pursue children through Internet chat rooms'.

There is a long history behind concerns about the dangers young people face from new technologies for distributing information and popular culture. We mention this history because we think it's very important to keep the concerns about threats to young people in perspective.

US scholar Judith Levine has written an internationally acclaimed book on this subject titled *Harmful to Minors*. She notes that:

> dire assessments of a morally anarchic world are not new. But they tend to crop up in times of social transformation, when the economy trembles or when social institutions crumble and many people feel they're losing control of their jobs, their futures, or their children's lives. At times like these, the child-molesting monster can be counted on to creep from the rubble.

Her point isn't that paedophiles are imaginary or that there aren't threats to our children. She's arguing that we sometimes displace our anxieties about social and technological changes.

We all want to make sure that Australian children are protected from the real dangers that they face. And so, as we say above, it is important that we don't get distracted from real threats by stereotypes and bogeymen. So what is the evidence for the claim that the average child or teenager has been placed at an increased risk of being stalked and sexually abused or harassed because of the internet? How, in simple terms, is the online digital world more dangerous than the world in which parents tell their kids not to take lollies from strangers in the park?

There is evidence that some paedophiles do use chat rooms to contact and attempt to 'groom' children and teenagers to take part in sexual activities. But we also know that the same group have also used scout clubs, schools, football teams, piano lessons and even churches to find children to prey on. Clearly, we need to educate children and young people about the risks of disclosing personal information to strangers online or offline and let them know that not all adults, virtual or real, can be trusted. Teaching our children to play in the information traffic is a lot like teaching them how to deal with real traffic. You start out by holding their hand and hovering over them and then you gradually allow them to strike out on their own.

Over the past decade, law enforcement officers across the Western world have devoted a lot of resources to entrapping people who try to engage young people in chat rooms in sexual banter. Their efforts have, thankfully, resulted in the detection and imprisonment of some sexual predators. But, as important as we believe this kind of policing is, we think it's critical, given the extent of the research we've done, to state that any politician or commentator who claims that they can comprehensively protect children from online predators or pornographers is exaggerating.

In his book *The Culture of Child Molesting*, US scholar James Kincaid argues that we have been so busy constructing children as 'at risk' of sexual predators that we now have no other way of seeing them. Worse, it is the would-be protectors of children who unwittingly perpetuate this notion of children as sexualised. 'We have made the child we are protecting from sexual horrors into a being defined exclusively by sexual images and terms: the child is defined as the sexual lure, the one in danger, the one capable of attracting nothing but sexual thoughts.'

Professor Kincaid reminds us that if we only think about children's online experiences as potentially dangerous, then we are at risk of ignoring all of the creative social and educational things kids can be doing with computers. Even pre-teens are increasingly using the internet as tool for communicating with friends and designing web pages, which they use to showcase their own interests, ideas and artwork. The now-ubiquitous personal blog has taken the diary to new creative heights.

Cyberporn

The third main concern about the internet and children is that children might be exposed to online adult pornography. There's certainly no question that the internet has made a much wider range of pornography potentially much more accessible to children and young teenagers, but it's important to remember that kids have always been curious about sex and the world of grown-ups.

The Australia Institute, for example, asked a market research company to conduct a phone poll. It found that 38 per cent of boys and 2 per cent of girls aged sixteen and seventeen had deliberately watched porn on the internet. Approximately 73 per cent of boys and 11 per cent of girls in this age group said they had watched an X-rated video and nine out of ten boys and a similar number of girls believed that it was common for boys their age to view sex sites online. But the study also found that only 4 per cent of boys viewed sex sites on a weekly basis and that it was far more common for boys to look at X-rated videos than at internet sites. The study also found that substantially fewer numbers of girls aged sixteen to seventeen regularly viewed pornography. The study did not include questions about what the teenagers enjoyed or didn't enjoy in what they viewed or why they used X-rated videos more than the internet to watch pornography.

The authors of the Australia Institute report acknowledged that there is nothing new about young people trying to access adult sexual material. As we saw in Chapter 2, almost 40 per cent of consumers born in the 1950s or earlier had encountered pornography before the age of sixteen, and this percentage has been increasing every decade since.

It's interesting to note that when we interviewed our sample of consumers, none of them said they felt harmed by coming across pornography at a younger age. Importantly, none had been given pornography by an adult. They had all discovered it for themselves. The main sources of this pornography were parents' collections, those of other relatives and of the parents of friends, or material discarded in public places such as parks or on the street. In discussing the uses of this pornography, the interviewees made a strong distinction between finding pornography when they were kids and finding it as teenagers. Those who had found pornography before adolescence tended to describe it as meaningless or as funny. By contrast, those who first encountered pornography in their early teens tended to express interest in it. Several described the use of pornography at that age as a rite of passage, often consumed as a group, with an element of competition about who had the most.

Of course, many of these porn consumers came across pornography before the era of the internet, in a time when pornography was much easier to censor. The authors of the Australia Institute report express a very deep concern that the teenagers who have been accessing porn online may be exposed to what they call 'extreme and "deviant" sexual practices'. While they don't tell us what they mean by 'deviant' practices, they do go on to talk about the fact that pornography featuring rape and bestiality exists online, and express concern that young teenage boys will copy what they see or come to believe that it's OK to degrade and assault women and force them to have sex.

These are alarming claims, ones that were (unsurprisingly) given wide media coverage. But as we have noted, it's actually difficult to find such material, and it's certainly not the mainstream of pornography on the internet. When people are looking at internet porn, they are mostly looking at amateur sites that feature a variety of female bodies and that often include material written from the perspective of the women involved. Yes, young people are being exposed to porn on the Net. Yes, it's possible to find disturbing materials on the Net. But it doesn't automatically follow that vast numbers of young people are actively seeking out disturbing materials on the Net or that they are developing a preference for it.

The interviews we did with consumers, and all the research that we've talked about in this book, confirm that the kind of people who are tolerant of sexually explicit material are actually very concerned about violence, including sexual violence. And there is no good reason to think that teenage boys differ wildly from other porn consumers.

Nonetheless, the authors of the Australia Institute study do highlight a very important issue: there is a small but real risk that young people will come across pornography online that shows people being assaulted or denigrated. And obviously, if we're talking about children and younger teens, there's some risk that some of them will be upset by any sexually explicit material they come across. The big question is what parents and other people who care for children and teenagers can do about these risks? What is the best way to protect children and young people?

Unplugging the computer is one response. But that's obviously not something many parents or educators are willing to do, given the enormous information databank represented by the internet. Installing filtering software has some benefits, particularly for primary school-aged children whose research online will be limited. The problem with using such software for teenagers is that it has the capacity to seriously limit their ability to get to important information they need for school or just for personal reasons. For one thing, the internet has become a source of really valuable information about sexuality and relationships. Nonetheless, we believe that public resources and voices should be encouraging the development of increasingly sophisticated filtering software that will assist age-appropriate uses of the Net.

Another frequently proposed solution is to make internet service providers legally liable for everything they carry. This is a solution that many researchers and consumer advocates involved in online media have rejected as impractical, but it is one that certainly requires more public debate.

So filtering software has its place and government regulation, in so far as it is possible, is also important. Monitoring young kids' use of the internet by putting the computer in the lounge room or staying with them is also a good idea. But ultimately, parents and others who care about young people need to come to terms with the fact that, at some point, young people will be online without intense supervision. Self-regulation, as much as government intervention, defines the online media era. Preparing older children and teenagers to feel safe online and to make good choices about what they opt to see inevitably means talking to them about the kind of stuff we're worried they'll come across or go looking for.

Pornography is a subject that lots of parents feel uncomfortable about discussing with their children. But it's something that is now impossible to avoid if you live in a typical Western democracy. The internet is not the only place that children and teenagers are going to come across porn and references to it. The authors of one of the most comprehensive studies ever done of young people, sex and media, Professor David Buckingham and Sara Bragg, write:

> As the pornography industry continues to expand at a phenomenal rate, porn itself has become a popular topic for talk shows, documentaries and movies, and many visual artists now use pornographic imagery in their work. Meanwhile, a greater frankness about sexual matters is increasingly deemed necessary, not just for the psychological health of individuals but also for the prevention of disease (most obviously in the wake of AIDS). Male bodies are now increasingly displayed in sexually charged ways in the mainstream media, alongside female ones. Gay men and lesbians have been recognised as significant (and lucrative) 'niche' audiences, and gay and lesbian 'chic' has been seen to be marketable to mainstream consumers.

If parents and educators aren't prepared to broach pornography's existence in an age-appropriate manner, then they are essentially leaving kids to work it all out for themselves. Information about pornography, we believe, should be part of a broader sex education program in schools and at home. Talking about pornography brings it out from under the bed and gives parents and teachers a chance to express their own political and moral views on the subject and to listen to what young people think about it.

Kids who have been upset about something they've come across online are far more likely to talk to an adult about it if the subject has already been broached. There's certainly evidence that one of the things that young people worry most about when it comes to porn is an adult getting angry with them for looking at it.

A good example from one study concerns a teenager who, knowing that her mother would 'freak out' at the online solicitations and invitations to view commercial sexually explicit material that she was receiving, simply set up an AOL account for her mother with parental controls set to 'young teen', thereby blocking her mother from receiving such material. Her mother, not knowing what was being blocked, expressed surprise that her online experience was much less intrusive than she had been led to believe.

Professor Buckingham, who is one of the best known international scholars working on children and media, and his colleague, Sara Bragg, interviewed and surveyed more than 1000 children aged nine to seventeen and talked to parents as well. Their study confirms that one of the things that most troubles young people about sexual material is that their parents might know they've been looking at it—very few expressed any distress about their own exposure. Even the younger children in the study said they were relatively unconcerned by sexualised images they'd encountered. Many of the young people in the study saw the media as part of a process of sexual learning. But, as the study's authors note, this didn't mean that they treated everything in the media as true: 'Their [the media's] veracity and authority were frequently challenged; and—despite the fears of some conservative critics— they did not seem to have produced a widespread abandonment of "moral standards" among the young'.

Their interviews with young and older teenagers also confirmed that while many of them had been exposed to pornography or actively sought it out, they were capable of expressing strong personal opinions about it. Other research claiming that young people felt intimidated or powerless in the face of sexually explicit material made no sense. On the contrary, both boys and girls talked at length about their moral and political views on pornography.

While we would never suggest that it's OK to be blasé about children being exposed to hardcore pornography, it's reassuring

Protecting Children from Harm

Here are five things you can do to protect your kids from being harmed by pornography or adults who want to prey on them:

1 Keep the computer in a public space in your home if you have children and young teenagers who are accessing the internet.
2 Install good filtering software and regularly run a history check on the websites that your child has been accessing.
3 Talk to your child about what sites they visit and remind them not to give personal information to anyone they don't know in either the real or virtual worlds.
4 Talk to your children from a young age about their bodies. Tell them that they have a say in who touches their bodies and encourage them to talk to you about any behaviour by other adults that makes them uncomfortable.
5 Give your children age-appropriate sex education. Talk to them in age-appropriate ways about the existence of material showing people naked or, when you judge them ready, about material showing people having sex. Encourage them to talk to you if they come across any material that upsets them in the real or virtual worlds.

to know that there's a long history of kids coming across porn and that the most comprehensive research into their reactions suggests that it's rarely a traumatic experience for them. It's also reassuring to note, based on our own study and from common-sense observations of the world around us, that young men raised in a culture where feminism has made real inroads have better attitudes towards women than their parents, and their grand-parents. This is despite the presence of the internet or the increasing presence of sexualised images in mainstream culture.

Pornography can form part of the sexual education of older teenagers, many of whom are sexually active. In our study, many of the participants talked about how much they'd learnt about the human body and how to give sexual pleasure to their partner from watching porn. And while some pornography shows people being hurt, mistreated or denigrated, it's not axiomatic that teen-agers who are exposed to this will feel obliged to copy what they see. Pornography, like any other media, doesn't exist in a social vacuum. Teenage boys will bring their own values and attitudes to it. If they've grown up in a family or community where they've been taught that women are subservient to men, then they may well see this kind of pornography as a reinforcement. But many young men today are, thankfully, being educated and raised to accept that women are their social equals and that sexual assault and harassment are wrong.

After looking at all of the facts, we would argue that the very best thing we can do to protect children from sexual abuse or exploitation online is to arm them with information about their bodies and the right to say 'no', and to resource initiatives that combat the distribution and production of any material documenting the abuse of children.

In the next chapter we look at the ethics of porn production and consumption. We explore the different kinds of work environments porn is made in, at how porn performers are treated and how conditions could be improved. We also look at how porn consumers can make choices that ensure they don't support porn which is made by producers who have no regard for the physical and mental health of performers.

8

Porn, Sex and Ethics

This is what it's like to make porn for the first time: Your agent calls you and tells you there's a job for you in a new video. You're nervous, but you need the money and you've gone too far into this porn business to back out now. You arrive at the location, an upscale house in Los Angeles. The filmmaker tells you the other girl he hired is sick, so you'll have to do the scenes she was booked to do, as well as your own. One will be a double penetration scene, with two men you've never met before. Although you've heard that you have a right to know the results of your co-performers' most recent HIV tests, no one mentions HIV or any other kinds of infection. There are no condoms on the set. During the scene, the men slap and choke you, while calling you a slut and a whore. You begin to cry. Although you've never had anal sex before, the filmmaker convinces you to do the anal scene the other performer was booked to do. By the end of the day you're exhausted. You feel bullied and used.

And this is what it's like to make porn for the first time: You're at your local health food shop, where you see a flyer inviting 'exhibitionist dykes to make porn'. When you arrive at the location, a neighbourhood home, the all-female filmmaking team ask you what kinds of sex you prefer and what kinds of things you'd like to do in their movie. You have coffee and chat with your co-performers and negotiate more about the sexual practices you enjoy. The filmmaker provides gloves, dams and lubricant for your scenes, and you talk about the sexiest ways to use them onscreen. When it comes time for the sex scene, one of the filmmakers notices that you're still a little nervous and asks you if you're sure you want to go ahead. When you confirm that you'd like to go ahead, she asks you if you'd feel more comfortable if she got naked too. You laugh and say yes. The entire film crew undresses but maintains a respectful distance while you and your co-star have sex on camera for the first time. Throughout the sex scene, you use dirty talk to communicate how you want your partner to touch you. By the end of the day you feel tired, but elated.

Both of these vignettes are based on real accounts by first-time porn performers. For those who are morally opposed to pornography under all circumstances—that is, who believe commercial sex is always wrong or that sex should always be conducted privately, behind closed doors—there may be very little real difference between the two scenes. For those who take an ethical approach, however, the two scenes are as different as day and night. The first example involves manipulation, bullying and a clear disregard for the performers' health and safety. The second example, which is based on the making of SIR Videos' *Adult Video News* award-winning *Hard Love and How to Fuck in High Heels*, involves consultation, negotiation and real concern for the performers' emotional and physical wellbeing.

These examples fall at two extremes of a wide spectrum of porn production. There are some male porn producers who believe in making porn ethically. There are female producers who do not. Yet to think of porn only in terms of morality—that is, to assume it must be either 'all good' or 'all bad'—leaves no room to consider what can be done to make pornography better, for men and for women.

The difference between ethics and morals is, of course, open to debate. There are some who would argue that any religious, political or philosophical value system is moral and that ethics are simply the means by which moral frameworks are applied in everyday situations. In our work, we have drawn on the work of French philosopher Michel Foucault, who argues that there are bigger differences between ethics and morals. For Foucault, morals are universal rules or non-negotiable prescriptions. Certain practices are good, healthy and right; others are bad, unhealthy and wrong. These rules apply regardless of context. In contrast, ethics take into account factors such as timing and context. They are negotiable and can alter according to factors such as time, place and the needs and wishes of those who are involved in a particular situation. For Foucault (and for us) ethics imply care—care of the self and care of others. They are not the same as an 'anything goes' or 'if it feels good, do it' approach. Nor do they dictate that the majority rules or that market forces are always right. An ethical approach does not rule out all forms of valuing or judgement, but it does demand that values and judgements are made clear and explicit.

Almost all of us have had to confront the limitations of a universalising moral blueprint. The view that it's wrong to take a human life plays a central role in many religious and secular moral codes. In practice, however, killing is often condoned in particular contexts—for example, in self-defence, in defence of others and in war.

What has taking an ethical approach to pornography meant for our research in practical terms? For us, taking an ethical approach to researching the production and consumption of porn has required us to conduct ourselves in specific ways. Since porn production is highly regulated in Australia and sex work is heavily stigmatised, we have taken care to protect the identities of interviewees, unless they specifically told us we could name them in our publications. From the beginning of this project, we liaised with the Eros Foundation, Australia's adult industry lobby group. We didn't do this because we wanted to audition for the role of porn industry spin doctor, and we certainly never promised to do anything other than report our findings—be they positive or negative—fairly and honestly. We wanted to make sure that when we invited producers and consumers of porn to take part in our research, we had demonstrated, as openly as we could, that we were genuinely prepared to listen to what they had to say.

An ethical approach to our project also required us to take the question of whether or not pornography harms its producers and consumers very seriously. In the course of our research, all of us have responded to numerous requests for media comment. Many of these requests have come from male journalists who openly express ambivalence, if not shame, about their own porn consumption. Like many men (and men are still porn's primary audience), they are afraid that their use of porn harms women. They worry about addiction and are concerned that increased access to online porn is impeding their ability to form relationships. They want to know whether porn is truly demeaning and addictive or whether it's just harmless fantasy fodder.

These are perfectly valid questions, but they are based in a moral framework that seeks to define porn, once and for all, as either 'all good' or 'all bad'. As this book has demonstrated, all porn is not equal. Like other forms of popular media, pornography is made up of genres. Some are cheap and nasty in every sense of the term; others conform to high standards of ethics and aesthetics. Some porn workplaces are unsafe and exploitative; others have policies in place to safeguard performers' physical and emotional health and safety. Some porn sets are not workplaces at all, but the domestic bedrooms and lounge rooms of amateur exhibitionists. Porn producers, too, are a diverse bunch. While some (like John Stagliano, aka Buttman) are on the record as enthusiastic consumers and fans of pornography, there are others (notably Rob Black) who have publicly said that they do not actually like porn. It is theoretically possible to run an ethical business where you dislike your own product, but it presents interesting questions regarding the producer's attitudes towards his employees and consumers.

In the United States, and possibly in porn industries in other countries, performers are not 'employees' but 'contractors'. This means that they are required to assume certain risks and responsibilities that employers would otherwise be liable for. This is particularly relevant, as porn performers are both glamourised and stigmatised. In the United States, shrewd female performers regard their appearances in actual porn films as a means of marketing their own brand of sex celebrity. Unless performers are contracted to a specific production company (and very few are), they can use any business acumen they may have to promote themselves, and keep the profits. While producers and distributors obtain the most profit from films, performers are able to generate independent income by means of their fan clubs and associated merchandising. Tours as featured exotic dancers, with associated merchandise sales, are another means of independent promotion. Some, such as Christi Lake, use their funds to launch their own production houses or extend their careers off-camera by taking work as directors. But, like performers in other entertainment industries such as music or acting, good performers do not always have good business sense and are vulnerable to exploitation by manipulative managers and partners. For this reason, even high-profile porn celebrities can wind up being disenchanted with the business side of the sex industry at the end of their careers.

Since all three authors of this book have had considerable Australian media exposure as 'porn researchers' and have developed a reputation for discussing the positive aspects of contemporary pornography, it would be easy to assume that we are either ignorant of the ugly or frightening aspects of porn, or that we have deliberately chosen to ignore them. This is not the case. In the course of our research, we have looked at aspects of porn production and distribution that we find both offensive and disturbing, although not always for the reasons we might have expected. We are all familiar with critiques of porn that argue that participation in porn is intrinsically dangerous and harmful to women, and that porn offers a kind of blueprint for misogyny and violence against women. In most cases we disagree with this proposal. We disagree in part because we believe that consensual sexual practices, and the depictions of these practices, do not constitute sexual violence. We similarly do not believe that the alternative sexual practices popularly depicted in porn, such as anal sex or group sex, are in themselves dangerous or harmful to men and women. We are *always* opposed to coerced or forced sex, whether it takes place on or off-camera. Coercion can include threatening, nagging, manipulating and bribing, or the 'ambushing' of a partner who has consented to one kind of sexual interaction (say, oral sex) but not another. We are concerned that perpetrators of sexual violence hide behind the 'I saw it in porn, so it must be OK' defence, in an attempt to absolve themselves of responsibility for their actions. All sexual acts, including the act of *viewing* porn, should be voluntary. Although our research indicates that porn can (and does) serve as sex education for many consumers, the vast majority of porn imagery is a poor teacher when it comes to sexual ethics, negotiation skills and sexual boundary-setting.

Most porn does a reasonably good job of showing the kinds of sex acts that consenting adults might choose to participate in, and the kinds of outfits and accessories that might assist them. Certainly, it makes tricky positions and 'edgy' sexual manoeuvres look easy. Given that porn depicts idealised fantasy or entertainment sex, sexual athleticism is a clearly necessary skill for porn professionals and it's logical that most of the warming up and technical preparation for sex happens off-camera.

There is, of course, pornography that portrays sexual negotiation and sexual interaction from an ethically questionable perspective. A good example is the 'reality porn' genre, which features scenarios where women are depicted as drunk and therefore easier to manipulate sexually (the *Girls Gone Wild* series), or as 'dumb' and 'slutty' and therefore deserving of aggressive, abusive or coercive treatment.

During our three years of formal, funded research, we subscribed to *Adult Video News* (*AVN*), the US trade journal for the porn industry. In her survey of all three years' worth of *AVN*s, Kath was struck by the images and language used to market porn to US buyers. Although an actual sexual fetish for humiliation is rare, even in the BDSM scene, a substantial amount of porn was marketed as if audiences and producers alike believe that sex is inherently degrading and that female performers should be humiliated for being sexual. 'Gonzo' or 'reality' videos and websites, which feature the gimmick of the documentary-style filming of women making their porn debuts, seemed particularly prone to representing female performers as disposable 'dumb sluts' who 'deserved' poor treatment. As US commentator Shauna Swartz observes, this style of 'humilitainment' porn seems to rely on the ugly gimmick of non-consensual or manipulative sexual interaction as a means of establishing its 'reality' factor. For example, the central conceit of the website BangBus is that 'unsuspecting' women are manipulated into agreeing to have sex with the filmmakers for a fee, but are then discarded without payment. As Swartz describes it, 'the producers of these sites position their works as erotic documentaries that capture real encounters with eager women who are dumb or desperate enough to fall for their trickery'. This form of porn relies on the eroticisation of unethical sexual practice and of the broader social stigma against sexually active women in general, and sex workers in particular.

The unethical aspect of 'reality' porn production and marketing has not been lost on industry insiders—in fact, it has been criticised in several articles and interviews within *AVN* and in other collections of commentary on contemporary porn.

And just as there are many different types of pornography and motivations for appearing in it or consuming it, so there are many different types of porn producers. Well-established, successful producers like 'gonzo pioneer' Ed Powers and John Stagliano (aka Buttman) are on the record speaking respectfully and admiringly of the ability of female performers to have sex on camera— a difficult task, especially over the course of a long filming day— while communicating a sense of passion and enthusiasm. Yet there are others, like Rob Black of Extreme Associates, who explicitly position themselves as porn 'outlaws', marketing their work with claims to a sort of outsider status, beyond the boundary of the increasingly mainstreamed US porn industry. Their films do not just feature oral and genital penetration, but also staged scenes of abduction and beatings, the extreme stretching of vaginas and anuses with multiple penises or sex toys, and choking, gagging and slapping. It is this pornography that lives up to the claim made by some sections of the feminist movement that porn is the living embodiment of a deep-rooted patriarchal desire to humiliate and subjugate women.

It's clear that these films are deliberately designed to provoke a sense of revulsion and horror as much as (if not more than) an erotic response. They are, as porn reviewer Violet Blue refers to them, the *Fear Factor* of porn. According to producer Rob Black:

> it's no different than if you go into a video store and buy a 'Banned from TV, Caught on Video.' And they've got like five volumes, and all [of] it is news footage of these horrific accidents with people getting hit by trains (laughs), and a guy [in] a stand-off with hostages, and the cops blow his brains out, and his blood ... It's the same thing. You could go into Tower Records or Best Buy and buy a video where people are dying on camera ...

We are in no way sympathetic to Black's case. Since we believe that non-consensual filming and broadcasting (including the surveillance camera-style footage described above) is unethical in itself, we're especially critical of producers like Black and those responsible for the 'Banned from TV' reality programs, who profit from other people's risk-taking or actual physical distress. Although the beatings and choking featured in gonzo porn may well be faked (and Black has stated that it is in his films), there are some sexual stunts that can't be faked effectively. The reality factor in extreme porn relies on sexual 'stunt' performers who will *really* choke, gag and vomit during deep-throat sequences. Other stunts, like double anal penetration or 'gapes' (open, gaping anus shots), cannot be faked, nor can extended multiple penetration sequences or scenes where male performers deliberately ejaculate into a female performer's eye. We find this kind of pornography deeply offensive and abhorrent.

It should be emphasised that while *Fear Factor* porn is currently fashionable among 'rebellious' porn producers, it certainly doesn't cater to the tastes of the 'average' porn consumer. In a letter to the editor of *AVN*, self-proclaimed 'average Joe Six-Pack' reader Eric Ladamann commends the quality of a video he hired specifically because of the (in his words) 'catchy phrases on the box cover. They were: Absolutely [sic] No Anal, No Choking, No DPs, No Two Guys On One Girl, No Music and No Shaved

Pussies … just trimmed'. According to Ladamann, the video, made by Lexexx Productions, had a waiting list in his local video store and 'restored his faith in porn'.

Ladamann praised various technical and narrative aspects of the film:

> The picture quality was excellent, the positions and camera angles were viewer friendly … and the guys paid attention to the female bodies before they got head. [Ladamann] also saw some things you rarely see on adult movies these days: Eye contact, kissing, and dirty talking while having sex.

In their videos, and in the promotional material that accompanies them, extreme porn producers like Rob Black and Skeeter Kerkove dress like a cross between bikers, wrestlers and heavy metal musicians. They emphasise their distance from 'mainstream' or 'couples' porn by presenting themselves as outlaws. But unlike the men in those outlaw subcultures, extreme pornographers don't put their own arses on the line. They get young women to do that for them. Extreme sportspeople (and even the boys in *Jackass*) perform *their own* stunts and risk harming *their own* bodies in the name of entertainment. Extreme porn producers build their reputations by getting young women to take all the risks on their behalf.

We should emphasise that we accept that there doesn't seem to be a shortage of young women willing to perform in extreme films, and that we respect their right to make their own decisions, even when they seem to be unacceptably high-risk ones. However, the US porn production industry has not had a uniformly reassuring track record when it comes to ensuring performers' health and safety, and the risks can only be amplified when the producers are amped-up macho males and the performers are young women whose ongoing sexual and emotional health is not valued by their employers. Like any other worker, sex workers deserve consideration of their occupational health and safety.

There also seems to be a disturbing ongoing resistance to the use of condoms in the straight porn industry, with very few major companies maintaining consistent all-condom policies. In 2000, only two years after a well-documented series of HIV diagnoses in the Californian heterosexual porn industry, only 18 per cent of straight porn performers were on the record as 'condom only' players and 36 per cent were 'condom optional'. Currently, the external cum shot still rules in most porn, but there is a niche market for 'cream pies' (internal ejaculations). There is also a specialist market for fetishised facial cum shots where semen is deliberately directed into an actress' open eye. Since eyes have a very rich blood supply, it's possible to contract chlamydia, gonorrhoea, HIV and even herpes in this kind of scene. According to porn industry physician Colin Hamblin, these infections could lead to blindness if untreated.

The Adult Industry Medical Health Care Foundation (AIM) was established in 1998 as a response to a number of HIV seroconversions within the Californian porn industry. This non-profit organisation is largely funded by industry subscription and also accepts donations from industry and non-industry sources. AIM is headed by Sharon Mitchell PhD, a veteran of more than twenty years of onscreen and off-screen work in the industry. The Foundation sets the industry standards for HIV screening in the adult industry and also offers testing for a full range of STIs (sexually transmitted infections) and blood-borne viruses, including the highly transmissible gonorrhoea and chlamydia.

In addition, AIM runs a general practice for adult performers, hosts an industry-specific twelve-step meeting and offers a range of other services, including financial advice, 'pap smears, psychiatric assessment, drug and alcohol counselling, cosmetic surgery information, chiropractic healing and support groups such as *Relationships Group*, *Abuse Survivors Group*, *Women of Porn* and other special educational workshops'. AIM also offers new performers an 'induction' video, *Porn 101*, presented by Mitchell, along with porn performer (and trained nurse) Nina Hartley and current and retired male porn performers Mr Marcus, Hershel Savage and Richard Pacheco. As Mitchell describes it, the video covers everything 'from how to spot a scumbag producer—to safe sex and the psychosocial aspects of emotional and mental health for porn industry personnel'. Performers can also apply for AIM's

Life after Porn and Life after Sexwork scholarships, in which study is combined with individual counselling programs, which Mitchell describes as follows:

> Say you want to be out of porn next year. Let's say, for another month, you keep doing … hardcore scenes. Then maybe next month you stop working with guys; for the next three months only with girls. And then you just do single girl stuff. Then you just do your Internet stuff. All the while you're going to school, you're making a little more money, you're building your Website—it's all about long and short term goals that are for you specifically.

Since 2003, AIM has mandated monthly testing for gonorrhoea and chlamydia, in addition to monthly HIV testing and biannual screening for syphilis. In a 2003 interview, porn star Belladonna announced her 'retirement' at age twenty-two after performing in 250 films in three years, saying, 'A lot of the reason that I don't want to have sex on film is that I don't want to put up with any STDs ever again'. Describing her history of repeated gonorrhoea, chlamydia and 'several other' unspecified infections, Belladonna told *AVN* journalist Acme Anderson, 'It's draining on your body when you have to go to hospital every fucking day … I get STD tested every week'. Announcing her directorial video series *Bella's Perversions*, Belladonna said, 'No one will work for me unless it's a new test. It has to be no older than one day for … gono [sic] and chlamydia. Because the second you work after that, it's not a good test anymore'.

Sexually transmissible infections are an intrinsic risk in sex work, but they are easily contained in most instances by the use of condoms, regular testing and proactive treatment regimes. While some producers (like veteran performer/director Ed Powers) support regular testing and condom use, even on shared sex toys in girl–girl scenes, other producers still claim that condoms are off-putting to straight audiences. The two major objections we've seen to universal condom use in US-made porn are: condoms spoil the viewer's arousal by ruining the illusion of fantasy sex; and actresses find them uncomfortable after prolonged penetration.

The first objection seems odd when we consider that gay and bisexual porn has used condoms as an industry-standard practice since the 1980s. Clearly condoms haven't destroyed the illusions of gay men—although there is a niche market for bareback, or condomless, porn. While it is true that porn films depict 'fantasy' sequences, we cannot imagine that audiences really want to watch performers contracting STIs as part of their jobs. Indeed, a sizeable number of respondents in our consumer survey were troubled by depictions of sex that they felt posed a health risk to performers, notably in ATM or 'arse-to-mouth' anal sex scenes.

The problem of vaginal or anal chafing in prolonged penetration scenes could be addressed by trying different brands of condoms and better quality lube. The industry could also consider porn producer Alpha's recommendations that working hours should be capped and porn performers should be guaranteed standard rest breaks. In a letter to the editor of *AVN*, published not long after Belladonna's interview, Alpha wrote: 'We have no code of ethics to which adult filmmakers can subscribe and no means to ensure that any sort of industry standard is enforced. It is true that dogs, cats and bunnies have more legal protections on set than men and women'. Alpha observed that the issue hasn't yet been fully debated in the industry but that it needed to be, going on to list some 'basic things that are already being done by ethical studios'. These included compensating all adult performers fairly for their work, testing performers for STIs and HIV immediately prior to a shoot and ensuring that no performer 'is knowingly … exposed to any sexually-contagious disease'. Alpha also condemned 'extreme' filmmakers who market the 'surprises' they spring on inexperienced or unsuspecting performers, writing:

> No adult actor or actress should be coerced, bribed or begged into anything they don't feel comfortable with. Period. If dangerous or extreme are your thing, then find actors who are comfortable with your brand of kink. Performers should be fully advised before being hired as to what they will be expected to do.

In addition to endorsing testing, Alpha also suggests that safer-sex guidelines should be followed on the set. The issue of testing and safer-sex protocols is one that we believe can only be resolved from within the porn industry. To do that, however, porn producers, performers and audiences will need to see past the blind spot they share with most heterosexuals in the United States, Europe and Australasia. There is no evidence to support the idea that HIV, hepatitis and other sexually transmissible bacterial and viral infections only happen to 'bad' or 'dirty' people. People with such infections do not deserve to be shamed, stigmatised or excluded from the porn industry, or any other industry. At the same time, these infections clearly pose an occupational health and safety risk to porn performers, who should *never* be required to work without protection.

If the conditions of production are diverse, the condition of consumers can vary just as much. There's no doubt that the urge to collect pornographic images for masturbation can become painfully compulsive for some men. It can be distressing to find oneself drawn to explicit images and stories that provoke as much shame and fear as they do arousal. Then there are the men and women who feel that any form of sexual fantasy or masturbation is wrong and must be hidden at all costs. While we do not believe that masturbation or fantasy are harmful in themselves, we certainly accept that obsessive or compulsive sexual behaviours can lead to a great deal of suffering and are best dealt with in consultation with a sex therapist, psychologist or a similarly trained mental health professional. Many opponents of porn would suggest that the only way to resolve these issues is for men and women (but primarily men) to stop consuming porn entirely. While we don't discount that as an option, there is considerable evidence to suggest that the porn industry has been quite responsive to consumer demand in the past and that consumer activism might actually have a significant effect on the way porn is produced. The difficulty, of course, is that many porn consumers are relatively closeted, if not actively ashamed, when it comes to their porn consumption. Shamed, guilty consumers are not strong consumer advocates. With that in mind, we offer these possible solutions to the ethical dilemmas faced by porn consumers:

Dealing with Ethical Dilemmas in Porn: A Guide for Consumers

Dilemma: I feel bad about watching porn that primarily features female performers who have clearly had a lot of cosmetic surgery, or whose looks are obviously very 'high maintenance' (for example, fake tans, over-styled or over-coloured hair, long acrylic nails). I think I am developing unrealistic fantasy images of femininity that will leave me disappointed in my real-world relationships with women.

Possible solutions:

- Spend at least a month exclusively consuming 'all-natural' DIY amateur porn.
- You may also want to consider whether porn is the only source of idealised sexual imagery. Have the other forms of media you consume, such as Hollywood films, influenced your sexual tastes in any way? Is it possible that your peers or family members might also have influenced your ideals of feminine beauty?

Dilemma: I am concerned that some porn performers are forced or coerced into having sex for money. I do not want to support unfair or unethical work practices in the porn industry.

Possible solutions:

- Switch to consuming only non-commercial DIY or amateur porn.
- Do some background research in order to determine which commercial producers have work practices that you **do** support.
- Email production houses and ask them to answer your questions about their workplace practices. If you are satisfied with their answers, make an effort to consume their products exclusively. If you are not satisfied, boycott their products.
- Support your local sex worker peer-support organisations; for example, by making cash donations.

Dilemma: I am concerned that porn performers are putting their physical and emotional health at risk.

Possible solutions:

- Contact porn producers and request that they encourage performers to use condoms in their products.
- Ask your local retailer of DVDs/videos whether they can recommend porn featuring condoms.
- Ask the webmaster/mistress on your preferred websites whether they have any policies regarding safer sex.
- Let porn producers know that you think the health and safety of porn performers matters.
- Donate money to the Adult Medical Foundation and/or local sex-worker-run health and education programs.

- Avoid porn produced or distributed by anyone who has publicly declared their opposition to safer sex in porn, or to sexual health testing for porn performers.

Dilemma: Porn with 'rough' sex floats my boat but I worry that the performers are being harmed or injured.
Possible solutions:
- Make an effort to purchase porn made by reputable producers in the BDSM community who have a commitment to 'safe, sane and consensual' work practices. It is likely that anyone depicting a 'victim' in images made by these producers is either a professional sex-stunt performer or a person who self-identifies as a submissive and is part of a peer-support network within the BDSM subculture.
- Avoid the work of producers and distributors who are on the record as speaking or behaving in a dismissive, rude or predatory fashion about the people who perform in their films. For example, do filmmakers justify techniques that seem dangerous or unethical by claiming the women in porn are disposable? Do they claim performers are 'just dumb bitches' who 'deserve' to be treated badly?
- Contact producers and distributors and ask them what their policies are with respect to 'rough' sex scenes. Do they offer any formal or informal after-care or counselling services?

Dilemmas:
- I am worried because I have fantasies about the kinds of sex I see in porn. I don't know how to find a real-life partner who'll do those things with me.
- I am worried that my easy access to sexual satisfaction via porn is making me too lazy to work at building a mutually satisfying relationship with my partner. Frankly, I would rather masturbate on my own than go to the effort of 'making love' with him/her.
- My partner shames me and condemns me for liking porn.
Possible solution: Look for a relationship counsellor, psychologist or therapist who specialises in sexuality issues. You may wish to establish their general views on masturbation, pornography and/or alternative sexual practices before committing to a course of counselling.

In her 1979 monograph *The Sadeian Woman,* the late British feminist author Angela Carter suggests that there might be such a thing as a 'moral pornographer' who produces porn 'in the service of women'. The moral pornographer 'might use pornography as a critique of current relations between the sexes', producing porn that would 'begin to penetrate to the heart of the contempt for women that distorts our culture'. For Carter, moral pornography is porn that actively critiques political inequity between men and women. It is not necessarily nurturing, fair or egalitarian—in fact, she discusses the work of the Marquis de Sade as an example of moral pornography. Like some contemporary feminists, notably Laura Kipnis, Carter sees the graphic depiction of *in*equity as one of the key roles for moral pornography. This kind of porn, she implies, lays bare the foundations of contempt, resentment and fear of women's sexuality that underpin the debates, moral pronouncements and policy decisions that restrict women's freedom.

Carter's recommendation is clearly posed as a polemical challenge to both porn's supporters and its critics. Like many other feminists who oppose censorship, she implicitly rejects the assumption that banning images of inequality or exploitation will 'protect' women from the everyday experience of these things. However, she doesn't accept the proposal that all porn is 'harmless fantasy' that has nothing to do with our everyday lives. Carter's approach is challenging because it doesn't insist that porn is universally liberating *or* demeaning for the women who make it. She also avoids making final pronouncements on whether male consumption of porn is 'healthy' or harmful. Her approach acknowledges the role porn plays in our society *and* considers the contexts in which it is produced and consumed. It is, in our terms, an ethical understanding of pornography.

9

Afterglow?

When commentators talk about the content of pornography, they often refer to images of rape, bestiality and child abuse. Such images do exist in the world. But this is not the pornography that up to one-third of adult Australians who are porn consumers like to consume. While there are notable examples of unethical or dangerous porn production, the bulk of mainstream pornography depicts consensual sex and focuses on pleasure. There are two main strands: glossy, expensive couples porn, and boy/girl-next-door amateurs porn. Each has its own fans, but in both cases the fans are looking for images of people who seem to be genuinely enjoying themselves.

Although the image of the typical porn user in the media is often a sad, lonely man, addicted to the internet, who just can't get a girlfriend, the vast majority of Australians who like the genre don't fit this stereotype. Many of them do, in fact, have girlfriends. Many of them *are*, in fact, girlfriends. Some women like porn. Not as many as the men, but we came across plenty in our research for this project.

While it has been claimed that studies have proved that pornography causes violence against women, our research indicates that the link between porn and violence is murkier than this. Like other media forms, pornography depicts the range of social attitudes towards female sexuality. In some cases it celebrates sexual expression; in others it links sexuality with humiliation and violence. It is true that researchers have managed to create anti-women effects in the laboratory by showing violent porn to people who don't normally watch it, forcing them to watch it for hours, in public, in awkward situations, surrounded by strangers and researchers, and while not masturbating—that is, nothing like how porn works in the real world. In fact, there are far more dangerous issues out there correlated to negative attitudes towards women. And those of us who are concerned about sexual violence need to start with the most dangerous issues and ask what we can do about them.

It's been a long haul on this project—about five years from initial conception to finishing this book. And none of us has come away unchanged from the project. We've all learned a lot.

Alan, who oversaw the content analysis and ended up watching a lot of porn videos during it, learned a lot about sex. As a lifelong gay man, he had very little idea about what it was that heterosexuals did in bed together. His image of heterosex was mediated by the non-pornographic media. And it was interesting for him to realise that while watching television programs, reading magazines (even *Cleo* and *Cosmo*), listening to pop music and reading novels, he had never really seen representations of women who enjoy sex. In television programs, women want to talk about relationships. In magazines, they are interested in sex but want to manage it, control it, treat it like a challenge and still see it as something slightly dirty that men want more than they do. In pop music, only men want sex—women want love (white singers) or independence (black singers). And novels just don't have that much sex. So to see images of women enjoying sex in pornography was a revelation. So much so that at first it didn't seem real—surely these women couldn't really be enjoying themselves? To find out from interviews that many of them really do enjoy sex was an important breakthrough in his understanding of heterosexuality.

Catharine worked mainly on the cultural history of the regulation of porn, on child pornography and how to combat it, and on the exposure of young people to sexually explicit material. As a feminist with a long-standing interest in debates about how the representation of women in all media affects their social and political circumstances, she was fascinated by how little some of the debates have moved on. Despite the depth of contemporary knowledge about what causes violence against women and how important it is that men grow up seeing women as equals in every sense, she was amazed by how many contemporary commentators continue to assume that women and men are fundamentally different and that no sane woman could actually have any interest in watching or performing in porn. In Catharine's view, this approach points down a dangerous ideological slope: the view that any woman who performs in porn or expresses an interest in it deserves to be dismissed as irretrievably crazed or slutty. Catharine, like Kath, also became very interested in the question of how porn might be produced and consumed in a more ethical way: what would porn look like if performers were taken seriously as workers and not simply as fallen women? Given that porn is unlikely to go away, how can we work to make it safer for women and men working in the industry and what part can consumers play?

Finally, and most significantly for Catharine, writing the chapter on pornography and children forced her to really contemplate the horror of child sexual abuse and the trafficking of those assaults through images. Like the majority of Australians, her only exposure to the idea of child pornography came through media reports. When she did the research she found there was very little comprehensive and evidence-based work on the subject, but that what there is makes blood-chilling reading. The sexual abuse of children was around long before the internet. But the internet has made the distribution of child porn far easier. As the mother of two young children, Catharine grapples personally with the questions of how to protect her own children from abuse and of how to help them enjoy online experiences without exposing them to material they're not ready to cope with. Her research confirmed her view that the most important thing we can do for children is to give them age-appropriate information about the adult world, to talk to them about what they're viewing or experiencing, and to reassure them that they should always talk to an adult they trust about anything that disturbs them.

Kath, who focused on Australian porn production, interviewing amateur, fetish, feminist and DIY pornographers, also gave a great deal of consideration to sexual ethics. She learned that, to paraphrase cultural theorist Leo Bersani, the big secret about sex is that most people don't like it very much, even if they think they need it. She has also learned that sexual desires in general, and female sexuality in particular, is still a source of widespread shame and fear in our culture, and that this causes people to shy away from dealing with scary questions like, 'How *exactly* can we learn to negotiate safe, pleasurable sex?' Many, many people, even self-proclaimed feminists, seem to believe that sexual activity is intrinsically demeaning or degrading, and that those who 'flaunt' their sexuality (for fun or for profit) only do so because they are ignorant, stupid or have low self-esteem. A few even believe that sexually active women deserve to be humiliated and abused, simply because they are sexual. Kath is disappointed that although sexually explicit imagery has become increasingly available to younger people in the past decade, good quality, fact-based sex education that explicitly addresses the issues of sexual safety and sexual pleasure is still hard to come by. On the plus side, she learned that the job description 'porn researcher' could be a very handy icebreaker for a single woman in her mid-thirties.

In her 2003 book *Mommy's Little Girl: On Sex, Motherhood, Porn and Cherry Pie*, feminist porn pioneer Susie Bright compellingly argues that the current trend for what she terms 'rubbernecker porn' is a passing phase. She believes that while the traditional straight male porn consumer is still satisfied by 'poppin' fresh starlets sucking and fucking', the internet has offered the general population unprecedented access to sexual images. Porn is a novelty for most of these audiences, and producers of extreme porn are playing on the shock factor. She cautions against increased regulation, however, arguing that 'we have never had one genuine break from our heritage of sexual dishonesty and erotic hucksterism'.

While Bright is concerned by the trend towards *Fear Factor* pornography, as we are, she opposes increased censorship on the grounds that it will rob audiences of the opportunity to get through the sideshow phase of extreme porn to a point where they are ready to 're-examine the basics' and 'refresh [their] imagination'.

We hope so. We strongly support good pornography—and we absolutely condemn bad pornography. The recent history of porn has generally been one of moving away from the narrow masculine-centred genre of the 1970s to a much more inclusive form, with many different perspectives and sexual pleasures in more recent work. The blooming of amateur porn, and its huge popularity, is particularly encouraging from this perspective. We hope that this movement continues and that any remaining unethical practices in porn can be stamped out, as more people are more open and more honest about their engagements with the genre.

The Understanding Pornography in Australia Manifesto for Ethical Porn

Based on our research, we recommend the following:

- **Education:** We support sex education for young people that encourages literacy in sex-related media, including pornography. We believe that sex education needs to emphasise pleasure and safety, and also ethical sexual negotiation skills. In this context, pornography should be acknowledged as a diverse field of fantasy-based media of varying quality, not a literal document of the 'best' or 'worst' way to have sex.

- **Ethical marketing and distribution:** We support honesty and fair practice in porn marketing. Box covers should fairly represent the actual content of a DVD; key words and headings should accurately depict the actual content of a website.

- **Regulation:** Porn is not for everyone. No one should ever be exposed to porn (or any kind of sexual interaction) against their will. To this end, we support the regulated distribution of pornography. This includes restricting the distribution of porn to areas where young people below the age of legal consent are excluded (this may involve filters online). We oppose pop-up porn and 'mouse-trapping' (opening multiple porn sites that viewers are unable to click out of) for the above reason.

- **Ethical production practices:** We absolutely believe that porn should only be performed and viewed by consenting adults who are above the age of consent. Performers should be fully informed of the risks they assume in the course of their work and should be confident that employers have taken all possible precautions against workplace injury or trauma. To this end, we endorse the work of the Adult Industry Medical Healthcare Foundation (AIM) and support peer-based psychosocial and physical health and safety programs for sex workers (including porn performers). Since a number of porn performers also work in other areas of the sex industry, such as stripping and prostitution, we believe that the decriminalisation and unionisation of sex work would greatly enhance the health and safety of sex workers, in and out of pornography. We support the de-stigmatisation of STI testing, treatment and safer-sex practices, in and out of pornography. We support porn production that emphasises and promotes pleasure and consent. We condemn porn production that emphasises and promotes sexual manipulation, coercion or forced sex.

APPENDIX

The Understanding Pornography in Australia Project

Why Did We Do It?

As senior academic researchers with varying expertise in the fields of media, cultural and gender studies, all three authors of this book have taken part in debates about pornography. We all share a strong opposition to pornography, or any other media genre, that glamourises or portrays non-consensual sex, the humiliation or abuse of others or the sexual abuse of minors. What drew us together to do this research was a mutual concern that debates about pornography frequently proceeded as if all pornography automatically involves the degradation and humiliation of women and the eroticisation of rape and violence. We had all formed the view that the consumption and production of pornography was more complex than current debates allowed and that the idea that all porn is evil and that all porn consumers are addicted or morally corrupt was simplistic. Yet our evidence for this proposition remained, to some extent, anecdotal—it was largely based on what we ourselves had observed. It was clear to us that more empirical research was needed to find out the truth about what is in the most popular pornography and who consumed it. Regardless of our personal or political views, we all share a strong belief that public debate, policy and law should be based on fact, not solely on emotive or ideological responses to an issue.

What Did We Do?

We applied to the federal government's Australia Research Council, the body that administers funding for humanities and social sciences research on a highly competitive peer-reviewed basis, to fund a project to get some facts about the place of pornography in Australian society. The project was called Understanding Pornography in Australia. We got the funding and divided the project up along the lines of our expertise and interest.

Catharine's expertise is in the history of debates about censorship, with a particular focus on the way that women are portrayed in sexually explicit images. Catharine wrote the first chapter in this book, which examines the history of debates about pornography. Catharine has also done substantial academic research into children and media consumption, including the risks posed to them in an online environment. She wrote the chapter on children, teenagers and exposure to sexually explicit material. In doing so, she examined the substantial academic literature on how to protect children from exposure to inappropriate material and looked at the risks and benefits of teenagers being exposed to both appropriate and inappropriate material. She also reviewed the unfortunately scant academic material that looks forensically at the production and consumption of child pornography and drew conclusions about how we, as a society, can do more locally and globally to protect children from this heinous crime.

Kath's background has involved working in sexual health and sex education. Given the sensitive nature of social research in the sexuality field, Kath developed an early sensitivity to the fact that most people don't want to be treated like 'research subjects' when it comes to their own sexual behaviour or preferences. When she was doing work in the gay, lesbian and bisexual communities, she developed an alter ego named Nurse Nancy who dressed up in a nurse's uniform and latex gloves and carried a clipboard in a parody of the scientific 'this won't hurt a bit' intrusive style of social science research. Kath had already done a lot of research in alternative sexual communities and was particularly interested in non-mainstream porn. She knew that there were a lot of people producing their own porn because the mainstream stuff didn't appeal to them or seemed unethical. Kath's main interest, then, is in, chiefly, who makes porn in Australia and in the United States (where the majority of porn comes from), how the people performing in it are treated and what their motivations for performing are. Kath gathered her information primarily by doing interviews with local producers. She was able to interview a small number of photographers who produce locally made glamour and fetish pictures, and she also spoke to several local magazine editors and web administrators who commissioned photographic work. None conformed to the stereotypical image of the sleazy pornographer, and all of them could explain what they did to avoid making models uncomfortable. Kath also spoke to a very small number of performers, models and ex-models, although largely they were interviewed in the context of other roles; for example, as publishers or producers of porn. The producers, models and distributors were often introduced by other interviewees, although some responded to media coverage, or approached us after public-speaking engagements to offer their perspectives.

Interestingly, the more 'marginal' producers and performers—those who produced fetish porn, for example—were the most open about what they did and why they did it. Even those who produced material considered to be 'offensive' and which was refused classification under Australian classification guidelines were models of propriety before, during and after interviews. The only time a research assistant ever reported feeling personally uncomfortable was during an interview with the editor of a leading Australian soft-porn magazine affiliated with a mainstream publishing house. The oddest, and most inappropriate, event occurred after Kath had interviewed Carol Queen, the star of the anal sex instruction videos *Bend Over Boyfriend* and *Bend Over Boyfriend 2*. When Queen received an inquiry from a very mainstream soft-core Sydney-based men's magazine researching a light-hearted story on girl-on-boy strap-on sex, she referred them to Kath's sexpert alter ego, Nurse Nancy. In the email exchange that followed, it became apparent that the journalist in question was not seeking an interview or even a photo opportunity with Kath/Nancy. What he was looking for was a woman who would have anal sex with a stranger for no other reason than getting her name in a magazine. Kath declined the 'terrific' PR opportunity and recommended that the journalist seek out a commercial sex-worker and pay the appropriate rate (which, incidentally, is upwards of $400 in Sydney). Perhaps mainstream journalists could learn some ethical lessons from the producers of pornography.

Alan has always been more interested in the content of popular culture and its audiences. In his career, he's interviewed audiences of many kinds of popular culture and studied a lot of the actual culture itself, including television programs, trashy magazines, the internet, pop music and community newspapers. So he took on those aspects of the project. He organised a large-scale content analysis of fifty of the bestselling pornographic videos/DVDs in Australia. Getting information on popular titles was problematic. It's illegal to *sell* X-rated videos in any state in Australia (they can only be sold in the territories). However, it is legal to *buy* X-rated videos in each state, which is done via a massive mail-order market for pornographic videos and DVDs. The majority of these are sold by two companies—Gallery Entertainment and Axis Entertainment—and each supplied the project with copies of their twenty-five bestselling videos. Merging these samples allowed the analysis of fifty of the bestselling pornographic videos in Australia.

A number of key issues of concern about pornography were then identified. Bestiality, rape pornography and child sex abuse materials are thankfully all illegal in Australia. X-rated material is limited to films that 'contain real depictions of actual sexual activity between consenting adults in which there is no violence, sexual violence, sexualised violence, coercion, sexually assaultive language, or fetishes, or depictions which purposefully demean anyone involved in that activity for the enjoyment of viewers in a way that is likely to cause offence to a reasonable adult'. So the bestselling videos and DVDs were audited for violence and the objectification of women to see if the law was working. Careful guidelines were developed for these analyses. Alan followed standard social science protocols for content analysis and then published the information in highly reputable academic journals.

We've actually written two different kinds of material coming out of this project. First, in order to make sure that the research was all correct, we wrote academic versions of the papers, full of all the necessary jargon, statistical processes and caveats. Throughout the book, when we're discussing our own research, we often point you towards the more formal academic version if you're interested in reading this data.

Alan also organised a survey of more than 1000 Australian consumers of pornography and then conducted detailed interviews with forty-six of them from around the country. We accessed these consumers in two ways. First, we posted out a hard copy of the survey in the catalogue of Axis Entertainment, an Australian company that sells sexually explicit materials by post. Second, we put the survey online and publicised it in the media.

What Are the Limitations of Our Research?

The first limitation of our research is one that characterises any research in the humanities and social science fields, regardless of what any researcher tells you about their impeccably unbiased approach. We came to the project with the biases determined by our own educational backgrounds, personal experiences and moral and political views. As academic researchers, we all recognise our duty to put these biases aside. Certainly, we've all changed our views on the subject of pornography in subtle and, at times, radical ways in the course of this project. But the end result inevitably is one that is the product of our interpretation of data, both quantitative and qualitative.

In more specific ways, our research was limited by ethical constraints—those we imposed on ourselves and those imposed on us by the Research and Ethics Committees of Sydney and Queensland Universities.

The empirical heart of our research is grounded in the research done by the principal author of this study, Alan McKee. Alan relied on a self-selecting sample of porn consumers. In conventional media research terms this is a valid technique. The sample is substantial and the variety of socio-economic, age, gender and political differentials indicate that it is a broadly representative one. We would have preferred to work with a random sample but, interestingly, the sensitive nature of porn consumption meant that the ethical constraints imposed by our institutions prevented us from asking people who had not identified themselves as consumers about whether they consumed pornography. So the most important limitation of our survey is that only people who were willing to acknowledge their pornography use would respond to it.

It is also true that how we presented both versions of the survey had an impact on our results. It is not coincidental that there was a bias in the sample towards Australians with a higher than average level of formal education. One of the things that is taught at school and university is a familiarity and comfort with formal forms of writing, such as survey instruments. On this point, it's worth noting that we did attempt to reach different audience groups by circulating the survey in two different ways—as a hard copy sent out with catalogues and as an online instrument. The first method would reach people who had already self-identified as pornography consumers and who had been willing to sign up their names to receive a catalogue of pornographic materials. It would also be able to reach people who do not necessarily have internet access. By contrast, the online survey, although limited to people who have computer access, had the advantage of reaching consumers who were not necessarily signed up to catalogues of pornographic materials.

Notes

Introduction

Page xii: In March 2006, the Australian Labor Party: *Hobart Mercury*, 'Labor's Porn Shield'.

1. A Brief History of Pornography

Page 5, The term 'pornography': Heins, *Sex, Sin and Blasphemy*, p. 138.

Page 5, 'created over time by police and ...': Leonard, 'Pornography and Obscenity', in Houlbrook and Cocks (eds), *The Modern History of Sexuality*, p. 138.

Page 5, 'Pornography was not a given ...': Hunt, *The Invention of Pornography*, p. 11.

Page 5, 'names an argument, not a thing': Kendrick, *The Secret Museum*, p. 31.

Page 8: 'which professedly deal with ...': Leonard, 'Pornography and Obscenity', in Houlbrook and Cocks (eds), *The Modern History of Sexuality*, pp. 196–7.

Page 8, In eighteenth-century France, for example: Kraakman, 'Pornography in Western European Culture', in Eder et al. (eds), *Sexual Cultures in Europe*, p. 113.

Page 9, One prompt for this shift: Hunter et al., *On Pornography*, pp. 49–51.

Page 9, In his groundbreaking book: Marcus, *The Other Victorians*.

Page 9, In the United States: Heins, *Sex, Sin and Blasphemy*, p. 19.

Page 10, 'They are members of a society...': Travis, *Bound and Gagged: A Secret History of Obscenity in Britain*, pp. 5–7.

Pages 10–11, Nineteenth-century view that women had to be protected from sexually explicit material: Coleman, *Obscenity, Blasphemy and Sedition*, p. 51.

Page 11, As US historian Thomas Laqueur: Laqueur, *Solitary Sex*, pp. 339–40.

Pages 11–12, as Australian academic Barbara Sullivan writes: Sullivan, *The Politics of Sex*, p. 32.

Page 13, In one famous court exchange: Coleman, *Obscenity, Blasphemy and Sedition*, p. 32.

Page 13, As Barbara Sullivan, the author: Sullivan, *The Politics of Sex*, pp. 92–3.

Page 14, As Linda Williams records: Williams, *Hard Core*, p. 75.

Page 15, in a theatre Williams describes: Williams, *Hard Core*, p. 99.

Page 15, 'On the one hand ...': Sullivan, *The Politics of Sex*, pp. 129–30.

Pages 15–16, In Australia, a progressive Labor: Sullivan, *The Politics of Sex*, p. 138–9.

Page 16, The Williams Committee report: Travis, *Bound and Gagged: A Secret History of Obscenity in Britain*, pp. 263–4.

Pages 16–17, The Meese Commission: Heins, *Sex, Sin and Blasphemy*, p. 148.

Page 18, 'It has plagued us to understand ...': Dworkin, 'Against the Male Flood', in Cornell (ed.), *Feminism and Pornography*, p. 35.

Page 19, 'Gender is sexual ...': MacKinnon, *Feminism Unmodified*, p. 172.

Page 19, 'Pornography is the propaganda ...': Deitz, 'The Shackled Sex', p. 12.

Page 21, Accompanying this rapid growth: McNair, *Mediated Sex*; McNair, *Striptease Culture*.

2. Dirty? Old? Men?

Page 24, 'Mike likes to ...': Castles, 'In the Grip of a Guilty Pleasure'.

Page 25, According to a Roy: Roy Morgan, *Summary Report on Community Attitudes towards Censorship*; see also Richters et al., 'Autoerotic, Esoteric and Other Sexual Practises Engaged in by a Representative Sample of Adults'.

Page 25, 'booze, babes and balls': Di Mattia, 'Booze, Babes and Balls', accessed 2 December 2006.

Page 25, '[n]o man who ...': Hamilton, quoted in Symons, 'Torn on Porn's Net Effects'.

Page 26, Most research into pornography: A few exceptions are: Padgett et al., 'Pornography, Erotica and Attitudes towards Women'; Davies, 'Voluntary Exposure to Pornography and Men's Attitudes towards Feminism and Rape'; Smith, 'They're Ordinary People, Not Aliens from the Planet Sex!', accessed 9 June 2004; and Loftus, *Watching Sex*.

Page 26, In 1996, Hugh: Potter, *Pornography: Group Pressures and Individual Rights*.

Page 26, And in 2003: McKee, 'The Relationship between Attitudes towards Women, Consumption of Pornography, and Other Demographic Variables in a Survey of 1023 Consumers of Pornography'.

Page 27, A full 90 per cent: Lawrence and Herold, 'Women's Attitudes toward and Experience with Sexually Explicit Materials'.

Page 27, compared with an average age: *Asian Economic News*, 'Census Shows Australian Population Grew 6 Per Cent in 5 Years', accessed 14 November 2007.

Page 27, This was similar to the 2003 survey: Richters et al., 'Autoerotic, Esoteric and Other Sexual Practises', p. 186.

Page 28, The average annual income: Australian Bureau of Statistics (ABS), 'Average Weekly Earnings Australia', accessed 30 August 2004.

Page 28, In 1999, 27 per cent: ABS, 'Australian Social Trends 2002', accessed 30 August 2004.

Page 28, Another survey found that: Richters et al., 'Autoerotic, Esoteric and Other Sexual Practises', p. 186. See also Potter, *Pornography: Group Pressures and Individual Rights*, p. 149.

Page 29, In his 1996 survey, Potter found: Potter, *Pornography: Group Pressures and Individual Rights*, p. 86.

Page 29, (as George Pell once claimed): Pell, 'Crime Figures Prove We Live in an Age of Violence'.

Page 29, the 2001 Census found: ABS, 'Australian Social Trends 2004', accessed 14 November 2007.

Page 31, In 2001, 59 per cent: ABS, 'Age by Social Marital Status by Sex', accessed 2 November 2006.

Page 33, They are linked to a wider culture: See Potter, *Pornography: Group Pressures and Individual Rights*, p. 9.

Page 35, it seems that pornography consumers: See Loftus, *Watching Sex*, p. 305.

Page 37, So after we did the survey: McKee, 'The Need to Bring the Voices of Pornography Consumers into Public Debates about the Genre and Its Effects'; McKee, 'Censorship of Sexually Explicit Materials in Australia'; and McKee, 'The Aesthetics of Pornography'.

Pages 37–8, Gender and geographic location: According to Smith et al., 'Sex in Australia', p. 103, these are the key variables in differing sexual practices.

Page 40, 'Academics would have us ...': Trad, 'Save Kids from Porn'.

Page 40, 'just because a self-selecting ...': Gilding, 'Book Review: *Virtual Nation*', accessed 7 September 2005.

Page 40, We are often accused: *Canberra Times*, 'Need for Bottle to Put Porn Genie Back in Place'.

3. What Does Debbie Do?

Page 48, Estimates of sexually explicit material on the internet: Ropelato, 'Internet Pornography Statistics', 'Top Ten Reviews, 2006', accessed 30 November 2006.

Page 48, A Roy Morgan survey: Roy Morgan, *Summary Report on Community Attitudes towards Censorship*.

Pages 48–9, 'We're talking about ...': Hamilton, 'Guarding Our Kids from a Perverse Twist'.

Page 49, What kind of pornography is the most popular in Australia: McKee, 'The Objectification of Women in Mainstream Porn Videos in Australia'.

Page 49, Authors' 2003 survey of pornography consumers: McKee, 'The Relationship between Attitudes towards Women, Consumption of Pornography, and Other Demographic Variables in a Survey of 1023 Consumers of Pornography'.

Page 49, The South Australian Industrial Relations Commission ruling in 2006: Castello, 'Sack over Mail'.

Page 51, There is widespread public concern: AC Nielsen, *Film and Video Content*.

Page 52, Many previous academic studies: Palys, 'Testing the Common Wisdom'; Dietz and Sears, 'Pornography and Obscenity Sold in "Adult Bookstores"'; Barron and Kimmel, 'Sexual Violence in Three Pornographic Media', p. 163; Cowan et al., 'Dominance and Inequality in X-rated Videocassettes', p. 304; Monk-Turner and Purcell, 'Sexual Violence in Pornography', p. 62.

Page 52, That didn't make sense to us: By the same token, we didn't follow Andrea Dworkin and Catharine MacKinnon's argument that the very existence of pornography is an act of violence against women—see MacKinnon, 'Pornography as Trafficking'. This is a logical and coherent philosophical argument, but once again, it doesn't match up with the common sense definition of violence that most Australians are concerned about.

Page 52, 'Any form of behaviour …': Donnerstein et al., *The Question of Pornography*, p. 18.

Page 52, If it was absolutely clear: Even this is controversial. Some philosophers claim that women can never really consent to appear in pornography. They might say 'yes', but it really means 'no'. The argument is that appearing in pornography is such a horrific act that nobody could rationally agree to do it. Any woman who does do it must be acting under some kind of influence. This might be drink or drugs. Or it might be that they are so desperate for money that they have no other options but to do pornography. Or, finally, it might be that women think that they enjoy it, but they have been brainwashed by the patriarchal society surrounding them into eroticising their own oppression—see Jeffreys, *Anticlimax*. Again, this argument is consistent and logical. But it doesn't match up with what most Australians mean when they talk about consent in sex.

Page 53, So if you scream obscene abuse at a person: Cowan et al., 'Dominance and Inequality in X-rated Videocassettes'; Cowan and Campbell, 'Racism and Sexism in Interracial Pornography'.

Page 53, Various surveys of American: Yang and Linz, 'Movie Ratings and the Content of Adult Videos', p. 39; Barron and Kimmel, 'Sexual Violence in Three Pornographic Media'.

Page 53, Some included spanking: Barron and Kimmel, 'Sexual Violence in Three Pornographic Media'.

Pages 57–8, And it's interesting: Albury, 'The Best Straight Male Porn Star' in McKee, Beautiful Objects in Popular Culture.

Page 58, But people are also concerned: Rantzen, 'Does Erotica Really Turn Women On?'.

Page 58, For some people: Donnerstein et al., *The Question of Pornography*.

Page 58, Other people say: Zillmann, 'Effects of Prolonged Consumption of Pornography', in Zillmann and Bryant (eds), *Pornography: Research Advances and Policy Considerations*.

Page 58, For other people: Hamilton, 'Guarding Our Kids from a Perverse Twist'.

Page 58, For still others: Dworkin, *Pornography: Men Possessing Women*.

Page 58, For still other people: Donnerstein, 'Pornography: Its Effect on Violence against Women', in Malamuth and Donnerstein (eds), *Pornography and Sexual Aggression*.

Page 59, Whenever you take a photo: Kappeler, *The Pornography of Representation*.

Pages 59–60, There's a common concern: Patriquin, 'Addicted to Porn'.

Page 60, Our coders counted: We have rounded off numbers to the nearest per cent for this book. The precise figures are given in the academic journal versions of this research; see McKee, 'The Objectification of Women in Mainstream Porn Videos in Australia'.

Page 64, 'are uniformly portrayed …': Hamilton, 'Guarding Our Kids from a Perverse Twist'.

Page 66, 'Sex, a word …': Dworkin, *Pornography: Men Possessing Women*, p. 23.

Page 66, And, as 1970s feminism: Dell'Ollio, 'The Sexual Revolution Wasn't Our War'.

4. Does Pornography Cause Masturbation?

Page 74, When we surveyed: McKee, 'The Positive and Negative Effects of Pornography as Attributed by Consumers'.

Page 75, Negative effects commentators claim are caused by exposure to pornography: Fewster, 'Guilty Pedophile Sobs as Judge Revokes Bail'; Rantzen, 'Does Erotica Really Turn Women On?': Coffman, 'Pornography Victimizes the Vulnerable'; Hamilton, 'Guarding Our Kids from a Perverse Twist'; Pell, 'Crime Figures Prove We Live in an Age of Violence'; Anon., 'Lust Junkies Flooding Cyberspace'.

Page 76, Some aggregate studies suggest: Abramson and Hayashi, 'Pornography in Japan', in Malamuth and Donnerstein (eds), *Pornography and Sexual Aggression*; Gentry, 'Pornography and Rape: An Empirical Analysis'; Kutchinsky, 'Pornography and Rape: Theory and Practice?', pp. 51, 58; Kimmel and Linders, 'Does Censorship Make a Difference?'.

Page 76, But other studies suggest: Baron and Straus, *Four Theories of Rape in American Society*; Scott and Schwalm, 'Rape Rates and the Circulation Rates of Adult Magazines'.

Page 76, We should note that: Zillmann and Weaver, 'Pornography and Men's Sexual Callousness toward Women', in Zillmann and Bryant (eds), *Pornography: Research Advances and Policy Considerations*, p. 119.

Pages 76–7, Some researchers have managed: Donnerstein and Berkowitz, 'Victim Reactions in Aggressive Erotic Films as a Factor in Violence against Women'; Malamuth and Check, 'The Effects of Mass Media Exposure on Acceptance of Violence against Women'; Malamuth, 'Rape Fantasies as a Function of Exposure to Violent Sexual Stimuli'; Check, *The Effects of Violent and Non-violent Pornography*; Zillmann and Bryant, 'Effects of Massive Exposure to Pornography', in Malamuth and Donnerstein (eds), *Pornography and Sexual Aggression*.

Page 77, Other researchers have been unable: Baron and Bell, 'Effects of Heightened Sexual Arousal on Physical Aggression'; Fisher and Grenier, 'Violent Pornography, Anti-woman Thoughts, and Anti-woman Acts'; Linz et al., 'Effects of Long-term Exposure to Violent and Sexually Degrading Depictions of Women'; Malamuth and Centi, 'Repeated Exposure to Violent and Non-violent Pornography'; Padgett et al., 'Pornography, Erotica and Attitudes towards Women. See also discussions in Fisher and Barak, 'Sex Education as a Corrective', in Zillmann and Bryant (eds), *Pornography: Research Advances and Policy Considerations*; Donnerstein et al., *The Question of Pornography*; Fisher and Barak, 'Pornography, Erotica and Behaviour'; Fisher and Grenier, 'Violent Pornography, Anti-woman Thoughts, and Anti-woman Acts'; Linz, 'Exposure to Sexually Explicit Materials and Attitudes towards Rape'.

Page 77, These studies have consistently: Abel, 'Effects of Exposure to Violent Erotica'; Abel et al., 'Sex Offenders'; Gebhard et al., *Sex Offenders*; Goldstein and Kant, *Pornography and Sexual Deviance*. See also Johnson et al., and Walker, cited in Donnerstein et al., *The Question of Pornography*, p. 34.

Page 77, There is agreement among: Padgett et al., 'Pornography, Erotica and Attitudes towards Women'; Davies, 'Voluntary Exposure to Pornography and Men's Attitudes towards Feminism and Rape'; Potter, *Pornography: Group Pressures and Individual Rights*, p. 143; and our own survey. For an exception, see Crossman, 'Date Rape and Sexual Aggression by College Males', cited in Malamuth and Donnerstein (eds), *Pornography and Sexual Aggression*.

Page 78, the simplest possible explanation involves: See debates in Fisher and Barak, 'Pornography, Erotica and Behaviour', p. 72; Davies, 'Voluntary Exposure to Pornography and Men's Attitudes towards Feminism and Rape', p. 15 (Expanded Academic); Fisher and Barak, 'Sex Education as a Corrective', in Zillman and Jennings (eds), *Pornography: Research Advances and Policy Consideration*, p. 298; Kutchinsky, 'Pornography and Rape: Theory and Practice?', p. 48; Donnerstein et al., *The Question of Pornography*, p. 12; Brannigan, 'Obscenity and Social Harm', p. 5; Fisher and Grenier, 'Violent Pornography, Anti-woman Thoughts, and Anti-woman Acts', pp. 26, 35.

Page 78, The scientists have found: Zillmann and Bryant, 'Effects of Massive Exposure to Pornography', in Malamuth and Donnerstein (eds), *Pornography and Sexual Aggression*, pp. 130, 131; Donnerstein, 'Pornography: Its Effect on Violence against Women', in Malamuth and Donnerstein (eds), *Pornography and Sexual Aggression*, p. 62.

Page 79, In the experiments, the people watching: Zillmann, personal communication, 'Query about Methodology', 30 July 2004.

Page 79, This is somewhat different from the real world: Potter, *Pornography: Group Pressures and Individual Rights*, p. 111.

Pages 79–80, we also asked the consumers a series of questions: See also Spence and Helmreich, 'The Attitudes towards Women Scale', p. 66; Peters et al., 'Women as Managers Scale (WAMS)', p. 27; Burt, 'Cultural Myths and Supports for Rape'; Dreyer et al., 'ISRO'.

Page 80, 'You never know when …': Christensen, 'Sexual Callousness Re-examined', p. 178.

Page 80, This is because: Zillmann and Weaver, 'Pornography and Men's Sexual Callousness toward Women', in Zillmann and Bryant (eds), *Pornography: Research Advances and Policy Considerations*, p. 121.

Page 81, most surveys of porn users: Padgett et al., 'Pornography, Erotica and Attitudes towards Women'; Davies, 'Voluntary Exposure to Pornography and Men's Attitudes toward Rape'; Potter, *Pornography: Group Pressures and Individual Rights*.

Page 84, The closest we could find: Flood and Hamilton, 'Youth and Pornography in Australia', p. 24; Duggan et al., 'False Promises', in Caught Looking Inc (eds), *Caught Looking*, p. 82; Winick, 'A Content Analysis of Sexually Explicit Magazines Sold in an Adult Bookstore', p. 209; Kimmel, 'Introduction: Guilty Pleasures', in Kimmel (ed.), *Men Confront Pornography*; MacDonald, 'Confessions of a Feminist Porn Watcher', in Kimmel (ed.), *Men Confront Pornography*.

Page 87, Paul Hill quotes: Agence France-Press, 'ADDS with Identities of Victims and Earlier Hill Quote'.

Pages 87–8, The group Religious Tolerance: Religious Tolerance, 'Violence and Harassment at US Abortion Clinics', accessed 6 December 2006.

Page 88, The consumers that we interviewed: McKee, 'The Need to Bring the Voices of Pornography Consumers into Public Debates about the Genre and Its Effects'; McKee, 'Censorship of Sexually Explicit Materials in Australia'.

Page 90, Several researchers have pointed out: Gauntlett, 'Ten Things Wrong with the "Effects Model"', in Dickinson et al. (eds), *Approaches to Audiences*.

5. On Our Backs

Pages 101–2, Levy's description of *Girls Gone Wild* producers: Levy, *Female Chauvinist Pigs*, p. 12.

Page 102, 'the feminist project ...': ibid., p. 3.

Page 102, '*empowered* enough to get ...': ibid., p. 4.

Page 103, Feminists as diverse: Hollibaugh, 'Desire for the Future', in Vance (ed.), *Pleasure and Danger*; Califia, *Public Sex*.

Page 103, 'Here's the irony ...': Bright, 'Andrea Dworkin Has Died', accessed 11 April 2005.

Pages 103–4, The 'politics and values' Bright refers to: Loe, 'Feminism for Sale'.

Page 104, 'We were reclaiming ...': Royalle, quoted in Nagle, 'First Ladies of Feminist Porn', in Nagle (ed.), *Whores and Other Feminists*, p. 157.

Page 104, 1970s texts that aimed to demystify female sexuality: This movement within feminism was not universal, however, even among feminists who were 'pro sex' in other respects. In her 1983 article 'Sensual Uncertainty, or Why the Clitoris is Not Enough', Lynne Segal questioned what she saw as an uncritical overreliance on the behaviourist psychology of Masters and Johnson. See Segal, 'Sensual Uncertainty, or Why the Clitoris is Not Enough', in Cartledge and Ryan (eds), *Sex and Love, New Thoughts on Old Contradictions*, p. 34.

Page 105, 'consisted of intense discussions ...': O'Sullivan, 'Dangerous Desire', in Matthews (ed.), *Sex in Public*, p. 116.

Page 106, 'Why, when abuse ...': Sundahl, quoted in Nagle, 'First Ladies of Feminist Porn', in Nagle (ed.), *Whores and Other Feminists*, p. 159.

Page 106, 'because both gay and straight ...': Nagle, 'First Ladies of Feminist Porn', in Nagle (ed.), *Whores and Other Feminists*, p. 163.

Page 106, Both *On Our Backs*: O'Sullivan, 'Dangerous Desire', in Matthews (ed.), *Sex in Public*.

Page 107, 'without a sign ...': O'Sullivan, 'Five Years of Infamy', p. 7.

Page 108, 'I decided there was nothing ...': Nagle, 'First Ladies of Feminist Porn', in Nagle (ed.), *Whores and Other Feminists*, p. 157.

Page 108, 'couples, the educated ...': Heidenry, *What Wild Ecstasy*, p. 384.

Pages 108–9, Although Royalle's videos: Nagle, 'First Ladies of Feminist Porn', in Nagle (ed.), *Whores and Other Feminists*. In offering these examples, we are not seeking to advance the claim that female-produced porn is fundamentally different from (or better than) porn made by men. We are, however, seeking to counter the implication in Levy's complaints against 'raunch culture' that mainstream porn producers have conjured the idea that porn can support feminist principles out of a simple desire to expand audiences. The assertion that women can enjoy watching (and making) porn comes from within feminism, and reflects not just a venal marketing claim but an expression of political activism.

Page 109, 'lesbian fiction was ...': Bright, in Juffer, *At Home with Pornography*, p. 124.

Pages 109–10, 'I'm embarrassed to describe ...': Bright, *Full Exposure*, p. 64.

Page 110, 'a commercial term ...': Bright, in Juffer, *At Home with Pornography*, p. 124.

Page 110, 'perverse Mills and Boon' although 'certainly not high brow clitera-ture': JoyStick MuffBunny, 'Cliterature Reviews'.

Page 110, 'one of the conditions ...': Juffer, *At Home with Pornography*, p. 141.

Page 111, An issue of *Cleo* magazine: Le Mesurier, Cleo Magazine and the Makings of Popular Feminism.

Page 111, *Australian Women's Forum* censorship battles: See Chapter 6 for an explanation of Australian classification laws.

Page 112, The internet played: Although there are no universal definitions for the terms first, second and third-wave feminism, they are loosely used to describe generational shifts in feminist theory and practice. In the broadest terms, first-wave feminism equates with the women's suffrage movements of the nineteenth and early twentieth centuries. Second-wave feminism could be epitomised by the women's liberation movement that reached its peak in the 1970s. Third-wave feminism describes the 'girl power' feminism popularised in the 1990s.

Page 112, However, with the parallel rise: See Bail (ed.), *DIY Feminism*.

Pages 112–13, 'Unlike our feminist foremothers ...': Cited in Goldberg, 'Feminism for Sale', accessed 4 May 2002.

Page 113, Riot Grrl culture: Kimberly O'Sullivan notes that she and other Australian feminist sex activists also combined feminism with sex work in her '25 years on the left'. See O'Sullivan, 'Good Girls Gone Bad', accessed 20 August 2004.

Page 113, 'Full of images ...': Goldberg, 'Feminism for Sale', accessed 4 May 2002.

Page 114, 'a new generation ...': Firefox, 'Finally! Real Lesbian Porn Balls to the Wall', accessed 10 July 2002.

Page 114, 'being communicative ...': Butler, 'What Do You Call a Lesbian with Long Fingers?', in Williams (ed.), *Porn Studies*, p. 190.

Page 114, 'What we do ...': Firefox, 'Finally! Real Lesbian Porn Balls to the Wall', accessed 10 July 2002.

Page 114, '"We're like the punk rock company" ...': Queen, 'Yes SIR!', accessed 15 October 2004.

Page 115, 'I think the problem ...': Taormino, *True Lust*, pp. 98–9.

Page 115, 'the ultimate feminist gang bang.': ibid., p. 104.

Page 115, 'if lesbians attempt to ...': Butler, 'What Do You Call a Lesbian with Long Fingers?', in Williams (ed.), *Porn Studies*, pp. 191–2.

Page 116, SIR Video's *Hard Love and How to Fuck in High Heels*: Sullivan, 'Lesbographic Pornography', in Koivunent and Paasonen (eds), conference proceedings for *Affective Encounters*, accessed 15 October 2004.

Page 117: Those who like harder edged: See Chapter 3 for our analysis of content in porn.

Page 118, In fact, when we set out to interview: Unlike the survey, which was conducted during a short period, the interviews with producers were conducted over the entire duration of our project, from 2001 to 2004.

Pages 118–19, 'we made this mag because …': Stealth and Domino, Editorial, *Slit*.

Page 126, 'Feminist porn is irrelevant …': Cited in Newitz, 'Obscene Feminists', accessed 16 May 2002.

Page 126, 'One of the things …': Newitz, 'Obscene Feminists', accessed 16 May 2002.

6. DIY Porn

Page 128, 'WANTED, LADIES …': Ad in *Australasian Vixen* (a Melbourne-based swingers magazine), March 2002.

Page 130, Some agreed with: MacKinnon, *Only Words*.

Page 130, 'By the middle decades …': Scott, 'A Labour of Sex?', in Hawkes and Scott (eds), *Perspectives in Human Sexuality*, p. 236.

Page 131, 'It's just a hobby for me …': Galvin, 'The Pornstar Next Door'.

Page 131, 'I guess I wanted …': ibid.

Page 132, when researcher Rush Barcan interviewed 'Keith': Barcan, 'In the Raw', accessed 20 May 2002.

Page 133, 'the chat [on the sex-pic site] …': Rival et al., 'Sex and Sociality', p. 300.

Page 133, 'explore desires…': Rival et al., 'Sex and Sociality', p. 301.

Page 133, This finding was supported by: Kibby and Costello, 'Displaying the Phallus', accessed 5 April 2005; Kibby and Costello, 'Between the Image and the Act'.

Page 133, Indeed, as Kibby and Costello observe: Kibby and Costello, 'Between the Image and the Act', p. 361.

Page 134, 'pleasures and transgressions'; 'many logged …': Rival et al., 'Sex and Sociality', p. 304.

Page 134, Similarly, Kibby and Costello's: Kibby and Costello, 'Between the Image and the Act', p. 364.

Page 135, 'shows that the objectification …': Rival et al., 'Sex and Sociality', p. 316.

Page 135, As Slater has put it: Slater, 'Making Things Real'.

Page 138, 'the prize of one S/M aficionado's collection': Waugh, *Hard to Imagine*, p. 57.

Page 138, 'In the porn shops of …': O'Toole, *Pornocopia*, p. 22.

Page 146, 'Cute pin-up girls …': www.nofauxxx.com

Page 146, 'There are no specific scenes …': www.nofauxxx.com/dvd.htm

Page 146, 'If I change …'; 'The short (preventative) …': www.vegporn.com/modelinfo.html

7. The Pursuit of Innocents

Pages 152–3, Jenkins begins his book: Jenkins, *Beyond Tolerance*, p. 4.

Page 153, McKay's comments to the Australian media regarding the profile of child pornography users in Australia: Crooks, 'Caught in the Web'.

Page 153, 'scale of the enterprise ...': Jenkins, *Beyond Tolerance*, p. 32.

Page 153, 'the range of people involved...': Taylor and Quayle, *Child Pornography*, p. 5.

Pages 153–4, The bulletin board conversations: Jenkins, *Beyond Tolerance*, p. 121.

Page 154, 'The phrase neatly encapsulates ...': Jenkins, *Beyond Tolerance*, p. 127.

Page 154, Sadly, the great majority of sexual abuse: Mouzos and Makkai, Women's Experience of Male Violence.

Page 156, 'We started talking...': Grayson, 'No Right Not to Be Photographed', accessed 10 January 2006.

Page 157, 'Imagine a stranger ...': Dibbens, 'Monsters in Your Child's Bedroom'.

Page 157, There is a long history: Lumby and Fine, *Why TV Is Good for Kids*.

Page 157, 'dire assessments ...': Levine, *Harmful to Minors*, p. 29.

Page 158, 'We have made the child ...': Kincaid, *Erotic Innocence*, pp. 282–3.

Page 159, The survey on teenagers and cyberporn by the Australia Institute: Flood and Hamilton, 'Youth and Pornography in Australia'.

Page 159, The authors of the Australia Institute report: ibid., p. vii.

Page 162, 'As the pornography industry ...': Buckingham and Bragg, *Young People, Sex and the Media*, p. 92.

Page 163, 'Their [the media's] veracity and authority ...': ibid., p. 94.

8. Porn, Sex and Ethics

Pages 166–7, Accounts of the contemporary porn industry: For extended accounts of the contemporary porn industry in the United States, see McNeil and Osbourne's *The Other Hollywood* and Schlosser, *Reefer Madness and Other Tales from the American Underground*. Gaffin's *Hollywood Blue* provides a more anecdotal view of the Los Angeles porn scene in the 1990s.

Page 168, Discussion of Foucault's philosophies regarding difference between morals and ethics: Foucault, *The Care of the Self*; Foucault, *Ethics*, ed. P Rabinow.

Page 171, A good example is the 'reality porn' genre: This is not true of all reality videos. As Greta Cristina observes, even the *Girls Gone Wild* videos occasionally feature genuine exhibitionism and a focus on female pleasure.

Page 172, As US commentator Shauna: Swartz, 'XXX Offender', in Jervis and Zeigler (eds), *Bitchfest*.

Page 173, 'it's no different ...': *Frontline* interview with Rob Black, 2001, accessed 15 November 2006.

Page 174, 'The picture quality ...': Ladamann, 'Letter to the Editor'.

Page 175, In 2000, only two years: Mitchell, AIM Newsletter, accessed 10 April 2000.

Page 175, According to porn industry physician: Pike-Johnson, 'Risky Business'.

Page 175, The Adult Industry Medical Health Care Foundation: Legs McNeil and Jennifer Osbourne's exhaustive oral history of the US porn industry contains first-person accounts from AIM's Sharon Mitchell, the performers at the centre of the 1998 HIV outbreak and other high-profile HIV-positive men and women in the straight porn industry; see McNeil and Osbourne, *The Other Hollywood. AVN* ran an extended investigation of the controversies surrounding AIM's STD/HIV-testing programs in August 2003; see Kernes, 'Does Sex Kill?', p. 58. The issue became increasingly tense in 2006, when the Californian government proposed that occupational health and safety within the porn industry should be state-regulated.

Page 175, This non-profit organisation: In 2003 performers paid US$100 for all three tests, while production companies payed US$200 per month.

Page 175, In addition, AIM runs a general: AIM website, Sharon Mitchell profile accessed 10 April 2000.

Pages 175–6, As Mitchell describes it: Mitchell, AIM Newsletter, accessed 10 April 2000.

Page 176, 'Say you want to be …': Kernes, 'Does Sex Kill?', p. 58.

Page 176, Belladonna's interview with Acme Anderson: Anderson, 'Belladonna'.

Page 176, Producers' claims that condoms off-putting to straight audiences: Ramone, 'Powers'.

Page 177, 'No adult actor or actress …': Alpha, 'Letter to the editor'.

Page 180, Dilemma: Porn with 'rough' sex floats my boat but I worry: BDSM porn veteran Midori notes that the process of producing erotic photographs and/or videos can be emotionally and physically draining, even on 'professional' performers. See the 'Aftercare: Healing Better to Play Harder' chapter in her book, *Wild Side Sex.*

9. Afterglow?

Page 185, to paraphrase cultural theorist: Bersani, 'Is the Rectum a Grave', in Crimp (ed.), *AIDS.*

Pages 185–6, In her 2003 book *Mommy's Little Girl*: Bright, *Mommy's Little Girl*, p. 65. The discussion in the main text is a summary of Bright's argument.

Appendix

Page 191, Content analysis guidelines that were devised by Alan McKee and published: See the bibliography for full details of Alan McKee's 'The Objectification of Women in Mainstream Porn Videos in Australia'. It was published in *The Journal of Sex Research.*

Page 192, Alan also organised a survey: McKee, 'The Relationship between Attitudes towards Women, Consumption of Pornography, and Other Demographic Variables in a Survey of 1023 Consumers of Pornography'.

Bibliography

Books

Albury, Kath, *Yes Means Yes: Getting Explicit about Heterosex*, Allen & Unwin, St Leonards, NSW, 2002.

Bail, Kathy (ed.), *DIY Feminism*, Allen & Unwin, St Leonards, NSW, 1996.

Barbach, Lonnie, *For Yourself: The Fulfillment of Female Sexuality*, Doubleday, New York, 1976.

Baron, Larry and Murray A Straus, *Four Theories of Rape in American Society*, Yale University Press, New Haven, Connecticut, 1989.

Bashford, Kerry (ed.), *Kink*, Wicked Women Publications, Sydney, 1993.

Bright, Susie, *Full Exposure: Opening Up to Sexual Creativity and Erotic Expression*, HarperCollins, San Francisco, 1999.

—— *Mommy's Little Girl: On Sex, Motherhood, Porn and Cherry Pie*, Thunder's Mouth Press, New York, 2003.

Buckingham, David and Sara Bragg, *Young People, Sex and the Media: The Facts of Life?*, Palgrave, New York, 2004.

Califia, Pat, *Public Sex: The Culture of Radical Sex*, Cleis Press, Pittsburgh/San Francisco, 1994.

Carter, Angela, *The Sadeian Woman: An Exercise in Cultural History*, Virago, London, 1987.

Check, James VP, *The Effects of Violent and Non-violent Pornography*, Department of Justice of Canada, Ottawa, 1985.

Coleman, Peter, *Obscenity, Blasphemy and Sedition*, Angus and Robertson, Sydney, 1974.

Dodson, Betty, *Sex for One: The Joy of Selfloving*, Harmony Books, New York, 1987.

Donnerstein, Edward, Daniel Linz and Steven Penrod, *The Question of Pornography: Research Findings and Policy Implications*, Macmillan/Free Press, New York, 1987.

Dworkin, Andrea, *Pornography: Men Possessing Women*, Women's Press, London, 1982.

—— *Intercourse*, Simon and Schuster, New York, 1997.

Foucault, Michel, *The Care of the Self: The History of Sexuality*, vol. 3, Penguin, London, 1986.

—— *Ethics: Subjectivity and Truth*, Paul Rabinow (ed.), New Press, New York, 1997.

Friday, Nancy, *My Secret Garden: Women's Sexual Fantasies*, Pocket Books, New York, 1974.

Gaffin, Harris, *Hollywood Blue: The Tinseltown Pornographers*, BT Batsford, London, 1997.

Gebhard, Paul, John H Gagnon, Wardell B Pomeroy and Cornelia V Christenson, *Sex Offenders*, Harper and Row, New York, 1965.

Goldstein, Michael J and Harold Kant, *Pornography and Sexual Deviance*, University of California Press, Berkeley, 1973.

Heidenry, John, *What Wild Ecstasy: The Rise and Fall of the Sexual Revolution*, William Heinemann Australia, Melbourne, 1997.

Heins, Marjorie, *Sex, Sin and Blasphemy: A Guide to America's Censorship Wars*, The New Press, New York, 1998.

Houlbrook, Matt and Harry Cocks (eds), *The Modern History of Sexuality*, Palgrave, Basingstoke, UK, 2005.

Hunt, Lynn, *The Invention of Pornography: Obscenity and the Origins of Modernity, 1500–1800*, Zone Books, New York, 1993.

Hunter, Ian, David Saunders and Dugald Williamson, *On Pornography: Literature, Sexuality and Obscenity Law*, St Martin's Press, New York, 1993.

Jeffreys, Sheila, *Anticlimax: A Feminist Perspective on the Sexual Revolution*, The Women's Press, London, 1993.

Jenkins, Philip, *Beyond Tolerance: Child Pornography on the Internet*, New York University Press, New York and London, 2001.

Juffer, Jane, *At Home with Pornography: Women, Sex and Everyday Life*, New York University Press, New York and London, 1998.

Kappeler, Susanne, *The Pornography of Representation*, Polity Press, Oxford, 1986.

Kendrick, Walter, *The Secret Museum: Pornography in Modern Culture*, University of California Press, Berkeley, 1996.

Kick, Russ (ed.), *Everything You Know about Sex Is Wrong: The Disinformation Guide to the Extremes of Human Sexuality*, The Disinformation Company, New York, 2006.

Kincaid, James, *Erotic Innocence: The Culture of Child Molesting*, Duke University Press, Durham, North Carolina, 1998.

Kipnis, Laura, *Bound and Gagged: Pornography and the Politics of Fantasy in America*, Duke University Press, Durham, North Carolina, 2006.

Laqueur, Thomas, *Solitary Sex: A Cultural History of Masturbation*, Zone Books, New York, 2003.

Levine, Judith, *Harmful to Minors*, University of Minnesota Press, Minneapolis, 2004.

Levy, Ariel, *Female Chauvinist Pigs: Women and the Rise of Raunch Culture*, Schwartz Publishing, Melbourne, 2005.

Loftus, David, *Watching Sex: How Men Really Respond to Pornography*, Thunder's Mouth Press, New York, 2002.

Lumby, Catharine, *Bad Girls: The Media, Sex and Feminism in the 90s*, Allen & Unwin, St Leonards, NSW, 1997.

Lumby, Catharine and Duncan Fine, *Why TV Is Good for Kids*, PanMacmillan, Sydney, 2006.

MacKinnon, Catharine, *Feminism Unmodified: Discourses on Life and Law*, Harvard University Press, Cambridge, 1987.

—— *Only Words*, HarperCollins, London, 1994.

Marcus, Steven, *The Other Victorians*, Basic Books, New York, 1974.

McNair, Brian, *Mediated Sex: Pornography and Postmodern Culture*, Arnold, London, 1996.

—— *Striptease Culture: Sex, Media and the Democratisation of Desire*, Routledge, London, 2002.

McNeil, Legs and Jennifer Osbourne, *The Other Hollywood: An Uncensored History of the Porn Film Industry*, HarperCollins, New York, 2006.

Midori, *Wild Side Sex: The Book of Kink*, Daedalus, New York, 2005.

O'Toole, Lawrence, *Pornocopia: Porn, Sex, Technology and Desire*, Serpent's Tooth, London, 1998.

Potter, Hugh, *Pornography: Group Pressures and Individual Rights*, The Federation Press, Sydney, 1996.

Schlosser, Eric, *Reefer Madness and Other Tales from the American Underground*, Penguin, London, 2004.

Sullivan, Barbara, *The Politics of Sex: Prostitution and Pornography in Australia Since 1945*, Cambridge University Press, Cambridge, 1997.

Taormino, Tristan, *True Lust: Adventures in Sex, Porn and Perversion*, Cleis Press, San Francisco, 2002.

Taylor, Max and Ethel Quayle, *Child Pornography: An Internet Crime*, Brunner-Routledge, Hove and New York, 2003.

Travis, Alan, *Bound and Gagged: A Secret History of Obscenity in Britain*, Profile Books, London, 2000.

Vnuk, Helen, *Snatched: Sex and Censorship in Australia*, Random House, Sydney, 2003.

Waugh, Thomas, *Hard to Imagine: Gay Male Eroticism in Photography and Film from Their Beginnings to Stonewall*, Columbia University Press, New York, 1996.

Williams, Linda, *Hard Core: Power, Pleasure and the Frenzy of the Visible*, University of California Press, Berkeley, 1989.

—— (ed.), *Porn Studies*, Duke University Press, Durham, North Carolina, 2004.

Articles, Reports, Unpublished Manuscripts etc

Abel, Gene G, 'Effects of Exposure to Violent Erotica', paper presented at the Annual Meeting of the Society for the Scientific Study of Sex, Chicago, 1983.

Abel, Gene G, Judith V Becker and Mary S Mittelman, 'Sex Offenders', paper presented at the 11th Annual Meeting of the International Academy of Sex Research, Seattle, Washington, 1985.

Abramson, Paul R and Haruo Hayashi, 'Pornography in Japan: Cross-cultural and Theoretical Considerations', in Neil M Malamuth and Edward Donnerstein (eds), *Pornography and Sexual Aggression*, Academic Press, Orlando, Florida, 1984, pp. 173–83.

AC Nielsen, *Film and Video Content*, Sydney, 2006.

Agence France-Press, 'ADDS with Identities of Victims and Earlier Hill Quote', 29 July 1994.

Albury, Kath, 'The Best Straight Male Porn Star: Rocco Siffredi', in Alan McKee (ed.), Beautiful Objects in Popular Culture, a proposal for New York University Press, unpublished manuscript, 2002.

—— 'The Ethics of Porn on the Net', in Catharine Lumby and E Probyn (eds), Remote Control: New Media, New Ethics, Cambridge University Press, Melbourne, 2003, pp. 196–211.

—— 'Pornography', in G Hawkes and J Scott (eds), Perspectives in Human Sexuality, Oxford University Press, Melbourne, 2005, pp. 254–68.

Alpha, Letter to the Editor, Adult Video News, May 2003, p. 36.

Anderson, Acme, 'Belladonna: Riding the Pine', Adult Video News, May 2003, p. 144.

—— 'Harder, Ever Harder: Can Porn Get Any Nastier?', Adult Video News, October 2003, p. 42.

Anon., 'Lust Junkies Flooding Cyberspace', Gold Coast Bulletin, 31 July 2004, p. B68.

Australasian Vixen, 'Wanted! Ladies for Play', personal ad, March 2002.

Baron, Robert A and Paul A Bell, 'Effects of Heightened Sexual Arousal on Physical Aggression', in Proceedings of the 81st Annual Convention of the American Psychological Association, vol. 8, 1973, pp. 171–2.

Barron, Martin and Michael Kimmel, 'Sexual Violence in Three Pornographic Media: Toward a Sociological Explanation', The Journal of Sex Research, vol. 37, no. 2, May 2000, pp. 161–8.

Bersani, Leo, 'Is the Rectum a Grave', in Douglas Crimp (ed.), AIDS: Cultural Analysis, Cultural Activism, 9th edn, MIT Press, Cambridge, 1988.

Blue, Violet, 'American Sex Ed: Porn as Sexual Disinformation', in Russ Kick (ed.), Everything You Know about Sex Is Wrong: The Disinformation Guide to the Extremes of Human Sexuality, The Disinformation Company, New York, 2006, pp. 148–52.

Brannigan, Augustine, 'Obscenity and Social Harm: A Contested Terrain', International Journal of Law and Psychiatry, vol. 14, 1991, pp. 1–12.

Burt, Martha R, 'Cultural Myths and Supports for Rape', Journal of Personality and Social Psychology, vol. 38, 1980, pp. 217–30.

Butler, Heather, 'What Do You Call a Lesbian with Long Fingers? The Development of Lesbian and Dyke Pornography', in L Williams (ed.), Porn Studies, Duke University Press, Durham, North Carolina, 2004, pp. 167–97.

Canberra Times, 'Need for Bottle to Put Porn Genie Back in Place', 29 November 2004, p. 15.

Castello, Renato, 'Sack over Mail: Workplace Smut Ruling', Sunday Mail, 16 July 2006, p. 1.

Castles, Simon, 'In the Grip of a Guilty Pleasure', Sunday Age, 8 October 2006, p. 12.

Christensen, Ferrel, 'Sexual Callousness Re-examined', Journal of Communication, vol. 36, no. 1, 1986, pp. 174–88.

Coffman, Judith, 'Pornography Victimizes the Vulnerable', Washington Times, Letters page, 15 February 2004, p. B02.

Cowan, Gloria, Daniella Levy, Carole Lee and Debra Snyder, 'Dominance and Inequality in X-rated Videocassettes', *Psychology of Women Quarterly*, vol. 12, no. 3, 1988, pp. 299–311.

Cowan, Gloria and Robin R Campbell, 'Racism and Sexism in Interracial Pornography: A Content Analysis', *Psychology of Women Quarterly*, vol. 18, 1994, pp. 323–38.

Cristina, Greta, 'Girls Gone Wild', in Russ Kick (ed.), *Everything You Know about Sex Is Wrong: The Disinformation Guide to the Extremes of Human Sexuality*, The Disinformation Company, New York, 2006, pp. 164–9.

Crooks, Michael, 'Caught in the Web', *Who Weekly*, 18 October 2004, pp. 41–2.

Crossman, Leslie, 'Date Rape and Sexual Aggression by College Males', cited in Neil M Malamuth and Edward Donnerstein (eds), *Pornography and Sexual Aggression*, Academic Press, New York, 1984, pp. 26–91.

Davies, Kimberly A, 'Voluntary Exposure to Pornography and Men's Attitudes towards Feminism and Rape', *The Journal of Sex Research*, vol. 34, no. 2, 1997, pp. 131–7, also accessed via Expanded Academic, paginated 1–20.

Deitz, Melissa, 'The Shackled Sex', *Australian Women's Forum*, vol. 4, no. 36, 1994 pp. 12–14.

Dell'Ollio, Anselma, 'The Sexual Revolution Wasn't Our War', *Ms.*, preview issue, Spring 1972, pp. 104–6, 109–110.

Dibbens, Kay, 'Monsters in Your Child's Bedroom', *Sunday Mail*, 4 June 2000, p. 66.

Dietz, Park Elliot and Alan E Sears, 'Pornography and Obscenity Sold in "Adult Bookstores": A Survey of 5132 Books, Magazines and Films in Four American Cities', *Journal of Law Reform*, vol. 21, 1988, pp. 22–3.

Donnerstein, Edward, 'Pornography: Its Effect on Violence against Women', in Neil M Malamuth and Edward Donnerstein (eds), *Pornography and Sexual Aggression*, Academic Press, New York, 1984, pp. 53–84.

Donnerstein, Edward and Leonard Berkowitz, 'Victim Reactions in Aggressive Erotic Films as a Factor in Violence against Women', *Journal of Personality and Social Psychology*, vol. 41, 1981, pp. 710–24.

Dreyer, Nancy A, Nancy Fugate-Woods and Sherman A James, 'ISRO: A Scale to Measure Sex-role Orientation', *Sex Roles*, vol. 7, 1981, pp. 173–82.

Duggan, Lisa, Nan D Hunter and Carole S Vance, 'False Promises: Feminist Anti-pornography Legislation in the US', in Caught Looking Inc (eds), *Caught Looking: Feminism, Pornography and Censorship*, The Real Comet Press, Seattle, Washington, 1998, pp. 72–85.

Dworkin, Andrea, 'Against the Male Flood', in Drusilla Cornell (ed.), *Feminism and Pornography*, pp. 19–38.

Fewster, Sean, 'Guilty Pedophile Sobs as Judge Revokes Bail', *The Adelaide Advertiser*, 27 August 2004, p. 17.

Fisher, William A and Azy Barak, 'Sex Education as a Corrective: Immunising against Possible Effects of Pornography', in Dolf Zillmann and Jennings Bryant (eds), *Pornography: Research Advances and Policy Considerations*, Lawrence Erlbaum, Hillsdale, New Jersey, 1989, pp. 289–320.

—— 'Pornography, Erotica and Behaviour: More Questions than Answers', *International Journal of Law and Psychiatry*, vol. 14, 1991, pp. 65–83.

Fisher, William A and Guy Grenier, 'Violent Pornography, Anti-woman Thoughts, and Anti-woman Acts: In Search of Reliable Effects', *The Journal of Sex Research*, vol. 31, 1994, pp. 23–38.

Flood, Michael and Clive Hamilton, 'Youth and Pornography in Australia: Evidence on the Extent of Exposure and Likely Effects', discussion paper for the Australia Institute, no. 52, 2003.

Galvin, Nick, 'The Pornstar Next Door', *Sydney Morning Herald*, 10 January 2003, p. 27.

Gauntlett, David, 'Ten Things Wrong with the "Effects Model"', in Roger Dickinson, Ramaswami Harindranath and Olga Linne (eds), *Approaches to Audiences*, Arnold, London, 1998, pp. 120–30.

Gentry, Cynthia, 'Pornography and Rape: An Empirical Analysis', *Deviant Behaviour*, vol. 12, 1991, pp. 277–88.

Gold Coast Bulletin, 'Study Supports Marital Bliss', 9 October 2002, p. 31.

Hamilton, Clive, 'Guarding Our Kids from a Perverse Twist', *The Australian*, 17 August 2004, p. 11.

Harradine, Brian, Hansard, Senate, Employment, Workplace Relations and Education Legislation Committee, estimates, 5 November 2003.

Hobart Mercury, 'Labor's Porn Shield', 22 March 2006, p. 4.

Hollibaugh, Amber, 'Desire for the Future: Radical Hope in Passion and Pleasure', in Carol Vance (ed.), *Pleasure and Danger: Exploring Female Sexuality*, Pandora, London, 1992, pp. 401–10.

JoyStick MuffBunny, 'Cliterature Reviews', *Slit*, no. 1, 2002, pp. 150–1.

Kernes, Mark, 'Does Sex Kill?', *Adult Video News*, August 2003, pp. 40–76.

—— 'Porn 101 Grows Up', *Adult Video News*, February 2004, p. 74.

Kibby, Marjorie and Brigid Costello, 'Between the Image and the Act: Interactive Sex Entertainment on the Internet', *Sexualities*, vol. 4, no. 3, 2001, pp. 353–69.

Kimmel, Michael, 'Introduction: Guilty Pleasures—Pornography in Men's Lives', in Michael Kimmel (ed.), *Men Confront Pornography*, Crown, New York, 1990, pp. 1–22.

Kimmel, Michael and Annulla Linders, 'Does Censorship Make a Difference? An Aggregate Empirical Analysis of Pornography and Rape', *Journal of Psychology and Human Sexuality*, vol. 8, 1996, pp. 1–20.

Kraakman, Dorelies, 'Pornography in Western European Culture', in Franz Eder, Lesley Hall and Gert Hekma (eds), *Sexual Cultures in Europe*, Manchester University Press, Manchester and New York, 1999, pp. 104–20.

Krome, Margaret, 'Net Porn: Passion, Shame', *Capital Times and Wisconsin State Journal*, 17 September 2003, p. 8A.

Kutchinsky, Berl, 'Pornography and Rape: Theory and Practice? Evidence from Crime Data in Four Countries Where Pornography is Easily Available', *International Journal of Law and Psychiatry*, vol. 14, nos 1–2, 1991, pp. 47–64.

Ladamann, Eric, 'Letter to the Editor', *Adult Video News*, 20 August 2003, p. 20.

Lawrence, Kelli-an A and Edward S Herold, 'Women's Attitudes toward and Experience with Sexually Explicit Materials', *Journal of Sex Research*, vol. 24, 1988, pp. 161–9.

Laws, John, Interview with Fred Nile, Radio 2UE, 25 September 1984.

Le Mesurier, Megan, Cleo Magazine and the Makings of Popular Feminism, PhD, School of Media and Communications, University of Sydney, unpublished, 2006.

Leonard, Sarah, 'Pornography and Obscenity', in Matt Houlbrook and Harry Cocks (eds), *The Modern History of Sexuality*, Palgrave, Basingstoke, UK, 2005.

Linz, Daniel, 'Exposure to Sexually Explicit Materials and Attitudes towards Rape: A Comparison of Study Results', *The Journal of Sex Research*, vol. 26, 1989, pp. 50–84.

Linz, Daniel, Edward Donnerstein and Steven Penrod, 'Effects of Long-term Exposure to Violent and Sexually Degrading Depictions of Women', *Journal of Personality and Social Psychology*, vol. 55, 1988, pp. 758–68.

Loe, Meika, 'Feminism for Sale: Case Study of a Pro-sex Feminist Business', *Gender & Society*, vol. 13, no. 6, 1999, pp. 705–32.

MacDonald, Scott, 'Confessions of a Feminist Porn Watcher', in Michael Kimmel (ed.), *Men Confront Pornography*, Crown, New York, 1990, pp. 34–42.

MacKinnon, Catharine, 'Pornography as Trafficking', *Michigan Journal of International Law*, vol. 26, no. 4, 2005, pp. 993–1012.

Malamuth, Neil M, 'Rape Fantasies as a Function of Exposure to Violent Sexual Stimuli', *Archives of Sexual Behaviour*, vol. 10, 1981, pp. 33–47.

Malamuth Neil M and Joseph Centi, 'Repeated Exposure to Violent and Non-violent Pornography: Likelihood of Raping Ratings and Laboratory Aggression Against Women', *Aggressive Behaviour*, vol. 12, 1986, pp. 129–37.

Malamuth, Neil M and James Check, 'The Effects of Mass Media Exposure on Acceptance of Violence against Women: A Field Experiment', *Journal of Research in Personality*, vol. 15, 1981, pp. 436–46.

Malamuth, Neil, Tamara Addison and Mary Koss, 'Pornography and Sexual Aggression: Are There Reliable Effects and Can We Understand Them?', *Annual Review of Sex Research*, vol. 11, 2000, pp. 26–91.

McKee, Alan, 'Less Harm than Skin in X Flicks', *Sydney Morning Herald*, 2 June 2003, p. 15.

—— 'The Objectification of Women in Mainstream Porn Videos in Australia', *The Journal of Sex Research*, vol. 42, no. 4, 2005, pp. 277–90.

—— 'The Need to Bring the Voices of Pornography Consumers into Public Debates about the Genre and Its Effects', *Australian Journal of Communication*, vol. 32, no. 2, 2005, pp. 71–94.

—— 'The Aesthetics of Pornography: The Insights of Consumers', *Continuum: Journal of Media and Cultural Studies*, vol. 20, no. 4, 2006, pp. 523–39.

—— 'Censorship of Sexually Explicit Materials in Australia: What Do Consumers of Pornography Have to Say about It?', *Media International Australia*, no. 120, August 2006, pp. 35–50.

—— 'The Relationship between Attitudes towards Women, Consumption of Pornography, and Other Demographic Variables in a Survey of 1023 Consumers of Pornography', *International Journal of Sexual Health*, vol. 19, no. 1, 2007, pp. 49–76.

—— 'The Positive and Negative Effects of Pornography as Attributed by Consumers', *Australian Journal of Communication*, vol. 34, no. 1, 2007, pp. 87–104.

Miller, Dan, 'Keepin' It Real: The Reality Porn Rage', *Adult Video News*, May 2003, pp. 40–74.

Monk-Turner, Elizabeth and H Christine Purcell, 'Sexual Violence in Pornography: How Prevalent Is It?', *Gender Issues*, vol. 17, no. 2, Spring 1999, pp. 58–67.

Mouzos, J and T Makkai, Women's Experience of Male Violence: Findings from the Australian Component of the International Violence against Women Survey, Australian Institute of Criminology, Canberra, 2004.

Nagle, Jill, 'First Ladies of Feminist Porn: A Conversation with Candida Royalle and Debi Sundahl', in Jill Nagle (ed.), *Whores and Other Feminists*, Routledge, New York, 1997, pp. 156–66.

O'Sullivan, Kimberley, 'Five Years of Infamy', *Wicked Women: 1988–1993*, 1993, pp. 6–8.

—— 'Dangerous Desire: Lesbianism as Sex or Politics', in Jill Matthews (ed.), *Sex in Public: Australian Sexual Cultures*, Allen & Unwin, St Leonards, NSW, 1997, pp. 114–26.

Padgett, Vernon R, Jo Brislin-Slutz and James A Neal, 'Pornography, Erotica and Attitudes towards Women: The Effects of Repeated Exposure', *The Journal of Sex Research*, vol. 26, 1989, pp. 479–91.

Palys, Ted S, 'Testing the Common Wisdom: The Social Content of Video Pornography', *Canadian Psychology*, vol. 27, 1986, pp. 22–35.

Patriquin, Martin, 'Addicted to Porn', *Montreal Gazette*, 26 July 2006, p. B3.

Pell, George, 'Crime Figures Prove We Live in an Age of Violence', *Sunday Telegraph* (Australia), 8 August 2004, p. 83.

Peters, Lawrence H, James R Terborg and Janet Taynor, 'Women as Managers Scale (WAMS): A Measure of Attitudes towards Women in Management Positions', *JSAS Catalog of Selected Documents in Psychology*, vol. 4, 1974, p. 27.

Pike-Johnson, Heidi, 'Risky Business: Some Sexual Practices Can Be Dangerous', *Adult Video News*, August 2003, p. 52.

—— 'On Being the Chick in Your Rental Section', *Adult Video News*, January 2004, p. 26.

—— 'Ladies First: A Women Retailers Roundtable', *Adult Video News*, April 2004 pp. 36–48.

Ramone, Mike, 'Powers: "Rogue Elements" Threaten Health of Industry', *Adult Video News*, August 2003, p. 62.

Rantzen, Esther, 'Does Erotica Really Turn Women On?', *Daily Mail* (UK), 1 January 2004, p. 56.

Richters, Juliet, Andrew E Grulich, Richard O de Visser, Anthony MA Smith and Chris E Rissel, 'Autoerotic, Esoteric and Other Sexual Practises Engaged in by a Representative Sample of Adults', *Australian and New Zealand Journal of Public Health*, vol. 27, no. 2, 2003, pp. 180–90.

Rival, Laura, Don Slater and Daniel Miller, 'Sex and Sociality: Comparative Ethnographies of Sexual Objectification', *Theory, Culture and Society*, vol. 15, nos 3 and 4, 1998, pp. 295–321.

Roy Morgan, *Summary Report on Community Attitudes towards Censorship*, Roy Morgan Research, Braddon, ACT, 1999.

Scott, John, 'A Labour of Sex? Male and Female Prostitution', in G Hawkes and J Scott (eds), *Perspectives in Human Sexuality*, Oxford University Press, Melbourne, 2005, pp. 233–53.

Scott, Joseph EL and Loretta Schwalm, 'Rape Rates and the Circulation Rates of Adult Magazines', *Journal of Sex Research*, vol. 24, 1988, pp. 240–50.

Segal, Lynne, 'Sensual Uncertainty, or Why the Clitoris is Not Enough', in S Cartledge and J Ryan (eds), *Sex and Love, New Thoughts on Old Contradictions*, The Women's Press, London, 1983, pp. 30–47.

Slater, Don, 'Making Things Real: Ethics and Order on the Internet', *Theory, Culture and Society*, vol. 19, nos 5/6, 2002, pp. 227–45.

Smith, Anthony MA, Chris E Rissel, Juliet Richters, Andrew E Grulich and Richard O de Visser, 'Sex in Australia: A Guide for Readers', *Australian and New Zealand Journal of Public Health*, vol. 27, no. 2, 2003, pp. 103–5.

Spence, Janet F and Robert Helmreich, 'The Attitudes towards Women Scale: The Rights and Roles of Women in Contemporary Society', *JSAS Catalog of Selected Documents in Psychology*, vol. 2, 1972, p. 66.

Stealth and Domino, Editorial, *Slit*, no. 1, 2002, p. 3.

Swartz, Shauna, 'XXX Offender: Reality Porn and the Rise of Humilitainment', in L Jervis and A Zeisler (eds), *Bitchfest: Ten Years of Cultural Criticism from Bitch Magazine*, Farrar, Strauss and Giroux, New York, 2006, pp. 318–21.

Symons, Emma Kate, 'Torn on Porn's Net Effects', *The Australian*, 17 August 2004, p. 4.

Trad, K, 'Save Kids from Porn', *The Australian*, 19 August 2004, Letters page, p. 14.

Winick, Charles, 'A Content Analysis of Sexually Explicit Magazines Sold in an Adult Bookstore', *Journal of Sex Research*, vol. 21, 1985, pp. 206–10.

Yang, Ni and Daniel Linz, 'Movie Ratings and the Content of Adult Videos: The Sex-violence Ratio', *Journal of Communication*, vol. 40, 1990, pp. 28–42.

Zillmann, Dolf, 'Effects of Prolonged Consumption of Pornography', in Dolf Zillmann and Jennings Bryant (eds), *Pornography: Research Advances and Policy Considerations*, Lawrence Erlbaum, Hillsdale, New Jersey, 1989, pp. 127–57.

—— Personal communication, 'Query about Methodology', 30 July 2004.

Zillmann, Dolf and Jennings Bryant, 'Effects of Massive Exposure to Pornography', in Neil M Malamuth and Edward Donnerstein (eds), *Pornography and Sexual Aggression*, Academic Press, Orlando, Florida, 1984, pp. 115–38.

Zillmann, Dolf and James B Weaver, 'Pornography and Men's Sexual Callousness toward Women', in Dolf Zillmann and Jennings Bryant (eds), *Pornography: Research Advances and Policy Considerations*, Lawrence Erlbaum, Hillsdale, New Jersey, 1989, pp. 95–125.

Electronic Sources

Adult Industry Medical Health Care Foundation (AIM), Sharon Mitchell profile, http://AIM-Med.org/profile.html, accessed 10 April 2000.

Asian Economic News, 'Census Shows Australian Population Grew 6% in 5 Years', 24 June 2002, http://findarticles.com/p/articles/mi_m0WDP/is_2002_June_24/ai_87697048, accessed 14 November 2007.

Australian Bureau of Statistics, 'Age by Social Marital Status by Sex', ABS Census tables, 2001, www8.abs.gov.au/ABSNavigation/prenav/ViewData?action=404&documentproductno=0&documenttype=Details&order=1&tabname=Details&areacode=0&issue=2001&producttype=Census%20Tables&javascript=true&textversion=false&navmapdisplayed=true&breadcrumb=TLPD&&productlabel=Social%20Marital%20Status%20by%20Age%20by%20Sex&method=Place%20of%20Usual%20Residence&, accessed 2 November 2006.

—— 'Australian Social Trends 2002: Education—Educational Achievement', ABS, 2002, www.abs.gov.au/Ausstats/abs@.nsf/94713ad445ff1425ca25682000192af2/457f7f94fe83c8b6ca256bcd008272fe!OpenDocument, accessed 30 August 2004.

—— 'Average Weekly Earnings Australia', ABS, 2003, www.abs.gov.au/ausstats/abs@.nsf/b06660592430724fca2568b5007b8619/01e915eafa3e74eeca256e45007d8909!OpenDocument, accessed 30 August 2004.

—— 'Australian Social Trends 2004: Religious Affiliation and Activity', ABS, 2004, www.abs.gov.au/ausstats/abs@.nsf/1020492cfcd63696ca2568a1002477b5/fa58e975c470b73cca256e9e00296645!OpenDocument, accessed 14 November 2007.

Barcan, Ruth, 'In the Raw: "Home-Made" Porn and Reality Genres', in *Journal of Mundane Behaviour*, vol. 3, no. 1, February 2002, http://mundanebehaviour.org/issues/v3n1/barcan.htm, accessed 20 May 2002.

Bright, Susie, 'Andrea Dworkin Has Died', *Susie Bright's Journal*, 2005, http://susiebright.blogs.com/susie_brights_journal_/2005/04/andrea_dworkin_.html, accessed 11 April 2005.

Di Mattia, Joanna L, 'Booze, Babes and Balls', *Hecate*, vol. 13, no. 2, 2001, www.emsah.uq.edu.au/awsr/recent, accessed 2 December 2006.

Firefox, LaSara, 'Finally! Real Lesbian Porn Balls to the Wall—Pedal to the Metal', 2001, www.spectator.net/EDPAGES/hardlove2.html, accessed 10 July 2002.

Frontline, 'Interview with Rob Black', 2002, www.pbs.org/wgbh/pages/frontline/shows/porn/interviews/black.html, accessed 15 November 2006.

Gilding, Michael, 'Book Review: *Virtual Nation: Australian Journal of Emerging Technologies and Society*', vol. 2, no. 2, 2004, www.swin.edu.au/sbs/ajets/journal/issue3/GildingReviewAJETS3.pdf, accessed 7 September 2005.

Goldberg, Michelle, 'Feminism for Sale', *AlterNet*, 2001, www.alternet.org/print.html?StoryID=10306, accessed 4 May 2002.

Grayson, Russ, 'No Right Not to Be Photographed—Councils Overreact', *Online Opinion*, 12 July 2005, www.onlineopinion.com.au, accessed 10 January 2006.

Kernes, Mark, 'Fears of Health Inspectors on Set Premature', 2005, www.avn.com/index.php?Primary_Navigation=Articles&Action=View_Article&Content_ID=240865, accessed 16 November 2006.

Kibby, Marjorie and Brigid Costello, 'Displaying the Phallus: Masculinity and the Performance of Sexuality on the Internet', 1999, www.newcastle.edu.au/discipline/sociolanthrop/staff/kibbymarj/maledisp.html, accessed 5 May 2005.

Ladendorf, Martina, 'Pin-ups and Grrls: The Pictures of Grrlzines', paper presented at the Crossroads in Cultural Studies Conference, Birmingham, UK, 21–25 June 2000, www.jmk.su.se/digitalborderlands/inas/pinups_grrls.htm, accessed 26 November 2002.

Mitchell, Sharon, AIM Newsletter, January 2000, http://AIM-Med.org/newsletter-jan00.html, accessed 10 April 2000.

Newitz, Annalee, 'Obscene Feminists', 2002, www.orlandoweekly.com/util/printready.asp?id=2684, accessed 16 May 2002.

Nofauxxx websites: www.nofauxxx.com and www.nofauxxx.com/dvd.htm.

O'Sullivan, Kimberly, 'Good Girls Gone Bad: Lesbians and Sex Work', *word is out e-journal*, no. 3, June 2002, www.wordisout.info, accessed 20 August 2004.

Queen, Carol, 'Yes SIR!: S.I.R. Video's Shar Rednour and Jackie Strano', 2001,www.goodvibes.com/cgi-bin/sgdynamo.exe?HTNAME=magazine/features/sex_and_culture/2001041.html, accessed 15 October 2004.

Religious Tolerance, 'Violence and Harassment at US Abortion Clinics', *Religious Tolerance*, 2004, www.religioustolerance.org/abo_viol.htm, accessed 6 December 2006.

Ropelato, Jerry, 'Internet Pornography Statistics', 'Top Ten Reviews, 2006', http://internet-filter-review.toptenreviews.com/internet-pornography-statistics.html, accessed 30 November 2006.

Sixty Minutes (online), 'Porn in the USA' (transcript), 2003, http://sixtyminutes.ninemsn.com.au/sixtyminutes/stories/2003_05_11/story_831.asp, accessed 19 May 2003.

Smith, Clarissa, 'They're Ordinary People, Not Aliens from the Planet Sex! The Mundane Excitements of Pornography for Women', *Journal of*

Mundane Behaviour, vol. 3, no. 1, 2002, http://mundanebehavior.org/
index.htm, accessed 9 June 2004.

Sullivan, Moira, 'Lesbographic Pornography', in Anu Koivunen and Susanna
Paasonen (eds), *Conference Proceedings for Affective Encounters: Rethinking
Embodiment in Feminist Media Studies*, University of Turku, School of
Art, Literature and Music, Media Studies, Series A, 2001, no. 49, e-book
at www.utu.fi/hum/mediautkimus/affective/proceedings.pdf, accessed
15 October 2004.

Taormino, Trisan, 'Porn Faces Reality', *Village Voice Online*, 30 April 2004,
www.villagevoice.com/issues/0418/taormino.php, accessed 24 June 2004.

Veg Porn site: www.vegporn.com/modelinfo.html

Index

abortion clinic murders, 87–8
Action Sports Sex, 50, 54
actors: ages, 60–1; amateur, 128, 130–1;
    attractiveness of, 35, 117; body types,
    61–2, 68; diversity, 146; pay rates, 46;
    penis size, 63; performer/producers,
    113, 115, 143, 172, 176; support
    services for, 175–6
actresses: ages, 60–1, 71; amateur,
    70–1, 102, 128, 130–1, 134, 144–5;
    attractiveness of, 35; body types, 61–2,
    68, 102; breast size, 61–2; business
    skills, 170; diversity, 146; exploitation,
    102, 166, 170, 174; history, 136–7;
    pay rates, 46; performer/producers,
    101, 103–4, 108–10, 113–17, 139,
    145, 170, 175–7, 185–6; stereotypes,
    60; 'stunt' performers, 173; support
    services for, 175–6
addiction to pornography, 18, 25, 86,
    169, 178
Adult Industry Medical Health Care
    Foundation, 175–6, 187
Adult Video News, 143, 167, 171–3,
    176–7
Adult Video News awards, 114
Adultshop, 48
Agrey, Aer, 123–4
AIM, *see* Adult Industry Medical Health
    Care Foundation
Aizura, Aren, 121–2
Albury, Katherine, 185, 189–91
Ally McBeal, 138
Alpha, 177
'alternaporn', 146
Amateur Movies, 71
amateur pornography, 128–48; age
    specific, 71, 143; BDSM, 141, 143;
    body types shown in, 70, 132; chat
    rooms, 133–4; collages, 138; connection
    to everyday life, 134–5; 'crotch-cam'
    in, 133; fan cultures, 138–43; fetishes,
    141–2; handicams used to make, 21;
    history, 135–8; interactive, 133;

mobile phones used to make, 15;
    'ordinariness', 132; popularity, 69, 132;
    webcams, 132, 134; zines, 138–41;
    see also actors, amateur; actresses,
    amateur; lesbian pornography
Amateur's Homepage, 71
American Psycho, 6
Anabolic World Sex Tour, 50
anal sex, 35–6, 58, 67, 114–15, 122, 166,
    170, 173
Ancient Secrets of the Kama Sutra, 50,
    55–7
Anderson, Acme, 176
Anderson, Pamela, 134, 147
Angry Penguins, 12
Animal Locomotion, 135
anti-porn feminists, 4, 17–23, 44, 103,
    126–7, 130, 147, 172
'arse-to-mouth', 177
art and pornography, 3–7, 11–13, 23
'assaultive language', 53
Australasian Vixen, 128–9
Australia Institute, 159–61
Australian Idol, 131
Australian Women's Forum, 110–11,
    123–4, 139
availability of videos/DVDs: Australia,
    50; Australian Capital Territory, 21, 50;
    Northern Territory, 28, 50–1
Awesome Asians, 50, 64
Awesome Asians 2, 50
Axis Entertainment, 51

'bad' pornography, 43, 97, 102, 127, 186
Bad Wives, 50, 54, 57
Bambi, 139
Band, The, 124
BangBus, 172
Barakat, Nicole, 121
Barbach, Lonnie, 104
Barcan, Ruth, 132, 145
Baron, Robert, 52
Baroque, Leah, 122–3
Barrett, James, 87